Student Mobility and Narrative in Europe

Bringing together case studies and theory, this book is the first in-depth qualitative study of student migration within Europe. The author examines the experience of students who spend a year abroad in a European country, examining the social status of the traveller and exploring the student experience of mobility.

Using the key concept of 'the stranger', defined in Simmel's seminal essay of 1908, as a starting point, the author outlines the characteristics of the stranger as a social type. Examining the works of Park, Wood, Stonequist, Schütz and Siu, she presents a conceptual framework for the analysis of a new stranger, the European student traveller.

The empirical data have been obtained from interviews with students representing three types of study abroad programmes: Erasmus, assistantships and a European business school programme.

These interviews have produced rich narratives, bringing to light the constituents of the students' formative experiences: their mobility capital, their motivations, the arrival as a rite of passage, their definitions of culture shock, the discovery of new spatial conditions, the participation in a new social scene, the creation of a social fabric and the process of adaptation. By examining these, the author is able to demonstrate how the experience of mobility alters the concepts of 'space' and 'home', indicating that they are no longer perceived as being tied to specific geographical environments, but rather part of a mobile and changing life space.

Essential reading for anthropologists and sociologists interested in issues of mobility, migration and ideas and experiences of 'the stranger', this work will also be of vital interest to those working in education and to students about to spend a year abroad.

Elizabeth Murphy-Lejeune is a Lecturer in the French Department, Saint Patrick's College, Dublin. She has written extensively on Language, Culture and Intercultural Issues in a variety of European publications.

Routledge studies in anthropology

Student Mobility and Narrative in Europe
The new strangers
Elizabeth Murphy-Lejeune

Student Mobility and Narrative in Europe

The new strangers

Elizabeth Murphy-Lejeune

London and New York

First published 2002
by Routledge
11 New Fetter Lane, London EC4P 4EE

Simultaneously published in the USA and Canada
by Routledge
29 West 35th Street, New York, NY 10001

Routledge is an imprint of the Taylor & Francis Group

© 2002 Elizabeth Murphy-Lejeune

Typeset in Baskerville by Taylor and Francis Books Ltd
Printed and bound in Great Britain by Biddles Ltd,
Guildford and King's Lynn

British Library Cataloguing in Publication Data
A catalogue record for this book is available from the British Library

Library of Congress Cataloging in Publication Data
Murphy-Lejeune, Elizabeth, 1948–
Student mobility and narrative in Europe: the new strangers/
Elizabeth Murphy-Lejeune.
p. cm.
Includes bibliographical references and index.
1. Foreign study – Europe. 2. Foreign Students – Europe – Social
conditions. I. Title.

LB2378.E85 M87 2002
370.116–dc21

ISBN 0-415-26179-1

To Antoin, Nathalie-Anne and Alexis

Contents

Tables

Acknowledgements

I wish to express my gratitude first of all to the fifty students who agreed to be interviewed. Their narratives provided the substance of a rich fabric on which to base this work.

I am also indebted to Pat Little and Bertrand Dubois, who diligently read substantial parts of this work. Their recommendations were always judicious and helpful.

I am very appreciative of the support which I received from the President of Saint Patrick's College, Dr S. Clyne, and my Head of Department, Gay Barry, who facilitated my research activities. I wish to acknowledge the financial support from the College towards the cost of indexing.

Introduction

Foreigner: a choked up rage deep down in my throat, a black angel clouding
transparency, opaque, unfathomable spur.

(Kristeva 1991)

The stranger has been an object of inquiry high on the agenda of Western civili-
sation. The ubiquity of the theme vouches for a permanent questioning of
otherness across centuries, across genres, across disciplines. Yet, its place in
Western thought remains paradoxical. From the Greek world where 'Barbarians'
and other aliens named the unthinkable and the eccentric to medieval peregrina-
tions, from the cosmopolitism of the Enlightenment to the global village of the
present and the virtual mobility of a world in constant expansion, the same questions linger on. What does it mean to be a stranger, other than the same? What
are the social conditions which create strangers? What are the boundaries distinguishing strangers from others? How does an individual experience being a
stranger? What relationship do foreigners have with the languages in which they
come to live? More specifically, what is the meaning of such questioning in the
context of European mobility?

The particular form of stranger analysed here is the travelling European[1]
student. Student mobility is understood as the short-term stay abroad, usually
one academic year of nine to twelve months duration. This experience,
posited as an instrument of European construction, represents an ambiguous
venture in university education. The stay abroad induces direct contact with a
language and culture, qualitatively different from institutional learning, transcending it in a way. Its impact and outcomes are still perplexing and difficult
to assess. As a small minority, mobile students are indeed undefined, little
known. Who are these young people who take up the challenge of mobility
when the vast majority of their peers disregard it? What are the characteristics and circumstances of their experience in their overall biographical
trajectory and other learning experiences? The paucity of research, particularly qualitative, in this area (Admit, 1999) leads to questions concerning the
uncertain status of this research topic. If the number of student travellers is
meant to increase, a more appropriate knowledge of their experience is
required.

This study originates from questioning the movements which drive individuals or communities outside their own national borders. Migration and mobility are envisaged as two facets of the same phenomenon. Migrations on a world scale usually correspond to economic and political instability and volatility. Traditional migratory flows, borne out of specific geopolitical relations, seemed somewhat stabilised. But, since the late 1980s, major changes in the economic, social and political structures of most countries have given rise to the globalisation, acceleration, differentiation, and feminisation of migrations (Castles and Miller, 1993). New migratory spaces and new diasporas are emerging (Van Hear, 1998). Nowhere have these changes had more impact than in Europe (Koser and Lutz, 1998). Moreover, the forms of migration are changing, giving rise to new types of migrants. One of the most significant new migrant profiles is that of the highly skilled worker, seeking professional added value or moving for study reasons, and whose migration may be only temporary (Eurostat, 2000). The mobile European student paves the way for this new type of migrant.

Tectonic societal changes, in particular the transition from the local to the global, and the momentous opening up of spaces for communication, are producing new forms of migration of a more individual type, where mobility is conceived as a continuous and multiple process rather than as a one-way ticket. Cross-cultural movements have become the norm, with departures from one's native country no longer as traumatic as in the past (Hoffman, 1999). To approach transnational movements through the study of a population which embodies the future in Europe, and in the general context of globalisation, brings to the fore these changes in contemporary migrations and calls attention to a new category of Europeans, the 'student travellers'.

The development of the European Union (EU), in particular through the Maastricht and Amsterdam treaties, has instituted a redefinition of the status of 'foreigner'. Citizens of member states have acquired a new political status, that of citizens of the EU, half-way between nationals and foreigners (Hen and Léonard, 1998). Among the rights which European citizenship confers, in first place comes the right to live freely in the territories of other member states. Notwithstanding this, statistics relating to intra-European migratory movements reveal a paradoxical situation. The number of EU citizens living in other member states seems extremely small given the official discourse encouraging Europeans towards mobility today and the measures adopted to facilitate such movement. EU non-nationals represent about 2 per cent of the total EU population (Eurostat, op. cit.).[2] Even though emerging demographic trends show that mobility between member states is on the increase, Europe today is still overwhelmingly sedentary. The vast majority of its citizens are 'immobile' nationals, settled within their national borders which they only leave for short trips. The discrepancy between rights and reality[3] is blatant in the area of European citizenship (Close, 1995). In this context, what is the social, cultural and symbolical status of a European residing temporarily in another member state? Can European students consider themselves as strangers inside Europe or do they promulgate a new way of being in Europe? The new forms of mobility emerging in Europe contribute to new ways of being and thinking about it (Morin, 1987).

A further development is that international contacts have become more diverse with the progress of virtual mobility. Video-conferencing or electronic communication, video correspondence, inter-university agreements, transnational research cooperation, and the increasingly intensive use of the internet, open up the media through which intercultural contacts may come about. However, the physical move abroad, as study period, work placement or work experience, represents an unmediated form of international contact which sets the specific learning experience it produces directly into the student's life as a whole. The lived relation to strangeness perturbs the nature of exchanges and the relations between cultures and languages. It certainly promotes many competences. But its impact as a holistic experience remains somewhat obscure.

Student mobility is considered here as a particular case of migration, a choice which may surprise. Indeed, the study of travellers journeying in the context of programmes and agreements which facilitate their movements, within a relatively homogeneous cultural area, for a duration fixed in advance, might appear rather distant from the often dramatic problems besieging international migrants. Yet, given due consideration to the extreme diversity and complexity of these movements, it is legitimate to view students, even in the European framework, as belonging to the political category of 'non-nationals', who have a different nationality. Their migratory route must be different from that of other 'non-nationals' – the immigrant, the exile, the refugee, the asylum seeker, and even more so the undocumented migrant. These categories of migrants have dominated research on migration in which ethnic contacts were viewed primarily as a group phenomenon affecting multicultural societies (Sollors, 1996). To take into account a new category means extending the research context. It allows for a new perspective on migration, no longer examined from the point of view of receiving societies, absorbed by the presence and potential integration of sometimes unexpected newcomers, nor from the point of view of migrant communities. Rather, this new vantage point considers the issues from the perspective of the individuals at the heart of the migratory process, giving them a voice to express their own narrative among other similar narratives.

Migrants of all kinds share a special position, that of strangers who, on the boundaries of sameness and otherness, provoke a sometimes unsettling awareness in their interlocutors and test the permeability of borders. Similar properties preside over their destinies. The decision to leave, the arrival in a new space, the progressive appropriation of a linguistic and cultural environment, the new professional roles, the acquisition of social relations, the identity transformations required to adapt successfully, are part and parcel of each experience. As such, the nature of the initial process of entry and of the effort required to adapt and potentially integrate may be considered as common to diverse strangers. The process of contrasting different migrant trajectories leads to the question of invariants. To what extent are these experiences comparable, or is there a radical distance between disadvantaged and privileged migrants due to differing socio-economic contexts? In other words, is it all pain and no gain for some, all gain and no pain for others (Hoffman, op. cit.), or indeed a bit of both? Certainly, the degree and intensity of adaptive experiences vary depending on a multiplicity of social and personal variables. Nevertheless, it could be assumed that 'on one level, exile is a universal experience' (ibid.: 39). What then are the properties which migrants of all kinds share?

The very meaning of migration has also changed. Whereas it elicited in the past a kind of social and psychological death, flexible borders and communication facilities give more and more migrants[4] the capacity to choose. Migration was seen as the enforced departure towards spaces infused with economic and political expectations and 'leaving was more important than arriving' (Goldring and Mac Einri, 1989: 173). Migration today is seen as the longed-for arrival in spaces carrying new promises, but home or newer possibilities are never too far away. The new migrants attract attention because they represent a group claiming its visibility and difference, unlike the immigrant of the past trying to fade into the masses. The post-modern world induces more fluid and diversified contacts.

More specifically, migration patterns have changed radically in EU member states, presenting a novel migratory context. New poles of attraction within Europe have surfaced. The Irish example in the late 1980s is indicative because it draws attention to two significant permutations. First, newer destinations towards European countries gradually extended the pattern of traditional emigration towards English-speaking countries (Mac Einri, 1989). Secondly, more temporary forms of migration created a new category of expatriates, in transit between societies, provisional passengers, called in a particular case the 'new Irish' in New York (Corcoran, 1993). More recently, Ireland and other European countries underwent a demographic sea change when they became countries of immigration, both for their own emigrants returning home and for immigrants from abroad. These tendencies show that people are increasingly sensitive to rapid economic or social changes. They uproot themselves with greater ease. This is why the term 'traveller' was chosen to designate these new migrants. It draws the line between traditional migrants and the contemporary mobile individual. The traveller is a modern nomad[5] who comes and goes, circulating between spaces and times for variable durations.

The student traveller heralds this new type of migrant, which the transition from migration to mobility symbolises. Migration denotes movements outside one's country of origin[6] into another for a variety of reasons, leading to changes in residence and legal status. By contrast, mobility is a more general term which applies to phenomena other than movements from one national territory to another. It emphasises first and foremost change. It refers to a specific quality or condition, that of being 'capable of movement, not fixed, characterized by facility of movement, easily changing, free' (*Oxford English Dictionary*). Mobility is the quality of those who can easily move and adapt to different environments. It may be conceived principally as a geographic condition. It may also extend into the linguistic, social, psychological, intellectual, professional, cultural domain.

Migration, as a decisive final movement leading to long-term social integration or assimilation, implies a slow but intense transformation of the individuals concerned. Mobility implies a shorter kind of integration, where personal transformations may be more peripheral.

Focusing on the new category of European travellers should contribute to a better understanding of the 'migratory elites' (Chédemail, 1998; Musgrove, 1963). An invisible category, deleted from migrations statistics because of its reputed lack of problems, it nevertheless exists and becomes more diverse as the impact of globalisation becomes more widespread. A long-lived category, it embraces several populations of travellers who crossed history: monks and other itinerants in the Middle Ages, merchants during the Renaissance, bankers in the burgeoning capitalism of the nineteenth century, modern business and sports people, and of course thinkers and artists of all times. The globalisation of many human activities favours the expansion of this population. The mobile European student belongs, up to a point, to a migratory elite. But her/his membership is only potential since her/his destiny is still wide open. Whether s/he opts for a European, even international, route or for a national itinerary belongs to a future which is only being sketched. In short, within the category of 'culture travellers' (Furnham and Bochner, 1986), the mobile student is in between the tourist's transient passage and the migrant's long-term stay in terms of length of stay. The prominence of the professional motive brings the student traveller closer to the expatriate, also a temporary traveller on a mission, but her/his linguistic and social situation is different.

Consequently, the student traveller's trajectory may be understood as situated at the intersection between two migratory models: the traditional immigrant and the 'golden' expatriate (Wagner, 1998). Traditional migration usually refers to a durable settlement, return to the home country being in a state of suspense. The constraining, sometimes distressing, circumstances which surround departure and arrival into a country whose welcome may be unfavourable accentuate nostalgia for home and the emergence of a bipolar world. Transition from one environment to the other and the concomitant language and culture learning process may be painful. Contrastingly, travellers from the international elite are but temporary expatriates and their return home is scheduled. The privileged circumstances of their departure and the favourable welcome extended to prestigious, sometimes sought after visitors exempts them, if they wish, from involvement in the local society. Similarly, their relation to their national origin benefits from a certain detachment. Language and culture learning are left to their fancy.

The European student traveller borrows from these two categories some of their characteristics. If the student is unlikely to experience her/his passing into the new world as painfully as the permanent migrant, her/his relative inexperience of foreign living, the test which adaptation represents and limited personal resources may somewhat hinder a nevertheless coveted experience. Unlike the expatriate, s/he does not have access to professional services organising her/his material life, and her/his integration into local society is rather more pressing in terms of linguistic and social participation. As for the expatriate, the student stay is of short to medium duration and professionally motivated. Like the expatriate, the experience abroad may just be an interval in a life story while for the immigrant, the interval may not be so incidental and fortuitous. One of the main differences between expatriates and students is the greater flexibility which youth confers. Without family responsibilities or other ties, students are in a state of family and economic 'lightness' (Mauger, 1995) and their affective and mental horizon should be more unobstructed. As a result, their integration into a different environment might prove easier, faster and more comprehensive.

Part of a secular tradition whose main beneficiaries were privileged, the student stay abroad in Europe perpetuates age-old practices, often the preserve of language students as linguists or 'professional strangers' (Agar, 1980). A private or commercial affair for a long time, the novelty rests in the public efforts aimed at democratising these periods of education outside home and at officially integrating them into national university curricula. International authorities, such as Unesco or the Council of Europe through conventions on the recognition of qualifications (1997), and European Union policy provide the political and legal framework for the internationalisation of European institutions. Student mobility constitutes a major component of their international activities, and some member states have tried to facilitate this activity through bilateral and unilateral agreements (NARIC, 1993). The right of free movement within the EU, instituted in the Treaty of Rome, incited the EU authorities to reduce obstacles to student mobility, notably through recognition of qualifications, introducing the European Credit Transfer System (ECTS) for Erasmus students. The adoption of major European programmes in the late 1980s – Comett (1986), Erasmus (1987), Lingua (1989) and Tempus (1990), followed by Socrates (1995) – was seen as the beginning of a new era in European cooperation and exchanges. Article 126 in the Maastricht Treaty explicitly mentions the development of the European dimension in education, particularly through the teaching of languages, and the promotion of student and staff mobility as two major aims of EU educational policy. The rationale underpinning the policy is primarily socio-economic and political, i.e. the provision of 'an adequate pool of manpower with first-hand experience of economic and social aspects of other member states' (Admit, op. cit.). However, problems persist, obstacles remain and little research has been carried out to assess the impact of student mobility on either institutions or individuals.

Even if European programmes promote mobility as a method and a course of action for the construction of Europe, excessive optimism would be ill-advised. Statistics are notoriously unreliable or contradictory in this area (Gordon and Jallade, 1995). So, the exact number of mobile EU students is still imprecise,[7] partly because free movers are elusive and agreements too numerous, but also because definitions of 'foreign' students and accounting methods vary from country to country. EU mobile students represent a very small minority of the student population in most European countries, well below the 10 per cent official aspiration. An increase in numbers should not be an end in itself.

Nevertheless, authorities should wonder about the role in the construction of Europe of the more than 90 per cent non-mobile students. To study mobility issues within Europe should contribute to unveil some of the obstacles which mar these movements, and prove a useful starting-point so as to uncover the specificity of those who choose that option. For, quite obviously, mobility is not given to everyone: it must be learnt.

Nevertheless, worldwide student mobility concerns a growing amount of students whose total number was estimated by Unesco at 1,400,000 worldwide in 1996, and an increase of at least 50,000 students per year was projected. Among the major host countries for international students, the United States comes first with about 560,000, or 34 per cent of the world number (Claeys, 1999), while it is generally estimated that the UK receives about 200,000 and France about 130,000. However, 'international/foreign student' is a generic term that refers to different populations. Three main categories coexist. They are treated differently in academic discourses: as a social problem linked to ethnic migration in the first case; as a political and educational issue in the case of EU students; and as an economic concern in the third case. These differing perspectives reflect the diversity of responses to student mobility according to its type.

The earliest and numerically most important category includes students, mostly but not exclusively[8] non-Europeans, whose country may have had historical links with the host country. In this case, knowledge of the foreign language, sometimes even a parent educational system, are pull factors. For these, student mobility often led to student immigration. This explains the influx of students from India and Pakistan to the UK and from the Maghreb or Eastern Africa to France. Following a steady increase in France from 1970, this student population which peaked in 1984 has been regularly decreasing since, leading to what Slama (1999) called 'the end of the international student' in France. The reasons for this decline are mostly political and related to restrictions imposed by the host country. In other words, these students are no longer sought after.

The two newer categories to emerge are welcomed with varying attention by host countries. The first one is the European exchange student, deriving from EU programmes since 1987, whose freedom of choice for a place to study is a legal right. European exchanges are considered and managed with varying enthusiasm from one institution to another and from one country to another. In some countries, incoming students who do not have to pay fees do not appear as attractive as those who do. However small their overall number still is, it is growing. For example, EU students in UK higher education institutions have increased sixfold between 1981 and 1992, from 5,400 to 35,400 (Greenaway and Tuck, 1995). Moreover, the number of European students who have studied in another member state is naturally increasing every year, producing a large pool of ex-student travellers.

A category of foreign students which has received much attention recently is that of the international free movers, whose mobility is 'spontaneous' (Gordon and Jallade, 1996) in that they organise themselves without institutional help. These students come from all regions of the world, including some from within

Europe; Asia is a major provider. Increasing worldwide every year, they are actively, some would say aggressively, recruited in a new economic drive to gain places in the world education market. The expansion of this market adds an economic dimension to European higher education. This economic dimension represents a major challenge for countries where education rests on the principle of equal and free access to all, including foreigners. For others, where higher education is a source of revenue, if not a matter of survival, the objectives are clear: attract fee-paying foreign students or disappear. For example, in the UK, internationalisation in higher education institutions is expected to contribute to the international balance of payments (Elliott, 1997). In other words, the market for international students has become unavoidably competitive. Movements of students must be understood as 'part of the more general linkages which include professional migrations and capital flows' (Castles and Miller, op. cit.: 163).

In that context, it would be easy to lose sight of the European dimension to be developed in higher education systems. National and institutional policies are sometimes vague concerning the distinction between Europeanisation on the one hand and internationalisation on the other. It sometimes looks as if the latter is more attractive to some. A model where higher education would be treated as a commercial product and competition would be the law would be very far from the construction of the European 'learning society' heralded by EU authorities. It is opportune to remember that universities are a European invention where circulation led to productive intellectual cross-fertilisation. Openness to the outside is part of a long tradition in such institutions. In this perspective, the year abroad represents an asset for a future promising a more intense circulation of ideas and individuals. It is central to a European education and to future socio-professional mobility.

The present study is an attempt to meet the need to explore European student mobility, focusing on the mobile individual in a phenomenological perspective, to try and account for the definition of the experience by the actors themselves, an often neglected source of information. It implies recording and interpreting what they say about their European experience, adopting a subjective and qualitative perspective rather than an institutional or statistical perspective. The present study also provides a conceptual framework for the analysis of this specific experience in a broader setting, embracing and contrasting various categories of migratory routes. Finally, it meets the need to set out more clearly the parameters of intra-European mobility today, the new forms of migration and the forces which may lead an increasing amount of individuals to move… or not to move.

The approach adopted to construct our research object is twofold, bringing face to face two sets of data. The first set of a more theoretical nature hinges upon the key concept of 'the stranger' defined by Simmel in 1908, and integrates texts from the sociology of the stranger which outline the characteristics of this new social type. The experience of fifty student strangers (Murphy-Lejeune, 1995) is analysed in this light, the concepts from this body of research serving as working hypotheses. The second set refers to the experimental corpus collected emerging from individuals whose general situation is similar since they are spending a year abroad, but whose specific context of entry into the new society is different. Three case studies[9] were selected as representative of three types of study abroad programmes. The investigation follows a movement to and fro, probing the relationships between data emerging from the early context of American migration and empirical data reflecting contemporary social conditions in Europe. This movement from one pole to another explores other dimensions as well, notably the distinctions between individual and common experience or between the sometimes contradictory meanings assigned to their experience by students and the driving forces which emerge.

The presentation and analysis of the data follow the chronological sequence of the experience: the period of time preceding the actual move, the arrival and its consequences, the process of entering the new environment, and finally the outcomes of the experience. The principal properties which cross the diverse experiences vary according to contextual and personal factors, but constitute nevertheless a significant story line from which to observe the stay abroad. They also provide the drift of our interview schedule. What are the main characteristics regarding the experience of European students staying for a year in a country other than theirs? What happens during the process of adaptation to a new environment and what are its significant moments? The answers to these questions are an invitation to travel across time, space and disciplines in the fertile field of strangeness, inspired by a contemporary figure, that of the student traveller in Europe as a new stranger.

In chapter 1, we review the key characteristics of the stranger, which provide a new conceptual lexicology to analyse the particular experience of European student travellers. In chapter 2, European student travellers are posited as new strangers, their own narrative taking its place among a diversity of other migrant narratives. We review previous research on the student stay abroad and present the methodological framework, the rationale for a qualitative approach, the choice of three case studies and the profile of the students. In chapter 3, we suggest that a crucial feature of student travellers is their 'mobility capital', or how wandering potentialities are etched in a life story and feed on family experience, on previous experiences and on personality. In chapter 4, we go one step further in the genesis of the travelling project and review the reasons expressed by the students as to why they opted for the year abroad. In chapter 5, we examine how moving from one cultural world to another may constitute a rite of passage, signalling new social conditions and contributing to the arrival acquiring particular significance in the experience. In chapter 6, we turn to the issue of culture shock in a European context, more particularly how students define the term and its meaning as well as the stages which marked their year abroad. In chapter 7, the main dimensions of the students' discovery of their new spatial conditions are discussed, notably the specific geographic territory in which they find themselves, the way they stake out their habitat, and finally the crucial choice of accommodation. In chapter 8, we look at other dimensions of the new social setting, approached here in terms of the socio-professional roles the students are vested with and their participation in the social scene through leisure and other activities. Following on the two previous chapters, chapter 9 outlines the creation of their social network through a mix of social contacts originating from different groups. Chapter 10 appraises the process of adaptation and its outcomes in the way the students define the term, the personal qualities they identify with it, and the signs which reveal the degree of their integration into the new society.

1   The stranger's template

Introduction: the conceptual lineage of the sociology of the stranger

Three texts define the sociological template or the formal characteristics of the stranger as a social type.[1] They are Simmel's seminal essay (1908), developed by Park (1928) and the work of his colleagues in the Chicago school of sociology, and finally crowned with Schütz's essay (1944). These texts provide the core of an attempt to analyse a more specific case of the sociology of the stranger, that of student mobility. They represent a rich conceptual framework, highlighting central characteristics of individuals in situations of social change arising out of migration or mobility.

A second set of texts includes the works of Wood (1934) and Stonequist (1937), together with Siu's article on the sojourner (1952), which present various portraits of strangers in differing social contexts. Each text contributes to the analysis of the general social type of the stranger, following Simmel's lineage, by exploring the distinctive set of features embodied in the particular type they describe. Park's marginal/hybrid/cosmopolitan 'citizen of the world', Schütz's newly arrived migrant, Wood's newcomer, the marginal/international/cultural hybrid described by Stonequist, Siu's sojourner, as well as Harman's modern stranger (1988) represent as many variants of the kaleidoscope of the stranger. The mobile fragments forming the background are the general characteristics which, reflected in the mirror of reality, produce sets of images, variants of the social type described. Our hypothesis is that travelling European students represent another variant of the kaleidoscope and that contemporary student mobility may be conceived in this conceptual framework. The earlier sociological literature provides points of comparison and contrast for the analysis of a new sociological concept, the student traveller.

Simmel's essay was the foundation stone of what became the sociology of the stranger, which aimed at an epistemological break from the existing body of knowledge on the subject. Simmel established the natural membership of the stranger to the group and introduced the stranger into sociology as a legitimate object of study.

The state of being a stranger is of course a completely positive relation;
it is a specific form of interaction [...] The stranger is an element of the
group itself, not unlike the poor and sundry 'inner enemies' – an element
whose membership within the group involves both being outside it and confronting it.

(Simmel in Levine, 1971: 143–144)

Highlighting new forms of sociability, his description embraces other
sundry 'inner enemies', from whom the stranger differs nevertheless because of
previous membership to another language-culture. Cases of strangeness in
which certain groups are disallowed the most general human characteristics,
such as the relation of the Greeks to the Barbarians, are however excluded
from the description since they no longer consider the stranger as an element
of the group itself.

The concept of 'the stranger'[2] occupies a special place in the sociological
tradition. Dominated by the model Simmel constructed and illustrated later in
the works of many researchers from the Chicago school of sociology, it took on
diverse guises and was weakened as a result, according to Harman (op. cit.). In
the German idealist tradition, the main problem lies with the stranger: how will
individual actors deal with the experience of strangeness? Assimilated to the
American context of the early twentieth century, it is the host culture that is
problematised: what kind of impact will the new arrivals have on the community
and what can be done to receive them? Two main research traditions emerged
from this, the first focusing on the status of the stranger in the group, as a
newcomer or as a marginal, the second exploring and expanding the notion of
social distance. In the end, the fate of Simmel's concept follows that of the individuals it depicts and becomes a creation without a history, evolving between
those who seek to preserve its original form and those who seek to adapt it to
new social conditions (Levine, 1977).

Simmel defines the formal position of the stranger as constituting a specific
type of social constellation which joins together various paradoxes and
tensions, notably distance and proximity. His essay and the texts which
followed delineate some major areas of inquiry in relation to strangers' experience: position in space and in time, social and symbolic position, as well as
identity issues. Spatially, strangers represent the unity between wandering and
fixation, nomads caught in between places. In time, the stranger is defined as
'the person who comes today and stays tomorrow' (Simmel in Wolff, 1950:
402), a 'potential wanderer' accustomed to chronological discontinuities.
Socially, as an intruder challenging established relations, the position assigned
to him[3] is ex-centric, on the margins of society, and his status is at best inde-
terminate, often devalued. As someone who is both outside and inside, he
possesses a distinct type of objectivity which can be defined as freedom from
prejudice and convention. In the absence of organic ties with members of the
group, relations to strangers are more abstract and categorical. Finally, the
spatial, temporal, social and symbolic disorientation experienced by strangers

in their new environment may cause a personal crisis during which identity borders are disturbed and must be renegotiated. These characteristics signal the essential tensions which are the hallmark of the stranger's template: wandering and fixation, present and future, proximity and distance, familiarity and strangeness, inclusion and exclusion.

The spatial position of the stranger

The first characteristic of strangers is their physical position in space, or what Wood calls their 'attribute of mobility'. Strangers are mobile, having left a primary space and set foot in another space. Their spatial position is best expressed for Simmel by the synthesis of two conceptual opposites, wandering and fixation, nomadism and territorial attachment. As if suspended between two poles, this permanent tension inevitably introduces a to-and-fro movement into their destiny, a movement which may only be understood as the coexistence of places of belonging, as the to-and-fro of wanderers, and as the loosening of original affiliations.[4]

Mobility and dislocations in space

The physical or geographical move represents a minimal definition of strangers, that which distinguishes them from sedentary natives. By contrast, the attribute of established groups is stability of place and relationships among members.

> It is he who comes among us, perhaps from the far ends of the earth, perhaps, if we are city-dwellers, from the apartment across the hall. In any event it is the stranger who comes and the group who receives. The group is, as it were, at home.
>
> (Wood, op. cit.: 46)

The proximity inherent in the direct contact created by the arrival of strangers brings about a dynamic situation which calls for changes in the social environment. But physical proximity increases the intensity of reactions to the new intimacy initiated, demonstrating the fallacy of a conception of contacts as benevolent (Amir, 1969). Simmel, when he ascertains that spatial relations are not only the condition, but also the symbol of human relations, puts forward a spatial conception of human contact, highlighting the territorial basis of social contacts.

The stranger is 'in between' at least two geographical, linguistic, social, cultural, national spaces. As such, displacement induces duality and sometimes dislocation, in that a part joined to a contiguous whole may be disconnected from it, sometimes painfully, since that which one leaves buried in one's native land troubles one's memory for a long time: 'the very decision to leave family, friends, and countrymen produces some premonitory pangs of homesickness' (Stonequist, op. cit.: 84). Yet whatever the motives for leaving, breaking from one's native roots, not only physically, but above all mentally, is a prerequisite for crossing over to the other group (ibid.). As a result, depending on factors such as duration and aims of the move, migration may end up generating a multiplicity of references. Then space opens up and becomes more complex. Ultimately, space, be it physical, personal, affective, social, cultural or mental, must be redefined.

Distance and proximity: the paradox of the stranger

Simmel formulates the defining paradox of 'the stranger' by saying that 'in the relationship to him, distance means that he, who is close by, is far, and strangeness means that he, who also is far, is actually near' (1950: 402).[5] This communicates the essentially ambiguous position of strangers. Distance and proximity are experienced simultaneously in their case and frequently in a conflictual mode (Park, op. cit.). Obviously, the synthesis of nearness and remoteness must be understood beyond the spatial sense, embracing the psychological, social and symbolic dimensions as well.[6]

Conceived as a tension which evolves, it is a crucial feature of the experience of strangers because it relates to their membership orientation. Indeed, distance and proximity do not appear as rigid or fixed. Instead, they generate moving and fluid boundaries depending on the objective and personal circumstances which affect them. However, the very coexistence of closeness and remoteness is what makes the position of strangers problematic at all times:

> When those who should be close, in any sense of the term, are actually close, and those who should be distant are distant, everyone is 'in his place'. When those who should be distant are close, however, the inevitable result is a degree of tension and anxiety which necessitates some special kind of response.
>
> (Levine, 1977: 22)

Simmel also draws attention to the fact that the stranger is no 'owner of soil', not only in the physical sense, but also metaphorically 'as a vital substance which is fixed, if not in space, then at least in an ideal position within the social environment' (in Levine, 1971: 144). Strangers have traditionally been denied ownership rights and the social or civic rights which accompany them. Besides, as long as in the eyes of others they remain strangers, they will not have access to native rights, nor to their history or cultural heritage. This legal and symbolical status explains why, as a supernumerary, their designated functions in the group are the circulation of economic and cultural goods or the social roles of mediators or intermediaries.

European mobility: a new way of thinking about space

Historically, wandering and mobility are part of the construction of Europe. Land of immigration as well as of migration, Europe evolved through a constant mix of populations, a permanent ethnic and cultural melting-pot (Delouche *et al.*, 1992). Traditionally, pull and push factors led citizens to varying degrees of mobility within the European space. Notwithstanding this, as mentioned earlier, most citizens of the EU are, by and large, not travellers who have acquired the freedom of moving from one location to another and staying there for a while. Will trans-European mobility be sufficient to transform non-migratory habits? At a time when border-crossing is officially sanctioned, it seems fit to examine the possible passages from one status to another, and their effect on the mobile individual. For example, within the EU, how are statutes negotiated between nationals and non-nationals?

Beyond the European context, relations between geographic mobility, virtual globalisation and the home are being transformed. Spatial membership is put to the test. The globalisation of information via the internet is breaking down the barriers of geographical space. Time may become a substitute for space as the basis for social relations (Meyer, 1951). The main hypothesis, particularly in the literature on migrants, is that lasting mobility, whether voluntary or not, induces a trauma caused by the loss of origin and the need to rebuild a place, sometimes a homeland. The new social situation requires settling in a place: 'those who do not take root somewhere have no landmarks, the soil is moving under their feet, they have no place any more' (Fisher, 1981: 14, our trans.). 'Home' is here defined mainly as the place where affective roots, family or friends, are located. Consequently, narratives of 'homesickness' and 'homecoming' chronicle migrants' memories of the past, the heartache of those who are cut off from their primary location, their link with childhood (Hoffman, 1989). Similarly, analysts of modernity call attention to the growing sense of alienation resulting from life in societies where strangeness has replaced the old familiarity (Harman, op. cit.). To what extent can we transcend a dramatic approach to mobility as uprooting so as to account for the trajectories of those who participate in a space perceived more positively as a place where circulation and exchanges are fostered?

Indeed, the migratory nature of modern experience presents individuals with several possible biographies. 'Life careers' are no longer fixed. But the other side of this biographical expansion may be what Berger *et al.* (1973) call the 'metaphysical loss of self', which generates a nostalgia of 'being at home in society, with self, and eventually in the universe' (ibid.: 82).

As a result, the experience of mobility calls for a rethinking of space. Space used to be synonymous with a place of genetic or territorial ancestry, given, native, associated with heredity and origins (Wollen, 1994). In this approach to space, fixation, as understood by Simmel, was paramount. From the perspective of mobility, the traveller's space appears more hazardous, constantly reformulated, 'as the expression of a trajectory, as accumulated through space and over time. It can be seen as displaced, diasporic, nomadic, multiple or hybrid' (ibid.: 189). Then, wandering becomes a more legitimate way of living. Traditional definitions of home are challenged. What meanings does 'place' take on for the European mobile person? Is home what one leaves behind, moves to or carries along?

Discontinuities in time

The stranger's position in time is marked by a break with chronological linearity and by the discovery of the precariousness of his situation. His movements in time display distinctive signs punctuating the three diachronic forms of time. Departure disconnects from the past: the stranger becomes 'a man without a history' (Schütz, 1971a: 97). 'Potential wanderer' with an indecisive itinerary, he experiences the present as inflated, excessively dilated. Finally, the future for him is a permanent question mark, pressing on the issue of the length of the stay and of a potential return. The stranger, the metaphorical figure of precariousness, must then learn to manage the discontinuities inherent to his path. His reaction depends largely on whether the adventure is the result of a lasting desire etched in a personal life story or the unwanted outcome of an unbearable situation imposed by external circumstances.

Wandering and fixation: the potential wanderer

The stranger's position in time is essentially situated between today and tomorrow: he is 'the person who comes today and stays tomorrow. He is, so to speak, the potential wanderer' (Simmel, 1950: 402). The potential wanderer is defined by the chronology of his movements: arriving today and staying on for a certain time, he may equally leave tomorrow. Today for the stranger is shaped by his arrival in a foreign land. The future lies entirely in the indeterminacy of the duration of his stay. To stay or to go? The question might have been more critical in the past when travellers were either in transit with no desire to stay or conversely aspiring to permanent residence. Today's modern stranger may be closer to the potential wanderer who, if he settles in a new destination, maintains the freedom of leaving it.

Several figures of strangers illustrate this itinerant wandering which the post-modern discourse on nomadism has revitalized (Maffesoli, 1997).The cosmopolitan 'citizen of the world' who crosses borders with ease and lives in several worlds without settling in any one place is one such example. In her/his case, the process of identification is transcultural, mixed and supranational, not 'in between', but 'above' (Friedman, 1995): 'he lives on the surface of life, becomes blasé and easily bored, and restlessly moves about looking for new thrills' (Stonequist, op. cit.: 179). Her/his presence depends on spatial proximity, but s/he is absent socially and culturally. Such a position suits individuals wishing to observe the global away from local allegiances, settled in continuous otherness, navigators of space (Park, op. cit.). The sojourner described by Siu (op. cit.) is another variant of the modern wanderer, albeit a frustrated one since s/he did not cut off links from her/his primary attachments. S/he has acquired the freedom of going, but not of leaving. The expatriate who establishes roots for a certain time in a new place, mainly for professional reasons, but with no desire for permanency, is another figure of the potential wanderer. However, her/his membership of an original place is not questioned. S/he remains ethnocentred and her/his freedom of coming and going is still restricted.

The student traveller represents a special case of potential wandering, temporarily settled like the cosmopolitan and the expatriate, but for whom the stakes are uncertain. The uncertainties of youth open up her/his horizon. The duration of the stay may well be fixed institutionally, but it is not definite. The student stay abroad is governed by the rules of transition and passing. It is a border event between youth and adulthood, between an initial position, expressed by family and school orientations, and a coveted social position, professional and matrimonial. Whether the student's official task is study or employment, it is not just professional, and it also answers personal demands for novelty. Her/his temporary position in society does not constrain her/him to assimilate, as is the case for the migrant. Her/his story in respect of her/his native land is not summed up by a series of more or less failed returns, as it is for the sojourner. Above all, unlike the latter, the student traveller does not experience the to-and-fro movement between origin and destination as a cost, but as a benefit. S/he knows s/he may always move on again. S/he has made the first step towards freedom. For 'in exile, uncertainty meets freedom' (Bauman, 1996: 569). How far will they go? The ultimate step of this movement between today and tomorrow consists in conquering the mental and functional 'freedom of coming and going'.

A person without a history

Cut off from a segment of his life by his move into another time–space, the stranger becomes a person 'without a history' from the point of view of the approached group and remains excluded from its past.

> The culture of the approached group has never become an integral part of his biography, as did the history of his home group. Only the ways in which his fathers and grandfathers lived become for him elements of his own way of life. Graves and reminiscences can neither be transferred nor conquered
>
> (Schütz, 1971a: 96)

From a personal point of view, relations with his own history are painful. Biographical traces and collective memories are buried in his home ground. A stranger's past, both personal and collective, ceases to exist in the eyes of those around him. This is sometimes experienced as an amputation because a whole part of one's story becomes invisible to those who are now close. Doubly amputated from history, strangers are in no position to participate in the taken-for-granted pattern of the new group, nor in their heritage. Such severance from the past induces discomfort since it may be regarded by others as a deficiency. On the other hand, these first steps outside home also have the power to liberate individuals from the weight of custom (Park, op. cit.). Does freedom from the past generate liberation, amputation or feelings in between?

The relations strangers may have with the history of the host culture are essentially in terms of the present and future. If the intention to become a member is manifest, strangers will have access to the new history, but only from the outside as an external body of knowledge. As for the future, it is open, notably to the possibility of going away to new horizons. But the future is leaky, slippery, elusive. Does the empty space of the future represent for potential wanderers a wealth of promise or a cluster of uncertainty?

An inflated present

The stranger's temporal position is characterised by an inflated present because his personal chronology in the new context starts altogether with the here and now of his arrival. Strangers are the newcomers or the last arrivals,[7] and this newness presses them into the time of urgency. The experience of strangers multiplies the impact of immediacy. It is a time when each moment is an event, everything is an adventure, everything has to be negotiated on a new basis, including the most elementary forms of communication. The easy succession of events in a continuous and peaceful diachrony is interrupted. Personal time is suddenly compressed.

The stranger's time is also perturbed in its synchrony. In between two biographical moments, time-lags and discrepancies accumulate: discrepancy between self and self in two different time–spaces, discrepancy in personal and social links which are momentarily suspended, discrepancy in social routines. Established links are strained by distance, new links are to be formed, still on the horizon of the future. Routines attached to social practices built over the long term have not yet got under way (Giddens, in Cassell, 1993). Discontinuities in relations and routines may only be temporary when the newcomer actively undertakes to reconstruct a social universe. In other cases, they may persist.

In the transition, strangers discover a new facet of time: precariousness. Indeed, the new universe does not necessarily present itself as other than ephemeral and provisional. In this context, the evanescent time of encounters and conversations takes on a crucial role. Strangers are infinitely sensitive to the richness of a fleeting temporality where one becomes a navigator 'who is in between others, separated by the translucent wall of potential conversation; of otherness lying in wait' (Harman, op. cit.: 7). Experiences of mobility belong to the domain of precariousness, with the collective experience of migrations in the background. But more than mere stage settings, they produce new behavioural languages, new repertoires (Joseph, 1984).

The social eccentricity of strangers

The two-dimensional stranger, caught in between groups, is given a particular position in social space. First, his position in the unfamiliar group is 'determined, essentially, by the fact that he has not belonged to it from the beginning, that he imports qualities into it, which do not and cannot stem from the group itself' (Simmel, 1950: 402). A stranger is a person who has not been socialised in a given cultural space. Moreover, departure renders his position regarding the ancestral group suspect as if the membership pact was called into question due to participation, if only temporary, in other conventions. As such, his position in social space is doubly marked by distance. Being outside the social relations established by the groups he belongs to, his departure and his arrival shatter the common consent shared by members because he endorses different social practices. He also discovers that the acquired system of interpretation and action becomes worthless, even unproductive, since it interferes with the existing system (Schütz, op. cit.). This eccentric, asymmetrical position may induce a feeling of marginality (Stonequist, op. cit.) and a dilemma regarding potential status (Hughes, 1949).

Established social relations and membership

A stranger leaves a group and arrives in another where relations are based upon mutual recognition and a feeling of common belonging. These more or less permanent relations are the result of processes of adjustment, deriving from consent or tradition. Cohesion among members is essentially maintained by sentiment: 'those sentiments which are shared in common by all members of a group tend to form strong unifying bonds' (Wood, op. cit.: 31). So, 'a stranger who has entered a group for the first time is outside the system of relationships which unite the group, and, if he is to be included, these relationships must be extended to him' (ibid.: 8). An increase in outside contacts creates a tension which forces groups to rethink their system of relationships, their rules for inclusion and exclusion, and to discover adjustments, particularly if the presence of strangers persists and expands with new arrivals. The problem of integration of new relationships into the social structure is then posed. How will existing relations be extended? In which ways do societies open up or not to newcomers? Will they leave them outside or grant them, even temporarily, a social position and some rights?

In its social dimension, the relation between distance and proximity refers to the principles presiding over relationships among partners of the social body, or to 'the degree of reciprocal apprehension which is needed for the various relationships between human beings' (Simmel, in Small, 1905), notably the reactions of groups to strangers on the one hand and on the other the stranger's membership orientation. From the point of view of the group, the arrival of strangers requires adjustments manifested by specific behaviours. These vary according to the nature and relative stability of the relations uniting groups and individuals, the history of their mutual relations and dominant social representations, and the circumstances of the moment. From God to be adored to enemy to be exterminated, the status of the stranger has fluctuated across history and societies (Kristeva, 1991), underlining the ambivalence of collective reactions to this new presence. In Greek cities already, relations towards strangers were ambivalent. They represented both the sacred, since the unknown may have been of divine origin, and the other, intrusive and dangerous. Reactions ranged from fear, sometimes leading to rejection, to tolerance, even attraction. From the point of view of strangers, sociocultural borders will be perceived as more or less closed or open, particularly as long as personal relationships have not been established.

Social relations proceed from a reciprocal interaction during which the two parts must 'adjust' to each other. Wood insists on the double bind which invites the group to modify itself so as to open up to new relations and at the same time invites the newcomer to acquire 'feelings appropriate' for inclusion into the group. Forms of adjustment are dependent on the circumstances at the time the contact occurs, notably the characteristics of strangers, as groups or individuals, and in particular their reasons for leaving and their choice of host country, the conditions of entry into the host group, their desire for some form of membership, the aims and duration of their stay. These circumstances define the quality of the relationships hosts and strangers wish to establish either collectively or individually.

> Each relationship is therefore the resultant of a number of factors which belong in part to the social organization of the group and in part to special conditions of the meeting which are precisely never the same for any two contacts.
>
> (Wood, op. cit.: 245)

Individual factors do not appear as stable as factors related to the organisation of the group and, since they depend on the particular circumstances of each encounter, it is not easy to determine their impact. Each contact represents in a way a unique situation, and a factor which is influential in one situation may have the opposite effect in another.

The arrival of strangers

The arrival, and the departure, of strangers are experienced differently. Whereas the receiving group may experience unwanted outsiders as intruders and trespassers, travellers sometimes experience their new situation as a process of 'secularisation of society' and 'individuation of the person' (Park, op. cit.: 888).

The stranger is the person who enters where he does not belong, who arrives and disturbs. His coming is considered an intrusion because it shatters the tranquillity of social regularity and conformity and also because it lays bare the familiar by representing another strange realm of social reality: 'his knock is that of an outside social reality which suddenly impinges on the group and places its existence (and survival) in question' (Tiryakian, 1973: 48). Since a stranger does not share the basic assumptions of the historically defined cultural group where he arrives, 'he becomes essentially the man who has to place in question nearly everything that seems to be unquestionable to the members of the approached group' (Schütz, 1971a: 98). Troubling, the stranger is equally troubled, disconcerted, outside normal social systems. But, whereas strangeness is mutual, the established group does not perceive itself as 'other', but rather as already there. As previous occupants and owners, they fear the potential for expropriation represented by the newcomers.

At the same time, the individual who leaves 'learns to look upon the world in which he was born and bred with something of the detachment of a stranger [...] The effect of mobility and migration is to secularize relations which were formerly sacred' (Park, op. cit.: 888). Migratory individuals, who find themselves somewhat cast adrift from their own cultural moorings, are then in a position to become 'not merely emancipated, but enlightened'. On the one hand, the past is secularised, on the other, the new culture may never be vested with the same sacredness as the very first one anchored in a distant past for so long. As a result of this liberation from custom, the individual stranger may end up alone, but strengthened and invigorated.

The knowledge of the stranger

If strangers' movements perturb established members, it is because the acquired system of knowledge, although incoherent, inconsistent and only partially clear, 'takes on for the members of the in-group the appearance of a sufficient coherence, clarity, and consistency to give anybody a reasonable chance of understanding and being understood' (Schütz, op. cit.: 95). As a result, it imposes itself on consciousness as natural and obvious. 'Any member born or reared within the group accepts the ready-made standardized scheme of the cultural pattern handed down to him [...] as an unquestioned and unquestionable guide of all the situations which normally occur within the social world' (ibid.). In the absence of evidence to the contrary, this delusion of the obvious may persist. 'Thinking-as-usual' is maintained so long as its basic assumptions hold true, the first one being the absence of change in social organisation. Yet, the stranger is precisely the bearer of an 'evidence to the contrary', challenging the 'knowledge of recipes' whose function is 'to eliminate troublesome inquiries by offering ready-made directions for use, to replace truth hard to attain by comfortable truisms, and to substitute the self-explanatory for the questionable' (ibid.). Thus, the intrusion of strangers disconcerts the natives' mental peace of mind.

Besides, for travellers, their own thinking-as-usual ceases to be operational outside their own borders. The acquired cultural pattern no longer functions as a tested system of recipes and 'reveals that its applicability is restricted to a specific historical situation' (ibid.: 96). Strangers also discover the hurdles set in the 'field of adventure' which the new environment represents. Strangers, when they abandon the singleness of meaning, lose their feeling of security and are left hovering between worlds, bereft of their customary rules of thinking and acting and doubtful about the new ones. The experience teaches them 'that a man may lose his status, his rules of guidance, and even his history and that the normal way of life is always far less guaranteed than it seems' (Schütz, op. cit.: 104).

> Therefore, the stranger discerns frequently with a grievous clear-sightedness, the rising of a crisis which may menace the whole foundation of the 'relatively natural conception of the world', while all those symptoms pass unnoticed by the members of the in-group, who rely on the continuance of their customary way of life.
>
> (ibid.)

The move introduces a double disintegration: disenchantment regarding the validity of the native system goes along with lack of confidence in the new system. A profound discomfort ensues. The crisis, in Thomas's words, 'interrupts the flow of habit and gives rise to changed conditions of consciousness and practice' (Thomas in Schütz, ibid.). In this light, one of the first tests for strangers abroad is to take the full measure of the cognitive and linguistic limitations which separate them from others coming from a different culture.

An unequal social position

Social relations not only unite individuals, they also determine their position within the social structure (Wood, op. cit.). The main characteristics of the social position assigned to the newly arrived are, as stated above, eccentricity, marginality and loss of status. To start with, the ex-centric, inferior or insignificant position conferred on strangers usually occasions a feeling of social devaluation, all the more smarting in that the familiar position experienced until then would have been as a member of a majority, central group: 'the stranger loses the sense of security with which the familiar is associated. In his new environment, he has no recognized and respected status to maintain; he is outside the social group' (Wood, op. cit.: 10). Moreover, even though in principle social relations are based on reciprocity, the reality is that the new partners of the social scene are, in respect of the wanderer, strangers, but unaware of it. This is why the inequality of the relationship is double-edged.

The stranger, who discovers himself as a *déraciné*, is quite distinct from the individual who has 'but one tribal or national tradition to acquire, one language to learn, one political loyalty to develop, one moral code to which to conform, one religion to follow' (Stonequist, op. cit.: 2). The danger for him is to become a hybrid with an uncertain status, since there is a contradiction between the marginal status assigned to him and his own personal need for social esteem

(Hughes, 1949). In some people, this situation is what triggers the feeling of marginality: 'on the margin of each society, partly in and partly out, they experience mentally the contrasts, tensions, or conflicts of the two races or cultures and tend to become a characteristic type of personality' (Stonequist, op. cit.:121). One way or another, far from being static, the stranger's status is unstable and alterable.

Student travellers represent a specific case of mobility and strangeness. Do they experience the ambivalence of their social status or does the context of the EU enable them to transcend it? How do they confront the double dimension of their social space? Does the characteristic of non-membership disappear at some stage in their stay, and what are the factors which facilitate this process? When and under what conditions is it possible to change from one category to another without becoming native? What are the alternatives for the stranger who does not seek membership of the new group?

Symbolic ambivalence: the 'qualities' of the stranger

The stranger is a member of the group whose position implies 'both being outside it and confronting it' (Simmel, 1971: 144). This ambivalent position grants him certain 'qualities' and determines the specific roles bestowed on him. 'In' the group, but not 'of' it, among the qualities he imports, one of the most notable is a specific kind of objectivity between participation and detachment. As a result, relations with strangers are by nature different, more abstract and typified. From the point of view of the individual, ambivalence is two-sided, his relationship to the native context being equally thrown into confusion.

The objectivity of the stranger

The special position of strangers in the social field is best conveyed by the specific characteristic of objectivity and its corollary, the freedom it confers. By objectivity is not meant passivity or lack of participation, but rather a particular kind of attitude.

> Because he is not bound by roots to the particular constituents and partisan dispositions of the group, he confronts all of these with a distinctly 'objective' attitude, an attitude that does not signify mere detachment and nonparticipation, but is a distinct structure composed of remoteness and nearness, indifference and involvement.
>
> (ibid.: 145)

The stranger's objectivity is a product of the outside position which separates him from the factions and partial interests shared by insiders.[8] It is for Simmel 'a positive and definite kind of participation' (ibid.) resulting from the special proportion of proximity and remoteness which characterises him.

Stonequist sees this attitude as akin to the ironical or critical attitude of the observer who, because he combines the insight of the insider with the remoteness of the outsider, 'is skillful in noting the contradictions and the "hypocrisies" in the dominant culture' (op. cit.: 155). But he finds too much emotional tension underneath for this to be true objectivity. Schütz also indicates that the objectivity of strangers is restricted by their native knowledge, which functions as a ruling guide and a filter, creating its own distortions. In other words, the iconoclastic position of strangers may enable them to escape the most glaring ethnocentric oversights[9] and, to a certain extent, 'the myopia of the cave' which mistakes local superstition for truth. But 'the role of Outsider apparently no more guarantees emancipation from the myths of a collectivity than the role of the Insider guarantees full insight into its social life and beliefs' (Merton, 1996/1972: 349).

Objectivity with Simmel refers essentially to disentanglement from local collusions. As a result, the objective spirit is freer because it functions 'according to its own laws under conditions that exclude accidental distortions and emphases' (1971: 145). Since the objective person 'is not bound by ties which could prejudice his perception, his understanding, and his assessment of data' (ibid.: 146), he may liberate himself from subjective restrictions which hinder those whose actions are 'confined by custom, piety, or precedent' (ibid.). This relative autonomy grants him the intellectual bias Park mentioned in relation to emancipation. Indeed, for a reflective light to be triggered, a tribulation must take place, an event, an experience, an encounter. Something must help to untie the traveller from the regular unquestioned adherence to categories deemed normal. Migration and mobility create the necessary distance, a space from which it becomes possible to observe habitual assumptions from the outside. Energies usually bridled by tradition are unleashed. Thought and action are released from conventional inhibitions and creativity is enhanced (Kupferberg, 1998). If mobility and objectivity bestow upon strangers greater freedom from local prejudice, it is because the criteria with which they appreciate data are more general. The stranger is assumed to see things more clearly (Jansen, 1980). Of course, this outside, 'bird's-eye view' applies not only to relations of proximity, but also to those relations which are loosened by distance.

Crossing social borders may be experienced by some as a threat to their identity if the discrepancy between self-identity and ascribed identity is too disturbing. For others, it may be perceived as an exhilarating trip into a new social territory. Anonymous in the sense that their origin is unclear, strangers benefit from 'a certain ease to roam about in the social structure' (Tiryakian, op. cit.: 47). This relative anonymity enables them to enjoy a larger social approach and sometimes to have access to what may be denied to natives. Interactions may be more liberal precisely because they are disengaged. Attraction towards the unknown would only add to the charm vested in the stranger. However, a free spirit runs the risk of passing for an enemy importing viruses that have the potential to break up the group.

Abstract and typified relations

Strangers are not organically linked to the group. As a consequence, mutual relationships are of a 'more abstract nature', based on what is common to a large number and not on specific features. 'With the stranger one has only certain more *general* qualities in common, whereas the relation with more organically connected persons is based on the similarity of just those specific traits which differentiate them from the merely universal' (Simmel, 1971: 146). The same character of distance and proximity is to be found in these relations as in any other, but the commonality shared by a great many becomes preponderant in relations with strangers over the individual elements.

> The stranger is close to us insofar as we feel between him and ourselves similarities of nationality or social position, of occupation or of general human nature. He is far from us insofar as these similarities extend beyond him and us, and connect us only because they connect a great many people.
>
> (ibid.: 147)

The tension comes from awareness that only the general is common and that this accentuates the non-common. The feeling of strangeness is not necessarily due to differences or misunderstandings, but rather to the fact that the elements which contribute to proximity are so general that they lack connecting force: 'their remoteness is no less general than their nearness' (ibid.: 148). In this case, the relation lacks warmth: 'the connecting forces have lost their specific, centripetal character' (ibid.: 147). The dimension which is lacking for the relation to be personal and 'warm' is judged to be the commonality of specific individual traits.

In the stranger, individual traits are at first invisible. This is why strangers are not perceived as individuals, but as strangers of a certain type, not to be evaluated individually, but collectively. Schütz mentions that the greater the distance, the more general and typified the knowledge one has of individuals. A different origin prevails over the other dimensions of identity, working as a symbolic frontier. Wood stipulates that 'it is not so much the fact that the individual is judged to be a type that is to be deplored as the fact that the concept of the type is so often an erroneous one [...] Not infrequently, the concept of the type is a superficial one colored by prejudice' (op. cit.: 267). She adds that this tendency 'to evaluate the individual on the basis of the categories to which he is assigned' (ibid.: 265) might be regarded as a preliminary step, preceding the construction of more specific relations; as 'our acquaintance with a particular person advances, this category tends to become qualified. Its bounds are pushed this way and that until they break down' (ibid.: 266). However, individual traits are slower to be uncovered than categorical traits. In short, the symbolic dimension of the distance–proximity, which forms the basis for familiarity and strangeness as they are perceived by the actor and the other, is paramount in mutual interactions and representations.

One way or another, the symbolic position of strangers is far from comfortable. In the eyes of others, whether from their native social space or from the new space, strangers, bearers of otherness, are troublemakers. Having to consider reality from two points of view, their position may be perceived from the outside as ambivalence, because it manifests itself through fluctuations and contradictions. There is a double wound characterised by, on the one hand, social isolation, uncertainty of status and cultural doubt of the person who cannot take the new pattern for granted and on the other, misunderstanding, even ignorance, of the foreign experience at home. At best, the stranger's loyalty towards the new group, sometimes towards the old one, can only be ambiguous, mobile, alterable since his route poses in acute form the question of dual membership. He appears ungrateful. But, to him, the new culture is 'not a shelter but a field of adventure, not a matter of course but a questionable topic of investigation, not an instrument for disentangling problematic situations but a problematic situation itself and one hard to master' (Schütz, 1971a: 104). The discovery of a 'third place' where the dichotomy would be transcended and where the stranger would find 'his' place, may prove to be elusive for a long time in the traveller's story.

A particular relation

For strangers to be included as members, Wood points out, there must be some modification in the social landscape and the formation of new relations. The factors which will speed up or delay this process depend on the flexibility of the system of relations and on the personal qualities of individual strangers, as well as on the circumstances of the contact. One of the most important of these is the anticipated length of the period of mobility. For the objective of the visit, allied to its duration, temporary or permanent, largely determines the attitude of the strangers towards the new society and, reciprocally, the attitude of society towards them. Wood suggests that 'the degree of mobility which is present determines to a considerable extent the existence of all other attributes' (op. cit.: 247). For example, if the relation is to be permanent, the other features might change, even disappear. Objectivity will be of a different kind in the case of the passing tourist and in the case of the sojourner temporarily involved in the host society. If the stranger is only passing through, his eccentricity may be tolerated; if he is here to stay, his situation will attract more attention. In fact, strangers interest more when they take up residence. In that case, they may be granted economic and social rights, as human rights.[10] But the wandering of passing strangers, free from attachment, makes them suspicious, odd, vaguely unsound.

In his conclusion, Simmel reaffirms the position of the stranger as a *de facto* member of the group, drawing attention to that particular relation which remains somewhat mysterious since we know only its basic ingredients, the mix of distance and proximity and their reciprocal tension, but have yet to explore their special proportion.

In spite of being inorganically appended to it, the stranger is yet an organic member of the group [...] Only we do not know how to designate the peculiar unity of this position other than by saying that it is composed of certain measures of nearness and distance. Although some quantities of them characterize all relationships, a special proportion and reciprocal tension produce the particular, formal relation to the 'stranger'.

(1950: 408)

This statement regarding the mutual nature of the relationship between groups and strangers is one of the main contributions from the sociology of the stranger. The stranger is a product of membership, of what constitutes a member. He is defined by reflection, in the mirror of what membership is. 'The stranger is not a social nonentity; by bringing the unknown into our sphere of perception, he receives a social identity of prime significance' (Tiryakian, op. cit.: 48). Yet the literature on the subject has dwelled mostly on the meaning of the stranger to the host group, with the other side of the relationship remaining relatively unexplained.

Indeed, societies invest the stranger with contradictory roles, as emblem of objectivity and troublemaker at the same time. In the end, the stranger comes to represent the abstract relations which our imagination lends to virtues eluding common understanding. Host communities come to view strangers as the negative of the native, a symbol of otherness, sometimes threatening. This perception maintains distance between them. The stranger becomes the sign of what is incomprehensible, impossible to assimilate, a sublimated expression of inequality (Freund, 1981). The ambivalence of this representation in the collective imagination makes of him the representative of a certain strangeness of humans to themselves (Raphael, 1986). In these conditions, can one cease to be a stranger, both in the eyes of others and in one's own eyes? Under what conditions does the change in status come about? Is the gaze of those who either exclude or include on a par with the stranger's aspirations?

Fragmented identities

The spatial, temporal, social and symbolical disorientation which strangers experience may provoke a personal 'crisis' during which their identity appears somewhat fragmented or torn apart. The social tensions inherent in their marginal situation are reflected in their mind (Stonequist, op. cit.). Changes must take place so that strangers adapt to the new conditions, external and internal, of their existence. During that process of transformation, the situation of strangers evolves, the forms of adjustment adopted constituting as many solutions to their dilemma.

The personal crisis or the conflict of the 'divided self'

The most striking effect of mobility is, as mentioned above, the conflict or crisis which may affect individuals profoundly[11]: 'the conflict of cultures, as it takes place in the mind of the immigrant, is just the conflict of "the divided self"', the old self and the new' (Park, op. cit.: 892). 'It is as if he was placed simultaneously between two looking-glasses, each presenting a sharply different image of himself. The clash in the images gives rise to a mental conflict as well as to a dual self-consciousness and identification' (Stonequist, op. cit.: 145). This period of intense personal mobility, trademark of the initial period, makes the arrival in foreign territory a real rite of passage, 'a longer or shorter period of emotional strain and instability until adequate readjustments are made and assimilation finally effected' (Wood, op. cit.: 159). Having lost something of the old self without regaining full integrity, travellers find themselves as if suspended, in a state of psychological and social uncertainty.

The crisis does not necessarily follow a linear path, but on the contrary may be choppy or cyclical. At first, the feeling of strangeness predominates, one's own strangeness, even in its physical aspects, and the strangeness of the new environment. Travellers must accept the demise of the most intimate part of their identity, left behind and of no use in the new context. Moreover, what constitutes their identity in its most general dimension, their membership to a 'type', acquires in the eyes of others an excessive importance. Individuals feel themselves as homeless, statusless and rootless.[12] Solitude, sometimes alienation, of the person cut off from intimate relations dominates at that time a desolate uninhabited social landscape.

The experience of strangers described in the texts points to the crisis evolving in stages.[13] The first phase usually corresponds to lack of awareness of self as a stranger. It is in sharp contrast with the second phase, during which individuals take the full measure of the problematic situation they find themselves in. Later descriptions of culture shock focus on this second phase, conceived as a problem of mental health. However, the adaptation process develops then in an ulterior phase of adjustment during which identity, both personal and social, is reconstructed, leading eventually to some form of 'acculturation' (Acton and Walker de Felix, 1986; Berry, 1990a, 1990b; Park and Burgess, 1921). Once individuals manage to solve the conflict, the adaptation process is supposed to be over. In this light, the condition of strangeness appears as temporary. It is supposed to disappear as individuals adopt appropriate solutions with a view to a new socialisation.

Indeed, it has been suggested that the exercise in de-socialisation/re-socialisation which permeates the experience of mobility calls for the abandonment of the concept of social pathology which marked migratory studies and the adoption of the notion of partial, transitory disorganisations (Joseph, op. cit.). Instead of being haunted by what he calls the 'phobia of schizophrenia and subjective disintegration' which characterizes the sociology of migration, Joseph pleads for a redefinition of 'civilities', so that a new sociology of adaptation as a continuous life process may appear. However, the onus of redefining civilities rests with the stranger. Indeed, the formation of new social relations, and the efforts required to adjust successfully, depend essentially on the initiative of the newcomers. The natives because of their numerical force have the power to maintain them on the margins. This is why we speak of adaptation strategies in terms of 'social seduction'.

The experience of strangers is comparable to other social situations involving transitions or intracultural mobility. Its specificity, according to Park, is precisely this period of 'inner turmoil and intense self-consciousness', particularly the fact that in their case it may be 'relatively permanent': 'the result is that (the stranger) tends to become a personality type' (op. cit.: 893). For Schütz too, the distinctive sign of the migrant's experience of strangeness is the crisis, particularly the profound feeling of alienation caused by radical linguistic and cultural difference. Whatever the terms used, intercultural conflict, reflexive crisis, or later on culture shock, all refer to the obligatory passage through an interim period of maladjustment and unease which varies in intensity. In the case of a temporary mobility, what role and value will be attributed to this crisis?

A new personality type

The crisis results in personal transformations for the mobile individual compelled to modify at least some identity features in order to adapt. Schütz explains that a new state of consciousness is called for and new rules of interpretation and action must be defined. The first change involves moving from a position of observation into action as the newcomer enters the social scene as a partner: 'jumping from the stalls to the stage, the former onlooker becomes a member of the cast' (1971a: 97). Secondly, the 'new cultural pattern acquires an environmental character. Its remoteness changes into proximity; its vacant frames become occupied by vivid experiences; its anonymous contents turn into definite social situations' (ibid.: 98). Knowledge *in situ* gains contextual richness and distance progressively gives place to proximity. The empty, anonymous, imagined cultural frame becomes a personal place as strangers write in their own experiences. This in turn leads to the third transformation, the remodelling of previous representations of the foreign group. From an internal knowledge, individuals move on to an interactive intercultural knowledge. The insular 'ready-made picture', formed far away, proves to be a fallacy when relations with those represented are introduced.

It is only after some length of time and experience of the new cultural system that newcomers may transit from relative awkwardness to relative communicative, social and cultural ease. However, the wait which maintains them in a learning situation, listening and observing, formulating hypothetical interpretations may be judged as a period of frustrating infantilisation. The adult foreigner is not her/his age culturally. Efforts deployed to master the new system end up in the best cases in a new socialisation. The process varies in degree and in intensity depending on personal and contextual variables. For example, if the choice of departure and host country is deliberate and the stay of a short- to medium-term duration, the test will be lessened. On the other hand, in the case of the migrant who is there to stay, transformations are sometimes comparable to a second birth (Jensen, 1927, in Stonequist, op.

cit.). Most of the time, the degree of socialisation achieved by temporary sojourners is situated between a minimal degree of functional adaptation and a more advanced degree of social and cultural integration.

The modern world, 'with its large-scale communication and movement', is creating new roles for mobile individuals. A new personality type is appearing, symbolised by what Stonequist calls 'the international mind'.

> Each acquisition of a foreign language opens the door to a new way of life. The individual who penetrates deeply enough into a foreign culture becomes a richer personality. He readily shifts from one language to another; from one set of habits, attitudes and values to another. Thus he is in a position to look at problems from more than one viewpoint, and to see the essential ethnocentrism of each. This is undoubtedly what is involved in the creation of the 'international mind', if defined in its profounder meaning.
>
> (ibid.: 178)

The 'international mind', a sort of ideal intercultural personality, is at home in another space, capable of taking on an active role in it because s/he has acquired the competence which enables one to move from one world to another. Beyond the dichotomy or antagonism between cultures, these individuals are members with an identity rooted in place, from which they are free to come and go into other cultures. In contrast to the cosmopolitan mentioned earlier, these individuals recognise the need for nationality and regard their expatriation, and all its vicissitudes, as a positive step in self-development. As a matter of fact, in their case 'self-understanding promotes the understanding of others' (ibid.: 179). As for Simmel's 'stranger', spatial proximity without an aspiration to membership grants her/him a specific intermediary cultural space which those who seek membership may be denied. S/he is privileged in that the host group is not excessively demanding, even tolerant since her/his presence is assumed to be temporary. Stonequist adds that the best example of an international mind is the 'humanistic scholar' whose portrait is ubiquitous in centuries of European scholarship. Present-day student travellers within Europe may be deemed to carry on that tradition of education to otherness through studying.[14]

The knowledge and skills strangers acquire are many. If they import 'qualities', they also discover new ones in themselves. The experience of strangeness places individuals in a situation where adaptation and transformations are necessary if they are to maximise their new life conditions. Life abroad is a powerful experience of discovery of self and others because it shakes personal and social representations and introduces into identity processes perturbing elements, notably the notions of moving identities and flexible cognitive borders. This challenge of redefining self and others is open to a great many individuals now that Europe offers students a new stage on which to position their identity.

Redefining the modern stranger

Simmel's concept rests on a fundamental feature: the stranger is defined as such in a mutual interaction, in relation to a host. Constructing a sociology of strangeness where members of the relationship are symmetrically estranged from each other, whether individuals as in Lofland's world of strangers (1973) or ethnic communities, means extending the original concept considerably. However, changes in social conditions call for empirical and theoretical changes, and for a redefinition of the stranger in the context of modernity (Murphy-Lejeune, 1998, 2000a).

We saw that the stranger is conceived in the sociological tradition as an autonomous actor with a definite origin distinct from that of the group. The social group is itself formulated as a definite, homogeneous entity. But the external visibility of the stranger may not fit with the modern context where strangeness has become a growing reality for most members, where social membership rules are being questioned, as are cross-lines between strangeness and familiarity. Has strangeness become the rule in society? To what extent has the city produced new membership rules? What is the line between strangers and members? What does it mean to be a stranger today, and what impact does the experience have on individuals?

Classical descriptions of the stranger have ignored the pressing question of 'who' the host is and how strangers express their interest in the group. But 'assuming stranger and host can find each other, it does not automatically follow that they have concurring definitions of themselves and of each other', Harman argues (op. cit.: 42), pointing out that the most crucial element is 'one's ability to negotiate within a language of membership' since the world today is 'so strikingly organised in communicative terms' (ibid.). The assumption of sheer communicability previously held falls short of acknowledging the problematic character of the interaction between self and other. As such, Harman's definition of the stranger attempts to free the stranger from being a speechless outsider, whose function is to delimit the group's boundaries, 'that which is beyond', and to show that 'the stranger has become the most important member in a world in which the quest for membership has become a full-time preoccupation' (ibid.: 43). In this light, strangeness is no longer a temporary condition, but a way of life.

The new type of stranger offered is 'everyperson', the modern actor who must adapt to the disintegration of traditional social units. In the first place, strangeness is seen as mutual rather than as the preserve of the actor visibly outside the group. In other words, the quest for membership is from within as well: the modern stranger is 'an outsider on the inside, whose autonomy is only possible through a linguistic outward glance' (ibid.: 44). Secondly, there is another layer of strangeness besides the visible signs of language, customs and dress. The second-order degree of visibility 'tests the stranger's competence at joining' and the modern stranger becomes a 'semiologist who actively reads the social in an effort to achieve membership' (ibid.: 45). Finally, this competence is acquired through 'a fluency in the language of membership'. The main difference, though, between the modern stranger and previous descriptions is that, in the new social conditions which prevail, strangeness has replaced familiarity as the basis of social organisation. In this context, spatial and indeed social membership are being superseded by cultural proximity. Berger's 'homeless mind' (Berger *et al.*, op. cit.) is the epitome of the person capable of living anywhere, adapting to a world evolving constantly, an 'expert navigator who is in between others' and who can only adapt in acknowledging that communication is problematic. Extending the scope of the definition of 'the stranger' is regarded as crucial if one is to understand its impact in the present context.

In the classical tradition, strangeness was investigated as the property of a certain social type and role, that of the stranger. Both Simmel and Schütz conceived of strangeness 'as pertaining to an observable and delimited realm of social relations obtaining between a host society and a person who is not a member' (Gurevitch, 1988). Today, Bauman (1995), among others, argues that the post-modern world is characterised by the permanent condition of living with strangeness. This condition has produced a pervasive uncertainty which is irreducible. He contends that the only emancipatory chance in this world is to recognise the rights of the stranger rather than to fight over who has the right to decide who is strange.

Indeed, many of the traits and terms present in the post-modern debate have much in common with those found in the sociology of the stranger. Was Simmel one of the first to sense and articulate the characteristics of what became dominant features of post-modernism? Certainly, if the latter is understood as a conceptual reaction to the meta-theories of modernity, then Simmel did open up a different way of experiencing and interpreting the social world. His concept of the 'stranger' finds echoes in post-modern interests in plurality, in difference and otherness, in individuality. The nomadism and wandering of travellers, the experience of time as discontinuous and precarious, the social dislocations familiar to post-modern discourse may also be read in Simmel's concept, as if his 'stranger', '*dépaysé, déclassé et déraciné*', was some emblematic form of post-modernism.

However, it may be argued that much post-modern discourse, which relies on Simmel's metaphors and states for example that 'we live in a world of flux, where mobility, experimentation, and transgression have turned into core signifiers' (Pels, 1999: 63), has become a cliché. This post-modern discourse of nomadism, roots, boundaries and identity may well be 'a cognitive plaything of the educated elite' (ibid.: 64). The kind of vocabulary of travel, migration and movement which proliferates in cultural criticism must not hide that there is a need for empirical specification registering differences between the privileged migratory elites and the underclass strangers or between the relatively settled and the marginal and hybrid: 'social inequality also increasingly expresses itself in terms of mobility' (ibid.: 76).

The circulation of ideas follows many paths. Among the many paradoxes bequeathed by Simmel, those relating to the stranger have intrigued generations of researchers. The merging of poles conventionally understood as opposites – fixation and liberation, objectivity and participation, exclusion and inclusion, and most famously distance and proximity – has never ceased to attract attention. The ubiquity of the concepts forged by Simmel is tangible in many disciplines and theories, 'in nearly every methodological genre, from ethnographic reportage, cross-cultural comparison and historical reconstruction to laboratory experiment, survey research and mathematical model-building' (Levine, 1977: 16). Imported into America by Small and Park, adapted to different social contexts and extended in the empirical context of the American city through the Chicago school of sociology, some of them became singularly important. The enigmatic power of 'the stranger' can only be inferred from the ongoing interest it attracts and from the numerous attempts at applying it to specific types of actors.

Conclusion: the characteristics of the stranger

The conceptual heritage delineated in this chapter brings about two fundamental innovations to the research area. The stranger is posited as a full member of our societies and the situation is analysed from the perspective of the individual concerned. However, some issues remain hazy. With the exception of Schütz, the authors ignore the question of language and communication. The two exemplars on which their analyses are based are those of the traditional migrant and of the marginal. The fact that the group is considered as a distinct entity induces a tendency towards dichotomies: the monocultural situation is contrasted to the stranger's situation, the established group is opposed to the outsider. Classical descriptions have ignored the possibility of other positions.[15] Most communities nowadays consist of a continuum from home-grown natives going back many generations, through varying degrees of newness and assimilation, down to the stranger who has just arrived. Finally, a certain hesitation is noted as to the value of the experience. Park and Stonequist particularly seem to hesitate between a pessimistic vision and a messianic vision. Is the stranger 'condemned to live' in a painful in between or does this position allow her/him to gain larger horizons?

In this chapter, we present a synthesis of the main concepts emerging from the sociology of the stranger, summarised in Table 1. This summary identifies some of the key characteristics of the sociology of the stranger, helping to provide an insight into the specific anthropology of the student traveller. By embracing these works, one can provide a new conceptual lexicology to analyse the particular case studies of the student traveller.

The key concepts emerging from the sociology of the stranger are echoed, applied or developed in much subsequent research and have become currency, without always appropriate acknowledgement of their originating author. A genealogical effort in that direction may prove useful in providing a coherent interdisciplinary framework relevant to the field of interculturality (Murphy-Lejeune, 2001). The legacy of this literature is perceptible in many contemporary debates, in discussions on new migrations and transnational spaces, nomadism, diasporas and social change, in studies of social contacts, marginalisation, ethnic relations, intercultural communication and urban ecology, in research on socialisation, socio-cognitive learning and foreign language-and-culture education, as well as in the area of identity, citizenship, culture and politics.

Table 1   The characteristics of the stranger

Space:
mobility–nomadism
dislocations
in between distance and proximity
absence of territoriality
'no owner of soil' (Simmel, 1971: 144)
opened space

Time:
discontinuities
'potential wanderer'
a person 'without history' (Sch ütz, op. cit.)
an inflated present
transient and passing
precariousness

Social position:
a new socialisation
social membership suspended
arrival as an intrusion
between segregation and integration, inside and outside
eccentric and marginal
social status dilemma

Symbolic position:
objectivity and freedom of the stranger
abstract and categorical relations
troublemaker, ambivalence
contradictory roles

Fragmented identity:
disorientation
personal crisis: conflict of the 'divided self'
transformations
learning and growth
multiple identities
individuation of self
adjustment–adaptation–integration

Intended to translate a specific experience of strangeness, to what extent will concepts arising from the contexts of the Jewish diaspora or American immigration be relevant to account for a different experience of strangeness, that of mobile students spending a year abroad in a European member state other than theirs by birth? Our narrative follows the major directions outlined above, examining the student experience in terms of time, space, social integration, personal interactions and identity. The original concepts serve as provisional hypotheses. They are set in a new context, the contemporary world of European study programmes and confronted with the students' testimonies in a constant to-and-fro between historical and empirical data. The emerging concepts represent in a way the fragments of an inventory, chapters in the unfinished book of the stranger. Other chapters remain to be written to complete the book which will establish the conceptual and empirical basis for an anthropology of strangers.

2 Narratives of student travellers

Introduction: a diversity of narratives

The analysis of European student travellers incorporating their experience in a broader theoretical and empirical context provides a new conceptual approach to the research of the stranger. Reviewing previous research on the topic, both in and outside Europe, the European student stay abroad appears as part of a long tradition and at the same time as a new development, relatively under-researched. The student is only a temporary migrant, but considering the 'sojourn experience' (Berry, 2000) alongside a larger set of migrant experiences illuminates both the singularity and the universality of a phenomenon which is becoming increasingly common. The European student experience of mobility exemplifies the new forms which cross-cultural travel and temporary integration from one European member state to another may take.

In this chapter, we present the methodological framework for this exploration of a singular form of mobility. The choices made, notably the selection of a cross-European group and of three different cases of student mobility for observation, break with conventional practice. The fifty students interviewed are then profiled in terms of their age, gender, national origin, and destination. The research unites voices from various origins which, together with the students' fifty individual stories, create a polyphony exploring the experience of strangeness through a diversity of narratives.

International migrants form a highly complex group. Their movements are helped or hindered by countries of origin and receiving countries. The decisions made are subjected to fluctuating political and personal choices. According to Mukherjee, the major narratives of expatriation, exile, immigration and repatriation represent 'four ways of accommodating the modern restlessness, the modern dislocations, the abuses of history, the hopes of affluence' (1999: 84). To Mukherjee, the narrative of expatriation 'drips with respectability, or at least with privilege, but the narrative of immigration calls to mind crowded tenements, Ellis island, sweatshops, accents, strange foods, taxicab drivers, bizarre holidays, strange religions, unseemingly ethnic passions' (ibid.: 79). Furthermore, expatriation, as an 'act of sustained self-removal', allows for the 'dual vision of the detached outsider' (ibid.: 72). But, immigration is not an elegant narrative because you give up status. In the narrative of exile, the spectrum of choice is narrowed too, the stay is imagined as provisional and ties to the home country are a source of suffering. For Simic (1999), the role of the exile is to be forever homesick and misunderstood. However different they are, migrants' narratives present common features which need to be outlined so that particularities stand out. Against this background, this research addresses the issue of the specific narrative of the European student traveller.

The European student traveller, a new stranger

The kaleidoscope of the stranger embraces different narratives, emanating both from within and outside national boundaries. The migrant within refers to cases of social mobility or social marginality. The migrant outside national boundaries suggests a great many cases, which one could tentatively differentiate along four major lines: space, time, status, and most importantly choice. In each of these, individual trajectories may vary enormously.

Spatial issues highlight the distance or proximity, geographical and cultural, as well as communicative, between the countries involved. Here, the tendency is for migratory spaces to become international, rather than just regional, and increasingly interconnected due to easier transports and information flows. Some migrants are welcome while others meet with either reticence or rejection from host countries. Time issues are used by countries to differentiate migrants according to the expected duration of their presence. Some stay for relatively short durations, up to five years, like expatriates or students; others might stay more than ten years, like immigrant workers; many are uncertain of the duration of their stay. This latter category of those who are hesitant is the most volatile because more than time, it is the attitude of the migrant and the reaction of the hosts to their presence which matter. Migrants who refuse to consider themselves as part of the new group remain forever sojourners. To Aciman (1999), they are 'permanent transients' settled in exile. Those who opt for assimilation, on the other hand, emerge from the statistics on migration to become naturalised citizens (Mukherjee, op. cit.). Status issues are complex since shifts from one category to another are frequent. They range from status upon entry, as political refugee, asylum seeker, labour migrant, professional expatriate, international student or foreign resident. Depending on their degree of qualification and prestige, some migrants may be actively sought after. Force and choice in the migration decision draw the line between 'proactive' and 'reactive' migrants (Van Hear,1998). The latter refers to refugees and asylum seekers, deported or expelled migrants, various displaced people and to some degree to economic migrants. The decision to leave one's country of origin may involve not only an element of personal choice, but also a regional element, i.e. specific migration networks and presence of ethnic communities facilitating some itineraries more than others. It also depends to a large extent on the economic and political state of play on the international scene at a given time. The growth performance and demand for labour of wealthier, stable countries influences their recruitment behaviour, with poorer or strife-driven countries providing a natural reservoir of manpower.

So the conditions leading to migration vary enormously from one case to another and produce a diversity of narratives. As mentioned before, part of the experience of strangeness drawn from these narratives appears common to various types of strangers as they pass from one group to another. Another part is unique. Certain general properties[1] which make up the experience can be found across a variety of situations of strangeness. These follow the chronological order which punctuates the process of adjustment-adaptation to a new culture: the objectives and motives before the experience, the strategies used during the process of adaptation, and the outcomes and transformations as a result of the experience. Our hypothesis is that the experience of the student abroad may be analysed in this framework, allowing for a shift in interpretation from the context of migrations to more modern forms of mobility where displacement no longer involves a movement one-way, but rather the potential for a regular to-and-fro movement. In this light, even though experiences of migration and mobility follow a broadly similar progress in the initial stages, the end result may be qualitatively quite different, particularly in the context of the European construction.

The particular experience of strangeness studied here is the individual lived experience defined by the actors themselves. Our aim is to personalise a research area to try and understand it through what the members say about it. In other words, 'affective actions', what the teller feels and says, are as important as 'effective actions', what happened (Kohler Riessman, 1993). The focus is on how students narrate and interpret events, situations and feelings in their own language. The initial research question is both descriptive and comprehensive:[2] what are the main characteristics of the evolving experience of European students spending a year in another culture? Other more specific questions, detailed as the analysis proceeds, derive from this question. What are the parameters of the students' situation? Why does their stay evolve one way or another? What are the various factors, personal or contextual, which come into play in the adaptation process? What are the characteristics of the process and its impact on an individual trajectory? What are the specific learning outcomes which these particular circumstances produce?

European student travellers are defined as new strangers because their experience, close to that of other strangers, is nevertheless distinct. They are temporary strangers, mobile and moving, young, capable of adapting and changing. They are student strangers who integrate their experience abroad into their initial education and training. They are considered in their various dimensions, as individual subjects, social actors, foreign language and culture learners. The critical assumption is that student travellers represent an innovation in European research. There are several reasons for this assumption. Notwithstanding the phenomena of the travelling medieval monk or the grand tour for children of the nobility, the institutionalisation of student mobility open to all is a new phenomenon. The student stay abroad has rarely been studied in its lived entirety, but rather in fragmented segments. The individual perspective, the social actors and their subjective experience, has generally not been brought to light. Student mobility is usually studied from the point of view of one country, looking at incoming and outgoing students, or involves a comparison between a few countries (Admit, 2000). It has rarely been studied from a cross-European perspective and research has often been restricted to one form of mobility, e.g. university exchanges. Previous research, either quantitative or qualitative, has tended to be descriptive. No attempt has been made at theorising the field.

The student stay abroad, tradition and innovation in Europe

In Europe, the student stay abroad represents a hybrid research area, spread between social scientists, educationalists and other specialists in various human sciences. Demographers and sociologists will privilege the geo-political and social entry, international administrators and educationalists will favour the political or institutional study of mobility flows in higher education, and others will select specific aspects relevant to their own field, be it intercultural studies, language and culture education, social psychology, counselling, literature, geography, drama, etc.

In English-speaking receiving countries, cultural contact and change have attracted widespread attention since the 1980s (Ward and Rana-Deuba, 1999) and an impressive array of academic literature on student mobility exists. It has focused on the process of adaptation to the host culture, mostly from the point of view of incoming rather than outgoing students and has progressively steered towards two particular areas of research: the search for variables and the study of the stay as a learning experience. In Europe, research is more recent and tends to measure the results of the stay from various perspectives, mainly academic, linguistic, professional or cultural, and less frequently personal, cognitive or socio-psychological. The predominance of the Erasmus experience in these descriptions grants the institutional perspective a prime position.

Influenced by the literature on migrants' adaptation and integration and on ethnic relations, initial research on student mobility examined the 'adjustment' of students, distinct from 'adaptation', evocative of a longer term phenomenon (Brein and David, 1971). Two assumptions are manifest in this literature. First, adjustment-adaptation[3] is interpreted as an essentially psychological process and, secondly, it is assumed that the sojourner will experience difficulties. These assumptions have dictated most of the early research which deals with the 'cultural disease', granting it a 'clinical flavour' (Furnham and Bochner, 1986: 13). The search for variables likely to affect the experience aspired to measuring their relative weight, so as to explain individual variations in the degree of success achieved (Church, 1982). The multiplicity of variables, which may for example include individual factors, i.e. intrapersonal, interpersonal and biological, as well as contextual factors, i.e. spatial-temporal, geo-political and control (Lonner, 1986), underscores the multidimensionality of the phenomenon.

Similarly, some Europeans have listed factors likely to influence the stay (Coleman, 1997). Mübig-Trapp and Schnitzer (1997) produced a structural equation model of factors affecting student cross-border mobility. But research on these variables is uneasy. It highlights the complexity of the interaction between individuals, the situation and environment, and the difficulty of isolating factors which function in a circular fashion. The tendency to multiply and subdivide 'predictive variables' (Wiseman *et al.*, 1989) only serves to confuse the picture. As a result, these overlapping studies produce specific results on particular elements which are too varied to afford a coherent picture.

Another research trend consists in considering the experience abroad as a learning process (Bochner, 1972, 1982; Guthrie, 1975; Kim and Gudykunst, 1988). Adapting to a new environment activates certain dispositions in the individual, who experiences 'growth' as a result of the tribulations inherent in passing from home to host culture. Berry (1990a, 1990b) describes this transformative process in terms of 'acculturation', conceived in a cross-cultural psychology framework as changes resulting from first-hand contact between two cultures. He differentiates four acculturation attitudes or strategies: integration, separation, assimilation and marginalisation.[4] Others, bringing in language acquisition theories (Brown, 1980; Clarke, 1976; Schumann, 1978), explored the cognitive dimension of the process. Acton and Walker de Felix (1986) have presented a model of development in four stages[5] – tourist, survivor, immigrant-resident, citizen – which suggests that stages in a learning process follow a somewhat similar pattern which includes a critical point, here called 'the acculturation threshold', between the second and the third. It postulates that the first two stages are strongly linked to the first language, but that, with time, the central cognitive system opens up more and more to the foreign language schemes and structures. However, crossing the acculturation threshold is perceived to require immersion or *in situ* learning rather than a classroom situation. This learning perspective is new in that it implies a reversal of views: the experience is finally considered as an opportunity for the traveller's personal enrichment rather than just as a stressful period.

If the stay abroad is a special learning place, research needs to identify the outcomes of the stay on individuals (Murphy-Lejeune, 1997, 2000b). Outcomes studies vary according to the perspective adopted. Institutional research focuses on academic, communicative and cultural impacts[6] (Teichler, 1991). Educationalists, trying to establish a pedagogical framework for the stay (Parker and Rouxeville, 1995), may identify objectives and attainments in terms of the linguistic, cultural, intellectual, personal, interpersonal and professional competences the stay promotes (Convey, 1995; Duenas-Tancred and Weber-Newth, 1995). Linguists tend to look at itemised aspects of language acquisition in a live context (Coleman, 1995; Freed, 1995; Milton and Meara, 1995; Regan, 1995; Walsh, 1994), leaving everything else aside. So far few European descriptions exist of the range of specific competences activated through the experience (Byram, 1997a). Besides, hardly any attempt has been made at grounding the research in empirical observation. The tendency consists rather in defining ideal models of competence which can serve as curriculum guidelines in a top-down fashion. Moreover, existing definitions of the area embrace the live experience in a particular educational context, generally referring to language-and-culture learning in an institutional environment (Byram, 1997b). Behind the various terms used to describe this general competence – 'intercultural communicative competence' (ibid.), 'sociocultural competence' (Byram *et al.*, 1997), 'transcultural competence' (Baumgratz-Gangl, 1993), 'intercultural communication competence' (Martin, 1989) – the attempt to theorise the field within education is different in Europe in that it links language and culture discovery,[7] whereas previous research tended to neglect language issues. In any event, whatever little research exists in Europe on the outcomes of the stay is still partial or normative.

Fragmented data and a research topic scattered in many areas, with projects directed at specific aspects of the experience to the detriment of a coherent whole, characterise the research on student mobility. Kim's attempt (1988) at constructing a theory of intercultural adaptation through an integrative model which could be experimented with is a welcome opening, bringing in various disciplines and examining many aspects of the experience in a general framework. The multidimensional model she presents clarifies the relationships between four main elements of adaptation: individual and social communication, environmental factors, personal predispositions, and adaptation outcomes. As such, it accounts for both processes and outcomes. But the model is at once too simple and too ambitious. Adaptation is defined in general terms and includes any group of newcomers. The model differentiates the main dimensions of the experience and highlights a great many indicators on which to work, but remains abstract.

By comparison, two broad types of studies helped to progress towards a better understanding of European student travellers. The first type are large-scale[8] quantitative evaluations. The Study Abroad Evaluation Project examined 82 study programmes in the United States and four European countries[9] (Burn, *et al.*, 1990; Carlson *et al.*, 1990; Opper *et al.*, 1990). Academic, language, cultural, and professional impacts on students were examined. The most complete evaluation in this style concerns the Erasmus experience, surveyed regularly from 1988 (Maiworm *et al.*, 1991, 1992, 1993; Teichler, op. cit.). The main results indicate that students consider their study period abroad as a major component of their professional and personal development. However, research findings vary depending on the instruments used: data from self-reports reveal more impact than standardised measures (Kaufmann *et al.*, 1992). There are other limits to the Erasmus evaluations. The list of questions asked includes some which could apply to any student experience and others aimed solely at the evaluation of the Erasmus experience, the institutional perspective corresponding to the official mandate. The more personal aspects are treated cursorily since closed questions or statistical information exclude individual voices. Nevertheless, the broad canvas provided offers a quantitative background for the interpretation of qualitative data. The general tendencies outlined are sometimes echoed in the personal testimonies we collected with a smaller sample.

The second type of research analyses the experience on the basis of qualitative data, diaries (Pearson-Evans, 2000) or interviews with students (Martineau and Lusato, 1995). In the latter, the themes and chronological presentation are close to ours. The mobile minority of European students is seen as possessing a trump card for their professional future. Though institutional aspects, in particular studying abroad, are prominent, a prime position is granted to the idea of personal 'project', maturing over time from sometimes distant origins.[10] Mobility is considered as a personal adventure and 'whatever the context, the lived experience presents similarities: preparation for departure, adaptation on arrival, culture shock upon immersion into the host society, and return shock when old habits must be resumed' (ibid., our trans.: 11). The chronological development represents a sequence particularly apt to account for the experience. Interestingly, this longitudinal study is based on three interviews with each student, before departure, during the stay, and three months afterwards. Such a method, which requires a considerable human investment, allows for the dynamics of the experience and evolution of representations to emerge clearly, but requires a big investment.[11] It seems to be the case that qualitative studies are starting to appear in Europe[12] (Rosselle and Lentiez, 1999), staking out landmarks for descriptions of the student experience to be contrasted[13] so as to cross-fertilise empirical research in the area. The incentive is to reinstate the users' voice within a narrative from which individual substance was sometimes missing. However, the absence of a theoretical framework from much research projects somewhat restrains the interpretation of data and their significance.

To sum up, descriptions of European mobile students have dealt mostly with Erasmus exchanges, but ignored other forms of mobility. Empirical research is scarce and, even when attentive to the students' voices, focused on institutional aspects of the experience. Data are frequently analysed without reference to a conceptual background for a more comprehensive understanding of the phenomena. Although our research object is similar, different conceptual and methodological choices orient our work in a specific way.

Methodological choices

Our methodological choices are new, notably in terms of the selection of students and in terms of the analysis framework. The students represent three case studies, a 'case' implying several individuals in a similar situation. Their stay abroad is organised through three different institutional programmes, which form three different cases of social entry. The analytical approach tries to capture the process through a 'comprehensive' method. It fluctuates between the set of existing data presented above, which belong to another time and place, and the set of empirical data collected by present-day interviews in a contemporary context. This pendulum-like movement between working hypotheses and empirical data allows for our two main objectives to be pursued: to reveal the specific features defining European student mobility in the theoretical light of the sociology of the stranger, and to focus the analysis on the mobile individual in order to account for a definition of the experience by those concerned.

The phenomena under scrutiny naturally call for a qualitative approach which details personal accounts of the experience, in all its ambiguity and complexity. Migrants' life stories acquired an innovative value in the Chicago school tradition (Thomas and Znaniecki, 1918–1920), where they revealed the concrete substance of socialisation processes in their dual orientation, as a general tendency and as a singular illustration. The European students' testimonies may be interpreted in this light as slices of life, miniature stories of a socialisation process. The type of information elicited includes sets of representations or thoughts and descriptions of social practices or experienced facts. The narrative focuses on personal history, the students' actual experience abroad, the images they construct of people, places, groups of individuals or scenes, the relationships they entertain among themselves and within themselves, their explanations regarding their choices and their itinerary, as well as descriptions of their stay and its progress. Each story is understood as a narrative in the broad sense of an account of connected events revealed by narration rather than in the more technical sense. Nevertheless, in our approach, the language collected, seen as constitutive of reality and establishing meaning (Murphy-Lejeune *et al.*, 1996), is a central element of the observation. Personal narratives are valued 'because of their subjectivity – their rootedness in time, place, and personal experience, in their perspective-ridden character' (Personal Narratives Group, 1989, in Kohler Riessman, 1993: 5).

The aim was to gain a first-hand in-depth picture of student travellers and their experience. This is why the comprehensive semi-directive interview was selected as the principal method of data collection. Before the interview, a written questionnaire covering a similar range of issues was used as a way of making contact with the respondents, introducing them to the topics under discussion. It also provided detailed but limited information, useful for quantifiable or biographical data. The topics covered in the questionnaire[14] included motivations and objectives, previous experiences abroad, initial contacts with the foreign culture, preparation before leaving, ideal duration of the stay, entry into the host culture through activities and contacts, exposure to the local culture, personal assessment of the year abroad and learning outcomes. The questionnaire corresponds to a preparatory stage in the inquiry. Its results were partially used.

The interview schedule[15] follows the chronological progress of the stay, leading the students to trace retrospectively their steps from the origins of the project to the day of the interview. It recapitulates the parameters defining the experience of newcomers, reviewed in the analysis of the migrant situation and of the various figures of strangers. Organised in three parts, it brings to light the period before the experience, i.e. previous travelling experience and personal background and attitudes, the actual process of entry and adaptation into the new culture, including immersion into the environment, social networks, contacts home as well as phases and degree of integration, and finally the after effects of the stay in terms of personal development and intercultural learning. Some of the issues investigated are intermingled. Duration of stay and motivations are linked and together impact on membership orientation. In the case of a European study programme, the personal project is set in an institutional frame which governs to a point the modalities of the stay, particularly its length, and membership orientation is presumed to be momentary. Social entry refers to the strategies adopted in relation to accommodation, professional role, social activities and personal relationships in the new society. The modalities presiding over entry may determine relations to the original culture, for instance, withdrawal towards home groups or openness to the outside. The way travellers wish to enter a new culture is also a function of the distance – proximity between cultures, of evolving social representations – which in turn may determine the existence or absence of a culturally induced 'crisis'. The effects of the experience may be approached in terms of the processes and strategies set in motion as well as in terms of the outcomes or transformations individuals appraise. In short, the issues covered in the interview schedule include aspects of the experience which are often inter-dependent.

The interviews, carried out by the same person, took place in various places and countries, the main constraint being the moment of data collection since the idea was to obtain a retrospective look over the experience.[16] Consequently, the interview dates were either immediately before the students' departure from the host country or shortly after their return home, and took place over three summers.

The interview situation is a personal encounter, a face-to-face conversation which goes beyond mere information taking. A dialogic situation *par excellence*, it is an experience in itself for researcher and interviewee alike researching meaning together. The chronicle of a slice of life which forms a distinct biographical unit places the narrators in the position of witness of their own history. They recollect it by producing a constructed discourse on a period of life which may not have been verbalised previously. In that way, by giving sense to a period of their life, their discourse represents a crucial moment in the construction of self. Some had thought about it or had talked about it with others, and their testimonies are richer for it. For most students, even the most reticent, the interview was a welcome opportunity to divulge a lived experience and to try and give it sense. No encouragement was necessary. The open questions allowed them to talk willingly and freely, taking control to a large extent. The researcher, with her own subjective world, is listening to a singular voice while at the same time paying attention to echoes to be found from one testimony to another. She is involved in the process of discovery as much as the interviewee. For the two interlocutors, the encounter is an exploration and a reciprocal exchange, even if one progresses on an uncharted terrain which the other is marking out with beacons. The essential characteristic of qualitative methods lies in this special relationship which they create between humans. It is the analogy between observed and observer which makes comprehension possible.

The exploration of lived experience sets the stage for thoughts, mental states or social behaviours. The emerging discourse transforms the internal experience into an outside reality, recorded on a tape, over which the original author somewhat loses ownership. Several choices were made to insert the students' presence in the narrative. The many quotations, recalling their own voice in the language they chose, represents a way of giving back the narrative to its rightful author. The students' language was not 'normalised' or corrected during the transcription. It is presented in its original form, which includes the many idiosyncrasies and inaccuracies inherent in oral talk in an informal conversation. Finally, the narrative and the discussion are frequently in the present tense so as to communicate the immediacy of their tales.

However, the overall research process involves several linguistic transformations. Transcribing oral texts into written form constitutes a major aspect of these. An effort was made to report the oral language of each individual without any intervention other than punctuation. Punctuation, reinstated in the written transcription, breaks up in a given way the continuous flow of spoken discourse. However, intonation alone does not always signal when a sentence which follows a train of thought actually ends. Two features of spoken discourse were also noted. First, non-lexical expressions such as 'eh, heu, ya, well', which mark a pause or hesitation in the formulation of thought, leave to the listener the task of imagining an unfinished sentence. Secondly, in oral discourse, the locutor often stages other locutors through indirect speech, either self, when the teller recalling one's own words acts two parts, or others whose words are quoted. This type of discourse (in italics in the text) adds life to the tale and peoples it with ghost speakers.

The analysis of the interviews is a process which consists in breaking up data to reassemble them in a different order. Here, it means reconstructing the inner world of others from the discursive elements available. All classifications rest on theory. But raw personal documents have no theoretical value in themselves. In order for a theory to emerge from the data, individual stories must be scrutinised and interpreted into a whole, following the logic of analytic induction (Znaniecki, 1934). In our case, each text or interview was read and analysed for itself vertically, revealing a singular architecture. Recurring themes or significant fragments were then classified into semantic categories for the two sets of data and confronted to the others along those lines. Variations on the same theme, which take on a personal shade with different interviewees, were noted. At the end of this initial phase of identification, a tentative definition of the broad phenomenon in its essential characters and the main analytical categories became visible, at both levels. This first picture was reformulated as each text or interview was examined within the general framework. From one interview to another, a new horizontal organisation allowed for links to be made, for confirmation or contradiction of previous results as well as for subjective variations to appear. As a result, the theory, rather than being totally grounded in the empirical data (Glaser and Strauss, 1967), was confronted and counterbalanced by them, and a new theory emerged.

Working on the substance of language implies trying to identify the set of meanings which a concept takes on with different locutors, so as to establish a semantic field for it. This elaboration provides a cartography of 'the language of strangeness'. This kind of work highlights the plasticity and multiplicity of realities, the subjective perspectives adopted. These different stories about specific events, connected around the topic of 'the student stay abroad', are analysed as so many narratives which tell us about major parts of student travellers' lives.

Three case studies

The experimental corpus is organised around three case studies representing three distinct study programmes. The general situation of the students is similar, but the specific course of their entry into the new culture produces different outcomes. Programmes abroad have become more common over the last ten years to such an extent that in some institutions, as one of the students, Hugo, thought, 'you have to apply for not going abroad because everybody is going!'. Nothwithstanding, the stay abroad is neither a common experience, nor a compulsory element in most European students' route, not even for language specialists (with the exception of the UK). A period of residence abroad is sometimes perceived as elitist since some financial investment, which may act as a key obstacle, is usually necessary. Students who opt for this kind of education are generally aware of the added value this difficult choice confers.

The three European programmes selected – (1) Erasmus university exchanges; (2) bilateral language assistants programmes; and (3) a French *grande école* international study programme, the Ecole Européenne des Affaires de Paris or EAP[17] – differ in terms of the official status of the stay abroad in their curriculum.

The Erasmus programme, instituting student mobility within what was the EC, recognises and accredits periods abroad, but the Erasmus stay appears as the most volatile of the three, subjected to the greatest variations between countries. Information on exchanges and recruitment of students varies depending on the openness of each third-level institution and the interest of members of staff. The informal ex-Erasmus network often works more efficiently than official channels. Places are sometimes hard to get for sought-after destinations, as Marco reports about his university in Rome, or on the contrary not taken up when available, as Hélène and Régine report about their university in Paris. Recruitment is usually in between these two extreme positions and varies according to the goodwill of the teaching staff, in the absence of specialised administrative services such as international offices, according to the information available, and above all according to the students' plans. Indeed, personal initiative plays a role proportionate to institutional shortcomings. Three key barriers to mobility seem common to most European countries: language, finance, and recognition and/or admissions; others, attitudinal or cultural barriers, such as the ethnocentrism of some universities and fears of students, or the workload involved in the management of the programmes, were found to be more country specific (Admit, 2000).

The other two professional programmes reveal a greater continuity between initial training and the period spent abroad.

Assistants teach their own language in a country whose language they are studying and their stay may be linked to a postgraduate research project in the foreign culture. Recruited among language students, the relationship they entertain with the foreign language and culture is more passionate, as we will see, than is the case for non-language students. If the stay abroad is not always compulsory for them, it nevertheless represents a logical development in a professional route focused on the study of foreignness. Particularly interesting, and despite its long existence in Europe, this experience abroad remains relatively unexplored (Byram and Alred, 1993; Byram, 1993).

In the EAP programme, there is not one year abroad, but three, involving study and work experience in three European languages and contexts. The students study at both Paris and Oxford and have the option of studying in either Berlin or Madrid. The overall curriculum is built on the concept of residence abroad with a close correspondence between the personal project, the experience and the professional future it leads to. The European dimension is part and parcel of their life, and sometimes may include an international dimension since recruitment outside Europe is possible. The expected benefits accrued include European mobility, language competence, intercultural communication, ability to feel at home in Europe, capacity to adapt to and work with a range of individuals within different cultural contexts and networking with a very cosmopolitan group of classmates and alumni. The EAP students have all made the initial choice of professional internationalisation in their course of study.

Prior to the stay abroad, the three groups differ in their degree of language competence, the mobility capital they have acquired, and the openness to foreignness existing in their family environment, as we will see. During the stay, the principal difference consists in the social conditions relative to their contacts with natives and entry into the new culture. Erasmus students find themselves with other foreigners in varying proportion, but among a majority of native students. EAP students find themselves foreigners among a multicultural group where foreign and native students are mixed, in more or less equal proportion for the Parisian year studied. Language assistants find themselves generally as one single foreigner among a largely predominant group of natives. This quantitative difference draws attention to the interplay between minority and majority groups in social relations and undoubtedly sways the experience of the arriving lone stranger. The choice of three case studies facilitates research into fluctuations as well as regularities across groups.

The profile of the students

Fifty students took part in our study between 1993 and 1996: 15 Erasmus students, 15 language assistants, 20 EAP students. What is their profile? Individual variables discussed here include age, gender, national origin and foreign destination, but a more personalised portrait is presented in the profiles of interviewees.[18]

Age represents the least differentiating personal variable. The essential characteristic of the group is age: they are all between 20 and 26 years old, the majority being 20 to 22 years old, which corresponds to the Erasmus results showing the average age as 23 (Maiworm *et al.*, op. cit.). Young and free, they rarely have family responsibilities. The stay generally takes place in the third year of university studies for Erasmus students, after the initial degree as a postgraduate year for language assistants, and varies more for EAP students since entry may be in the third year of post-secondary studies for French students following the *grandes écoles* system or at the end of their graduate studies for some German students, older than most. As an example, the age distribution for the EAP group for the 1992–1995 Berlin strand indicated that out of a total of 128 students, 37 per cent were less than 20, 31 per cent were 20–21, 21 per cent were from 23 to 24, and 11 per cent were 25 years old or over.

In terms of gender distribution, our particular sample included 27 females and 23 males, with strong variations among groups. In the EAP sample group, there were only 4 females for 16 males, while the opposite applies to the assistants sample, with 14 females and only 1 male. The Erasmus group, as expected, is more balanced with 9 females and 6 males. Data for the whole EAP group that year showed that females represented 32 per cent of the student population and males 68 per cent. Data for the French assistants sent to Ireland in 1994 indicated that 33 candidates were female and 7 were male. The strong male presence in the EAP group and the strong female presence in the assistants group may be understood in terms of academic subject choice and concomitant professional orientation: international management and business careers attracting more men and language careers, sometimes as teachers, more women.

The scarcity of cross-European research on student mobility guided the selection of students on the basis of national diversity within the EU.[19] Efforts were made to contact students from the twelve European member states at the start of the interviews. Results are uneven between the three programmes, the greatest national mix being observed in the EAP group since the sample represents a multicultural group of thirteen national/ethnic origins.[20] By contrast, the assistantship programme, which is the result of bilateral agreements, includes only two national groups, here Irish and French. The Erasmus sample is in between in relation to national diversity, but citizens from countries with the most-taught European languages are easier to contact than those from countries with lesser-taught languages, presumably less numerous. For example, Greece is not represented in our sample, an absence made up by the inclusion of a Russian citizen and a New Zealander. As a result, distribution according to national origin within the overall sample is irregular, the Irish and French contingents alone representing 50 per cent of the total. National origin is far from straightforward though: some students possess more than one, for example several passports. Many of them have foreign origins, mobility being part of a family history before its extension into a personal history.

Destinations are less varied. The most represented destination in our study, for 26 of the students, is France, since all the EAP students were based in Paris that year and the Irish language assistants were also in France. Next comes Ireland, host country for 19 students, the 9 French assistants and 10 Erasmus students. For the other Erasmus students, host countries were Belgium for Amin and Lucy, Germany for Julie, Spain for Maria and Italy for John, reflecting the weight of the languages taught in Europe. But their narratives sometimes stage previous experiences in other contexts. The conditions of the observation, based between Ireland and France, explain the lack of diversity in destinations. It also explains why a systematic study of the cultural perceptions related to a specific country was not possible.

The international nature of the group meant that two working languages were used, English and French, and switches from one language to the other were constant. Interviews were conducted in their first language for the majority, and in a foreign language, English or French, for others whose linguistic mastery varied. Oral data were gathered in the two languages and translated, where needed, in the written text. All in all, the empirical corpus includes 32 interviews in English and 18 in French. In short, the research adopts a cross-national and cross-language approach.

Beyond national, linguistic, cultural, social, professional and personal diversity, the fifty students with whom an interview relationship was set up spoke with the same enthusiasm and the same desire to convey their experience. None opted for the anonymity which was offered to them.[21] Their selection proceeded unsystematically and informally, as and when contacts were made possible through personal intermediaries. The interview gave them, and it surprised some of them, the opportunity to go back over their experience and to become aware in a reflexive way of their own social construction. Their voices continue to be heard, a few years on, and are echoed in the web of interpretations which reveal the fundamental heterogeneity of individuals. From a set of very diverse life stories, regularities may be found in the way they put into words the internal perception they have of their experience.

Conclusion: a narrative polyphony

Polyphony or the combination of parts which form an individual melody and harmonise with others refers both to the image of the choral model of communication celebrated in the Palo Alto school and to the concept created by Bakhtin to designate the multiplicity of voices which inhabit a language situation (Kramsch, 1993). The polyphony inside is manifest in several ways. Fifty individuals from three exchange programmes talk about their sojourn in six different European countries. Within each interview, themes interweave and the echoes are perceptible at various moments in a minor or major mode. Inside the written text, it comes in the form of a theme, furtively mentioned without being fully developed, which reappears in a new light elsewhere.[22] It comes in the shape of a student's individual voice, called upon to support a given issue, but disappearing only to reappear later in the narrative. For example, Matthew describing his difficult arrival appears in chapter 5, followed by the solitude attached to the beginning of his stay, and finally the different phases of his adaptation later. A same moment may be heavy with multiple meanings and repetitions underscore that a same event may be brought to light in different ways. Diversity nevertheless requires order. Looking for some explanatory coherence means that individual stories are looked into and segments are extracted from their original context for the general narrative. The difficulty of translating the many dialogic conversations which the interviews represent into a general interpretation is only partially assuaged by the place given to the students' voices in the report through extensive quotations.

This research is an account engaging voices of various origin: voices from the past emerging from the set of texts staging diverse figures of strangers, voices at the intersection of various academic discourses and disciplines, voices of the students collected and reported in two languages, speakers expressing a European experience anchored in several linguistic and national contexts, voices inside their discourse of locutors representing themselves or other characters, and finally inside the narrative reverberating voices of the themes intermingling and overlapping. The polyphony of the texts encourages consideration of the students' narratives, mirrors of a unique and plural experience, as transitory, hybrid, ever-changing, engaging processes of interaction, exchanges and borrowings at all levels.

The account on the meaning of the experience of strangeness is obviously unfinished. The search for meaning, contingent on the limits of intersubjective comprehension, is all the more fragile when one researcher is involved, when one take for collection of data is privileged, when one analytical approach is preferred, when one interpretative framework is selected. The richness of the interviews transcends one narrative. The unfinished score invites other voices to participate in the polyphonic work reported here.

3 Mobility capital: a taste for living abroad

Introduction: a migratory elite

EU citizens are by and large not accustomed to mobility. The right of residence in another member state offered to every European citizen is more an ideal, and European mobility more a dream, than a reality. Since mobility has only recently entered European discourse, it is conceivable that a certain delay is required between official policy and actual results, particularly where changes in lifestyles are concerned. The Student population reflects this general tendency. Like professional expatriates, student travellers are part of a minority significant enough to be distinct from the majority of their peers. This minority may be regarded as a migratory elite (Musgrove, 1963) in Europe, but not just for quantitative reasons. Our hypothesis is that they represent a qualitative elite as well. Ready 'to move', as they often say, they are open to changes in their environment: language, personal entourage, lifestyle, working style. They actually aspire to those changes, to this rift with the past which the desire for adventure signifies. They usually benefit from a high level of education. From an economic viewpoint, the stay abroad is sometimes perceived as a luxury, but it is frequently funded by the students' personal efforts. In what ways are they different from the sedentary majority of a similar age group? What are the forces which in a personal itinerary induce one individual to travel more than another? What individual events direct their route towards mobility?

We suggest that the main difference between student travellers and their peers rests in the acquisition of what we shall refer to as mobility capital. In economics, the term 'capital' is defined as a stock which has value as a source of current and future flows of output and income. Becker (1964) divided capital between human and non-human capital. Human capital comprises the stock of skills and productive knowledge that are embodied in people. Human capital enables an individual to improve her/his skills and earning capacity. Later on, Bourdieu (1980), borrowing from Weber, applied the term to other assets circumscribed in the notion of cultural capital. Mobility capital is a subcomponent of human capital, enabling individuals to enhance their skills because of the richness of the international experience gained by living abroad.

The students' mobility capital is composed of four main constituent elements. In this chapter, we analyse these elements: family and personal history, previous experience of mobility including language competence, the first experience of adaptation which serves as an initiation, and finally the personality features of the potential wanderer. Taken together, these various dimensions help to identify each student's mobility capital before departure. For, in time, the taste for travelling, *l'invitation au voyage* of Baudelaire's poem, precedes the actual experience in the imagination of the future wanderer. The urge to travel anticipates the experience so that the longer stay abroad is often expected in the end as a mandatory stage in a life story. It could even be said that one of the main features differentiating travelling students from sedentary students lies in this peculiar vision which makes them anticipate and prepare for the future, ahead of their counterparts.

Here, we look at the construction over time of a traveller's story. How does one become a potential wanderer, the person who will opt for a different course, breaking with chronological linearity, ready to experiment with precariousness? Wandering potentialities do not appear suddenly. Rather, they are etched in a life story and feed partly on family experience, partly on the traveller's own previous experiences and personality.

Family history and mobility

The experience of foreignness takes place in a historical and personal context. The historical context of our day lies in the construction of the EU and the necessity to encourage the mobility of human beings. The personal context refers in the first place to the role of families in facilitating mobility for their offspring. To what extent does family history influence individual trajectories?

Initially, the idea of establishing a determining link between certain family contexts and the desire to wander provides an attractive hypothesis. The families of our respondents appear open to foreign experiences if one is to judge by the relatively high number in our sample of families of mixed origin, of those having experienced expatriation, having travelled in dream or reality or having made international educational choices. The family links our students entertain with foreignness go from the most constraining, those of blood relations, to the most fortuitous, such as parental attraction to foreignness.

In a few cases, foreign links come in the shape of direct blood lineage, one of the two parents or of the four grandparents of the student having at one stage been a foreigner in the student's country of residence or one family member having married a foreigner.[1] Daniel's parents are Italian, but reside in Belgium. Hugo's mother is Polish and married to a German citizen. Eric's mother is Belgian and his father Italian, and they live in Luxembourg. Quantitative results show that six EAP students out of twenty, eight Erasmus students out of fifteen, and three assistants out of fifteen have some form of foreignness in their family background. They represent a total of seventeen students out of fifty or 34 per cent of the sample population. Of these, 22 per cent are the direct progeny of mixed marriages.

These family stories of migration and mobility come in many shapes and forms. In some cases, the grandparents emigrated. Marco from Rome has one Hungarian and one German grandmother who both married Italian men. Sometimes, the connection is less direct and involves a family member marrying outside the customary national compound. Sylvie's sister is married to an Irishman. Maria's family lived in Spain for ten years and two members of her family married Spaniards. It is also often the case that foreign connections breed foreign connections. For example, Marina's mother is Serbo-Croatian. Her father, whose father is from Luxembourg and whose mother is from Germany, was born in the Belgian Congo, studied in France, and settled back in Luxembourg. Young people born and bred in these hybrid families are accustomed to multiple nationalities, in particular to hyphenated identities, and crossing national borders is part of their everyday life scape.

Family mobility in the shape of a migration represents another connection. Tom's parents left Northern Ireland to settle in New Zealand. Eric's paternal grandparents left Italy when his father was 20 and his maternal grandparents left Belgium for Luxembourg. Mobility may also take the shape of a lengthy expatriation for professional motives, as is the case for Régine who spent seven years in Hawaii where her father worked as an astronomer, or in the case of Maria whose father spent ten years as a businessman in Spain. John too is used to this kind of professional mobility through his sisters and brothers who all work outside Ireland. Professional mobility is noticeable in families where seeds of strangeness already exist. For example, Marco's parents who are from mixed families themselves and who are fluent in four languages spent several study and work periods abroad. Another lever which may also contribute to this kind of route is internal mobility or the fact that within one's own country parents may have moved many times.[2] According to Jürgen, his family's numerous movements in Germany gave him a certain lightness whereby mobility experiences, even transcultural, become relatively customary and routine-like.

Because of their motley origin or their place of birth, some of these travellers possess several nationalities, sometimes several passports and usually more than one language. Difference, in the form of plurilingualism or pluriculturalism, is their natural habitat. Accustomed from an early age to travelling, they make up a special cohort of students. They describe themselves with phrases such as 'hybrid' (Damien, Eric), 'cosmopolitan' (Viktor), 'international' (Tom) or 'multicultural' (Christophe, Marina).

The practice of mobility, whether temporary or open-ended, varies from one European country to another. This is probably what Elena means when she interprets the word 'travel' in an Irish context as meaning 'emigration' and not 'stay abroad' since in Ireland for a long time travelling referred to permanent emigration rather than to journeying. She explains that her parents 'don't travel' because her father is the only one of a family of five children who has not emigrated, though in fact they do travel.

When I say they don't travel, I mean they haven't ever emigrated and come back... because they travel every year, you know, they... go on holiday, on holiday to different countries.

National traditions of migration, in particular the existence of diasporas in specific areas, create a natural climate enticing young people to go away or not. Many members of John's family live abroad and encouraged him 'to go and see the world' while young. In such a national context, potential wanderers find it easier to embark on their own personal journey.

Students who do not benefit from such connections abroad mention other signs demonstrating their family's openness in the absence of physical mobility. Welcoming foreigners to one's home corresponds to a form of virtual mobility. One becomes accustomed from a young age to physical proximity with strangers in one's domestic space. As a result, even when circumstances are not conducive to a real journey, this family practice opens up one's household borders. Lucy says that she always got on well with the foreign students who stayed in their house in the summer and that their presence contributed to her desire to travel. In Mathilde's home, visits by foreign groups in the context of town twinning produced a change of atmosphere and inspired a kind of magnetism: 'it made you feel like going to see what it was like in other countries instead of always having other people coming to your place'. Other people's visits to one's home-place and the intercultural contacts which they occasion are part of student travellers' mobility capital and many of them quote these as their 'first contacts with foreigners'. In our group, these contacts ranged from language courses abroad for foreigners staying in native families (for Suzanne, Lucy, Jose, Christian), to private exchanges (for Karine, Hélène, Lucy, Julie), or town twinnings (for Mathilde).

Prized in peripheral countries such as Portugal and Ireland, where distance relative to more central European countries represented an obstacle when travelling was still an expensive privilege, this type of virtual travel was valued by families seeking openness. The 'open house' symbolises the first step in a process of extending horizons beyond the domestic, progressing 'like a snowball', as Jose comments.

So it was always a very open house and that was very, very important for the openness, because you feel free to invite people when you are somewhere in Czechoslovakia, and you have someone that is going to Portugal, you can always tell them freely: '*well, stay in my place*', there's no problem because it's something that you are used to... And then progressively, we had those American friends, and then we started to go out a little bit, tourism and visiting some friends, you know it's like a snowball. My friends come and my friends go.

However, Jose adds that obstacles to European mobility arise not only from physical distance, but most importantly from what he calls ' inertia to travel'.

So in the Portuguese culture, there is a lot of inertia to travel, eh… especially to Europe because it takes a lot of time, it's costly, it's everything… a lot of international programmes, EEC programmes or university programmes… Portugal is one of the few countries where actually the number of scholarships available is bigger than the number of students who want to go because there is a little bit of inertia in our people… Plus it's a nice country, it has a nice climate with everything that you need, so why to move?

If in some countries, internal factors, historical or social, may create a climate of 'inertia to travel', entry into the EU is usually conceived as a positive social change triggering attitudinal changes such as greater enthusiasm for language learning. However, inertia or mental apathy would appear to be the norm for many Europeans today.

Living in a border area is also regarded as facilitating openness to foreign realities. Valérie mentions her life in three border areas as an influence: the area of the Jura where her Franco-Swiss mother comes from, the Ardennes area where her family lives, and Alsace where she lived as a student.

So I have always been like that, like that plunged into a, in a… besides, I always lived in a border area: at the Belgian border which many people cross daily, in Lille it's the same thing and in Alsace as well…

(our trans.)

When it becomes an ordinary practice, crossing borders loses its mystifying power. Residents of these border areas are used to a geo-cultural blend which Bruno as a resident of Turin, but originally from a village in the Alps close to the border, is also familiar with. Border areas are more permeable, particularly to linguistic cross-influences, and smooth the path to intra-European mobility for their residents. They may become flagships for European integration.

In the majority of cases, the students portray their parents in similar terms: pro-European, experienced travellers or eager to travel, curious, professionally open to internationalisation. Not all of them have had the opportunity to fulfil their longing for otherness, either learning a foreign language or living abroad. Some of them hand over to their children this unfulfilled dream of discovering other cultures. Juan's father in Spain has always had this interest, but speaks only Spanish.

Well, in my family, there was not really an international background at all. My parents… are from Leone and they have travelled, but just for holidays. So they were… very Spanish [he laughs] and they didn't speak any languages, just Spanish… and so my father always… he says that he always wanted to go out and get to know cultures that he couldn't because of his condition, so his situation and eh… he wanted his children to go out and know things and meet the people and so… he just… he sent us, my brother and I, away to England.

The father chooses an explicitly international education for his three children. They learn English at 4 years of age, they go for their first stay abroad at the age of 8 after which they go to England every year for language courses, followed by a month's stay in the United States at 14 years of age, then one academic year in an American high school as a teenager. Ania from Madrid and Kurt from the Black Forest area in Germany refer to the same unfulfilled 'dream' of their fathers, 'jealous of people who speak foreign languages' because they did not have the opportunity to study languages and consequently had to work in their native countries. The dream which could not become reality with the parents' generation affects the children's route. Christine highlights the frustration borne by parents with no language competence who, even on touristic visits, feel seriously restricted by their absence of linguistic knowledge. These testimonies from children whose parents regretted the absence of a European dimension in their school education give prominence to the road travelled since in the area of language provision to the benefit of young Europeans today. How many of them are aware of the opportunities at their disposal, which too often remain ignored?

The few students who declare that their family is 'not particularly international' are eager to draw the line between themselves and any potential parental impact. Iris is keen to state that she is the one with 'international objectives' and that the desire to travel comes from her only ('it's just me') as her enduring interest for foreign languages from an early age testifies.

> I... My family is not very international. We are all Dutch and I have got one brother who prefers to stay in Holland, but for holidays we went abroad. It is not that my family is very international, but I have got my international objectives. I think it is me who is just interested... and we travel with the family, but most of the time in Europe. No it's just me. It's something I always wanted, I don't know why. [From the beginning?] From when I did my High School I was always very into different languages and when we were in France, for example when I was twelve, I always tried to understand a bit and what I have learned at school and to use it at least. I took all the languages I could do at school for my A levels. For example, I was always very into other languages as well, learning about different countries. Not something for my family, it is just me. Not really anybody, not a nephew or something.

For Maria too, opting for an itinerary involving mobility is not just 'a family thing, it's more the person who is involved in it'. The taste for travelling is asserted here as an individual choice, a personal adventure, independent from possible family influences.

Travellers and others...: the travel bug

The hypothesis which links family context and taste for travelling seems too facile when student travellers are contrasted with their siblings. While students in our sample have opted for going abroad, their brothers and sisters have not necessarily followed the same path. A family context open to foreignness does not automatically produce the same effect among all children. In the same family, some will be more mobile than others. Our respondents have acquired what we call the travel bug. What forms do these variations take within a family history?

Personality is a key factor. Christine's sister does not like being away from her parents, goes back home every weekend when she is a boarder at school, and has never been to England though she loves the language. Matthew's brothers do not travel either. In Jose's family, the same conditions do not bring about similar travel plans. His sister finds it difficult to leave home: she does not possess the 'instinct' or the 'stomach' for adventure, which he acquired very early and which urges him to take on 'international options'.

> It was funny because for instance, my sister who had the same conditions, she is not at all... she is very open, she has a lot of friends all over, but she found it hard to leave, telling her to leave home sweet home, it's difficult. So, I think that it has a lot to do with personality. I have always been since very early a little bit adventurous: first, you do things and then, you think about them. So you tend to... since very early to, to... to have a very, eh... instinct, instinct, and stomach as they say in England, and you take a lot of decisions, maybe not all of them rational but out of feelings, out of emotions, and a lot of the international options that I did, if not all of them, were like that: you see something and you say '*why not?*' and you go.

Jose's choice of words like 'instinct', 'stomach', 'decisions... not... rational', 'feelings', 'emotions', stresses the role of the affective dimension in the genesis of the travel bug. The intercultural option requires a certain attitude on the part of the potential traveller in which feelings and emotions play a large part.

The contrast between Juan and his elder brother illustrates the possibility of totally different paths within a family. Juan notices that his brother, who came back transformed from a year in the United States ('he was more open-minded... he would dress differently and he would talk differently'), suddenly becomes anti-American and wants to stay in Spain.

> My brother had gone to the States for a year and he came back... he was slightly changed. [In what way?] He was different, he was more... eh... I felt he was more open-minded at the beginning, eh... he would dress differently and he would talk differently... then, he changed completely... but at the beginning, like the first days, he was like that, it was weird and then he started changing. And I remember when I came back from the States from that year, my brother was like... he was even worse... because he was anti-American and very, very... [What happened?] That's what I don't know. I mean I talked... I have eh... very close, very close cousins who know my brother pretty well [yes] and we discussed it and they didn't know. He doesn't want to go out at all and he just wants to stay in Leone.

On the contrary, Juan feels more American on his return. Similar experiences produced opposite results. According to Juan, this is due to their two different personalities. Two other factors may contribute to different reactions; age and positive impressions following the first contact abroad. Julie went on her first stay abroad at the age of 12 and 'liked what she saw', while her non-travelling sister went when she was 16 and did not enjoy herself. Personality, age and the type of experience one is exposed to appear as factors in relation to acquiring the travel bug.

Overall, the study of inter-family relations reveals two predominant patterns, the family identification pattern and the family differentiation pattern, the group of only children being considered apart. It is often the case that older brothers and sisters function as role models, inspiring their younger siblings. For example, Hélène's brothers all went to the United States with the same exchange organisation before she did. John's brothers and sisters live and work abroad and urge him to do the same. Marco's brother who had a very positive time during his Erasmus stay in Holland presses him to go as well. Lucy's two older sisters are 'accustomed to leave' and indeed one of them lives in Germany. Suzanne's five older brothers and sisters similarly represent a model of family mobility which stimulates her. In such households, the younger member tends to reproduce the older siblings' example. In a similar fashion, when travellers are the older members, they allude to the jealous fascination their experience provokes in their siblings too young to travel. Elena is 'the first to have tried something' and her younger sister envies her. The older member's footprints are in this case an invitation to imitate the family path.

On the other hand, others may select a path which is different to that of their siblings'. It may be the case of the youngest members when other family members are a generation older and may not have benefited from circumstances facilitating cheaper travel, as in Sylvie's and Hugo's families, both youngest of six children. Hugo explains that the post-war generation did not travel and that even his sister's departure as an au pair in the 1980s was regarded as 'a really big deal at that time'.

> My parents ... are very much the post-war generation and eh... about ten years or twenty years ago, there wasn't extensive travelling abroad and we are six children... I am the youngest... So at that time, it was not possible to go to travel with them. It was too expensive [And what about your brothers and sisters, do they travel?] Hum... well, my sister had like... ten years ago when it was a really big deal at that time, she went to... au pair in London, but that was... the others stayed in Germany. I was also the only person who was travelling a lot. I think it's times change.... Well, for us, it must... Like for my brothers and sisters, it was financial, not possible to travel, it was so expensive to travel and things have changed. Now, you just go to London, the flights are so cheap, the distances are coming together in Europe and that's a major change. Everybody is doing it.

The present economic climate is more conducive to travelling to the extent that young people in the 1990s feel that geographical distances are being reduced. In Hugo's story, this means that mobility practices within his family are modified. The travel bug should be contagious in such a positive situation. However, travel costs are not the only obstacle to mobility.

Factors related to individual educational choices equally bear on decisions. Julie draws attention to the role school subjects may play in the student's relation to mobility, contrasting her sister's interest in business, economics and geography, with her own in languages.

> Yeh, it's a bit strange because she sort of had a different attitude. She's more like… sort of things like business aspects, and economics and geography… whereas I sort of may be… because I was good at French and German in school, so when you're good at something it's easier to sort of like it and to want to know more about it… Maybe that's the reason.

Does this mean that language students are more prone to going abroad than other students? Even though, logically, studying foreign languages should contribute to stimulate the appetite for wandering,[3] mobility experiences were fewer among the linguists than among the non-linguists[4] in our group. Régine, a language student in the Erasmus group, observes that there were only ten language candidates for the three Erasmus exchanges which her French university offered, which to her means that, quite apart from financial constraints, 'people don't like to move'.

The eight only children in our sample all come from families which are themselves mixed or mobile. Their parents encouraged them to travel so as to extend a family horizon sometimes imagined as potentially restricted. This international orientation is visible in Damien's case whose parents opted for a European education early on: he spent six weeks in a French school at the age of 12 and four months at 15. Philip and Eric followed similar paths since both their fathers come from Italy originally. The boys spent their childhood holidays with their paternal family, extending their wanderings later on to other areas. Amin's mother who studied in Paris took him to stay with French friends when he was young. Ava's parents did not get a chance to travel outside Spain as adults, but encouraged her firmly to move on. The position of being an only child in these cases led to a pro-mobility family policy.

As a result, if our students' family history presents in many cases signs of real or virtual mobility and of cultural diversity which may be deemed above average, it would be too simple to draw the conclusion that the taste for travel is determined and shaped by certain family contexts. Personal factors intervene which predispose an individual to opt for adventure, when their siblings do not, and to exhibit a personal taste for travel. Parents withdraw to the wings while the main actor takes over the centre stage. In this respect, students' previous experiences may decisively alter the show about to be played.

Previous experience of mobility

The second element which contributes to the emergence of a mobility capital is based on previous experiences of mobility. By this, we mean any contact or stay abroad in a country other than the student's country and language of origin, implying national border crossing. Internal mobility is therefore normally excluded from this category. The data collected in our sample appear in detail in annexe 7, where each contact or stay abroad is indicated together with its respective duration and the destinations selected by the students. Two other elements which contribute to the general development of a mobility capital are also recorded: mixed origin and the event which generated the first experience of adaptation.

The table must be read with caution. The information was gathered in the course of the interview, prompted by one of the first interview questions: 'What kind of experience abroad did you have before leaving for your present stay abroad?' The table accounts for the students' main experiences, but not necessarily for all their experiences. A quantitative record was attempted wherever possible on the basis of the questionnaires.[5] The contrast between the two research instruments highlights the ambiguity of the phrase 'experience abroad'. For example, Caroline mentioned on the questionnaire her experiences outside Belgium, but not her numerous sojourns in a Flemish language school in Flanders, which stand out in the interview as the most significant experience of exposure to otherness in her story. Her compatriot Christophe clarifies the distinction: 'it is not an experience abroad, but rather the experience of another culture'. In other words, the experience of foreignness does not necessarily refer to movements outside one's own national borders, but should also include experiences sustained at home between parallel linguistic or cultural systems. This is why we draw a line between two kinds of experiences of foreignness: experiences of mobility abroad where a cross-national element is involved and experiences of adaptation where a cross-cultural element is involved. This cross-cultural element refers to a situation where young people are in transit between two differing worlds and have to adapt to their new environment. This kind of experience may take place in one's own country.

Students themselves are naturally inclined to clarify the meaning of 'experience abroad' during the interviews. What counts as an experience abroad? They quote three principal criteria as constituents of an experience abroad: duration ('So you also mean ten-day trips?', exclaims a surprised Daniel), quality of contacts with the natives deemed to be the distinguishing line between tourist holidays and sojourner experience, and autonomous travelling, i.e. travelling alone or not.

The main characteristics of the student travellers' experiences of mobility are indeed the age of the first stay abroad and the frequency of subsequent contacts, as the Erasmus study pointed out (Maiworm *et al.*, op. cit.), but also the proximity of their initial destinations. These elements are shared by the majority in our group, but variations within the sample population, both between the three sub-groups and according to the country of origin, are noticeable.

The majority of students had their first contact abroad at a young age through either family trips or language courses. For example, Iris or Karine went on several European family trips, then on a language course, when they were teenagers. Family trips reveal the degree of parental mobility mentioned above which is itself a function of family resources and national traditions. Language courses generally correspond to the beginning of foreign language education which, for this particular generation of students, did not include early language learning.[6] These early contacts abroad for pupils aged between 12 and 15 may be construed as demonstrating the parental aspiration for foreign elements in their children's education. Privately organised courses are sometimes concurrent with school trips, which help guarantee a minimum amount of foreign exposure during many young Europeans' school career. As a result, the university experience represented the first contact abroad for only one student in our sample. This first finding about the frequency of early contacts among our student population leads to questions relating to 'a critical age', as mentioned for early language learning (Singleton, 1989). Could there be a 'critical age' corresponding to a period of greater intercultural flexibility when young learners would be predisposed to greater receptivity to linguistic and cultural diversity? We can only infer from this finding the general tendency towards early contacts abroad in those who will become confirmed travellers.

This factor is cumulative: stays abroad start young and are then repeated at regular intervals during the young person's holiday time. Julie goes on a language exchange every year from the age of 12, alternating between France and Germany. So do John, Ania and Mathilde from the age of 14. Their mobility capital is varied. At the beginning of their itinerary, language stays coexist with short school visits or foreign holidays. This latter form of contact is conceived as being 'just holidays' (Louis) where 'you only meet tourists' (Daniel). The quantification of these experiences[7] reveals a total of stays abroad superior to four–five months for the majority of students, sometimes extending to more than a year in the shape of either many shorter periods (Jose mentions 'several stays of three months') or some long spells, as for Thomas with two experiences of a year and six months.

Language competence is obviously a significant part of the experience of mobility. Indeed, one of the main motivations for institutionally or privately organised student travel is language learning. Given their age, year of study and language learning past, the linguistic level achieved by departing students is generally high enough to enable them to pursue their study or work in the foreign environment. Many European studies on the year abroad point to the impact of a period of residence on students' language competence. This is why we will not elaborate on the specific issue of language development. Our discussion of the language issue will rather draw from the references made by the students about the major role played by language in their overall life abroad.

Mobility experiences accumulated to their benefit by our students represent a budding capital of which the year abroad may be judged a spontaneous development. As an extension of a journey which started much earlier on, the one-year stay also epitomises a more advanced stage in the development of their travelling capital. As they grow older, several transitions are noticeable, in the type of travel (from family holidays, language course, student trip, to summer job), in the traveller's degree of autonomy (starting with the family, then with friends, and finally alone), and in terms of geo-cultural distance for their selected destinations. In other words, learning mobility progresses at a steady, but cautious pace.

Learning mobility, a cautious progress

Young Europeans' destinations are noteworthy for their proximity and for the lack of diversity in the countries visited. Proximity may be of an affective nature for bicultural children whose holiday destinations are frequently the family in the other country. Even though these experiences add up to 'a lot of experience of travelling', the person who sees them from the inside is not quite certain whether they count as 'experience abroad' or not, as Daniel explains.

> Actually, eh, I had a lot of experience of, of travelling abroad, it was… in fact, my parents are Italian… and eh… I mean… every year in July or August, we went for a month to Italy and eh… in fact it was not even an experience abroad since we were all going as a family and it was in a village where I knew everybody…and eh… well I speak Italian fluently and it was, it wasn't really an experience of… foreignness because you see … my parents didn't go anywhere else since… we had a house there and we liked it a lot over there, my grand-mother still lives there… and eh… it was the experience abroad I had before Ireland (our trans.).

Though geographically located 'abroad', affective, social and linguistic familiarity reduces the foreignness of these experiences, but also limits the opportunity for experiencing more radically different locations, at least as long as the young people must follow their parents. For the others who travelled with their family, experience of remote places was also restricted because most European families of that generation commonly travelled within Europe, often towards sunny or border countries. In any case, being accompanied by their family singularly limited young people's exposure to strangeness.

When teenagers travelled on their own, the destinations reflected the language learning objective of the stay abroad. Here again distance is relative since language learning is designed to reduce the communicative gap between strangers and natives. The most frequently taught languages in Europe are but a few, and getting fewer with the dominating position of English. Thus, the most frequent destinations of young Europeans are language destinations where English, French or German may be learnt. The commercial basis of most language immersion programmes often leads to mediocre intercultural contacts. Caroline finds the asymmetry of these 'rather special' commercial relations embarrassing: she comes back from her classes, is served her dinner in front of television and then retires to one of the children's bedrooms. On the other hand, a few students were lucky enough to establish close affective links with their foreign partners, usually when a personal exchange was set up. In these cases, Karine explains, the learning process is like 'a total immersion' because the young foreigner who has been welcomed into a local family is transformed from spectator to participant of the social scene and goes from outside to inside.

Young Europeans' grasp of 'foreign' space is initially rather timid. It takes place mostly in Europe. For those who venture outside Europe, the main destination is again reassuring by its linguistic, even cultural, proximity since it mostly concerns the United States where European teenagers travel on their own when they are slightly older, generally around 15–16. In our sample, distant travels are the preserve of older students like Josef, Thomas and Jose, and are often related to work experience. Thomas worked in the Club Med for six months in Latin America. Jose made several business trips for AIESEC, an international economics students' organisation 'established in seventy-eight countries'. He took part in international meetings and was involved in a project with forty-three countries in the world. For many Irish students, a summer job in the United States represents a ritual practice punctuating their university studies. Régine, familiar with American culture, is regarded as an exception in the French context when she goes on a summer job. However, the summer job abroad is not a common practice in European countries where students are subsidised by the State or by their family.

Travelling practices differ in each country and in each family. Access to travel evidently varies with the cost involved, higher from countries at the periphery of Europe. European travels are more accessible to those families whose country shares borders with others. For others, the first trip abroad is frequently organised by the school, as was the case for Aoife, Fiona, Siobhan and Collette. For older European generations, travelling was not always easy for economic or political reasons, as Hugo outlined. It was a privilege rather than standard practice, as the parents' buried dreams of foreignness testify. Lastly, the number of children in a family induces a more or less abundant distribution of family resources. Our students' story of mobility takes place in a context which may not be understood fully outside larger socio-economic and historical factors which draw attention to variations inside each member state and between them in terms of the degree of mobility of their population.

The first experience of adaptation as an initiation

Two types of mobility exist: internal, within a national territory; and external, outside it. Is there even the slightest correlation between internal and external mobility? Some of our students mention specific episodes of their life as their first experience of adaptation to a different milieu.[8] Indeed, Schütz claims that his analysis is valid for many experiences of transition, which correspond to situations of intracultural mobility of a social, family, educational, geographical, professional, and economic nature. These situations have in common the fact that the individuals concerned are confronted with an unknown world whose social rules they do not master and which confers on them the status of temporary stranger. The specificity and hallmark of transnational mobility is due to the fact that language discontinuity is added on to socio-cultural dislocation.

The first experiences which the students identify as requiring an effort to adapt are diverse and emerge from different types of social change. One situation of internal mobility often quoted is that of the student who leaves the country to study in town. Maria mentions a young Spanish girl newly arrived in Cadix, who suffers from loneliness. According to Amin, a friend adapted easily to life on the Louvain campus because he had lived on his own before.

> He didn't go through the same... U curve as I went through... and that's because he's from the country and he's lived, he's lived, you know, by himself in Dublin for two years beforehand... and he never seemed to be worried by any... he adapted, I would think.

A change in school or university is frequently recalled as a dramatic and striking moment of transition, as Bruno and Hugo mention. The latter details the feeling of disorientation one experiences: 'school is a long process because, you know, children can be very nasty and they form a society... and this society changes because you grow all the time'. But, the transition is even more thorough and potentially traumatic when young people find themselves in a language boarding-school. These schools, established in bilingual countries such as Belgium or Ireland, proscribe use of the other language in order to foster language immersion. For Christophe, the change in linguistic regime, exacerbated by the separation from his family, was the 'hardest' experience he had known.

> So I did my... my primary schooling in French and my secondary schooling in Flemish... I changed linguistic regime at the age of 12 and that, that was more an experience than Paris because Paris doesn't... eh, France was not at all something special for me. I was feeling, I don't want to say I was feeling at home because the country and the culture are different,... eh... but, the language does a lot and is not going to make me feel uprooted [...]. But (the Flemish school) was the hardest because I wasn't... I couldn't speak a word of Flemish and eh... I was studying at home and I went to this boarding school and so, that, I had... I had everything together at the same time and... the medicine was swallowed (our trans.).

His evidence demonstrates the determining significance of language as a factor of dislocation and uprootedness. It puts into perspective what the students who share the language of the country they are staying in will be spared in terms of language adaptation, like the Irish in England and the students from Belgium or Luxembourg in Paris. However, if Christophe feels that his uprooting was overwhelming ('I had everything together at the same time'), in the end 'the medicine was swallowed'.[9]

Whether the move is individual or collective as a family, internal mobility is perceived as comparable to transnational mobility, because it often leads to other changes beside the purely geographical move. Inter-regional varieties in language or economic climate within a country may provoke a strong feeling of estrangement. Bruno explains that going from Lombardy to Piedmont ('only two hundred kilometres away'), from a 'very active' region to an area 'with just one main industry, Fiat, which dominates everything', disorientated him as much as moving abroad: 'In Italy, we are very different in each region... it may not be being abroad, but... there is a jargon as well, a jargon which is quite... quite different.'

Indeed, Nicolas compares the experience abroad to moving within one's country, without the language change.

> Yes, moving, moving... that's right. No, moving, but completely. Moving country is like moving houses. I mean you find yourself in a totally new place, you have to adapt to the weather, new accommodation, new neighbours, a new culture because often when you change from one region to another, you change from one culture to another... eh... to the new language, the new customs. Yes, it's like changing countries in the end with just language being the same! (our trans.).

Changing countries implies three different rifts: relocation (*déménagement*), since one leaves a geographical territory; disorientation (*dépaysement*), since one leaves a social and cultural territory; and uprootedness (*déracinement*), since one leaves an affective, personal, language territory. Moving from a town in southern France to a village in the Alps, where he feels as an intruder in a society he perceives as enclosed ('people with stupid prejudices'), caused Nicolas such a disruption that it took him seven years to adapt. 'Maybe in fact, I did not feel a problem later on [abroad] because... that particular experience was so severe, lasted so long...' As he did not feel at home in the mountain village, he established alternative 'homes' elsewhere, through repeated experiences abroad. Negative adaptation in France was transmuted into positive adaptation in Ireland, where he said he would like to settle in the end. Feeling inadequate in his native territory, he experienced the change as liberating, which is probably why he said that he did not have to adapt abroad. Similarly, Jürgen explained that his successive moves in his country had taught him what it was like to 'adapt to a different environment without leaving your country' and as a result, the idea of spending a year in England or in France does not alarm him ('no big deal'), while it scared some of his German friends.

The process of adaptation is not always abrupt and may even appear as the natural outcome of a progressive development. For Edwige, when sustained smoothly, moving does not lead to rifts or dislocation, but rather to detachment and adjustment. She 'did not miss home' in Ireland because she had already acquired a certain degree of autonomy when studying in France. She gradually left home for longer periods of time, eventually leaving for three months and then one year. The process of disconnection proceeded 'by stages', according to her own and her parents' rhythm, who now 'adapt very easily' to their daughter's wishes. Detachment is a two-way process. Parents who cling to their children make it all the more painful to get away. Marco did not encounter any problems either, because for him, separation 'was very progessive… from the age of 8'. He concludes that if before going for the year abroad, students have never left home and do not know the language, they will naturally go through shock and will want to go back home quickly. In short, previous adaptation through internal mobility prepares the ground for later experiences.

Nevertheless, the main adaptation experience for most of our students was their first stay abroad, generally a few weeks in the summer. This first experience functioned as an initiation and frequently coincided with culture shock. Some, namely Maria, Marina, John and Julie, went through this trial when they were quite young, around 12.

> Yeh, my first time in France, I was really… I was quite… I'd never been to Irish college. I went to tennis camps, and I went straight from there like over… thousand of miles away to France. Initially, it was quite hard, but the family I was staying with were very nice.
>
> (Julie)

Distance appears considerable to the young person, particularly if the ground has not been prepared by previous separations, like a language boarding school ('Irish college'). For others such as Hugo, Nicolas, Sophie or Juan, the first experience of adaptation took place later, when they were about 15. Does the age difference matter? In other words, is the impact of the shock greater or lesser when the traveller is younger or older? Several comments seem to indicate that the older the learner is, the more severe and lasting the shock is.[10] However, the duration of the stay must be taken into account. Younger students stay for short periods of a couple of weeks and their memories may not be as permanent. Subsequent stays are usually longer, from two or three summer months to eight or ten months, sometimes a school year. These longer adaptations are of a different kind, as we will see. However, the first experience of adaptation is an initiation in the sense that it introduces young people to the first elements of a more complex discovery and is the prelude preparing them for a prolonged learning route.

Is the experience of adaptation transferable to other contexts? Maria suggests that each country calls for a different adaptation and Julie confirms this when she says that the most difficult period is the beginning in a new environment.[11] After a while, familiarity with local cultural practices and behaviours provide a definite 'advantage'. Absence of familiarity is what causes the uneasiness or the shock of the beginning. However, even if each new context calls for a period of familiarisation, having gone through the experience once facilitates and lessens the next. Individuals know what to expect in terms of learning how to survive the shock of an environmental change. This specific type of knowledge is transferable. One experience of a profound social change prepares the ground for subsequent changes. The first experience of adaptation, whatever its nature or origin, has propaedeutic virtues: it represents a preliminary instruction for the more complete education ahead. We suggest that the context of the first adaptation may be other than a transnational situation, with no consequence for the capital of adaptation accumulated. When the experience of adaptation precedes the experience of mobility, the adaptation capital boosts the mobility capital.

Personality features of the potential wanderer

Personality features represent another constituent of the mobility capital. Those who acquire the travel bug have a different personality from their brothers and sisters, and consequently make different choices. What are the personal attributes which predispose an individual to be a potential wanderer? One broad characteristic, generally agreed upon, is that they are outgoing or extrovert, turned outside, like the sleep-walker 'whose relational life continues into his sleep' (Joseph, op. cit.: 13). This general characteristic manifests itself in several guises. Most students list curiosity, attraction for novelty or difference, and finally sociability or a desire to communicate and seek social contacts, as the three core elements of the travelling personality.

Curiosity is the attitude which confers the desire to learn new things, its opposite being intellectual apathy or indifference. Christine explains that she 'loves accumulating experiences' and is fascinated 'by civilisations, by people', just like Siobhan or Aoife, always keen to discover more about others and looking out for stories about other people's lives. At the opposite end, Siobhan is surprised by her English flatmate's 'ignorance' when, educated in Oxford and learning French and Italian, the latter did not know the colour of the Irish flag nor that a neighbouring country had an independent currency. Régine also notices that she only becomes observant when she is in 'travelling mode': 'I am very, very... not observant except when I am in "travelling mode"... I feel liberated when I am not in my home environment'. She finds herself 'rather fenced in' (*renfermée*) when at home: she has her group of friends and does not see other people. Travelling liberates from familiar circles because it offers opportunities for encountering different people. In a way, curiosity is there, but dormant, waiting to be awakened by outside stimulation. This is why she describes herself as 'rather curious, but lazy as well... and to get out of my laziness, I need a big jump, to go somewhere else...'. Here, curiosity is defined as both the condition and the outcome of travelling. As a cognitive disposition directed towards the outside, curiosity is the initial attitude required before getting to know different people. Amin talks about a 'broadness of perspective' which makes you question things and counterbalances one's tendency for intellectual stability and compliance. This free or independent spirit seems close to Park's emancipation which allows travellers to 'break the cake of custom' (1928.: 885) or indeed to the stranger's objectivity defined by Simmel as freedom from prejudice. Activated and energised by a new environment, a curious mind is ready to relax the stronghold of the ready-made wisdom received through early socialisation and to open up to a new world of knowledge.

Interest for the other rather than for the same is another feature quoted as characteristic of the potential wanderer. Instead of seeking people who are like her/him, act like her/him, have the same ideas, the travelling personality will be seduced by difference or the 'new' in the environment. The call to travel crystallises around the enticement of a totally different social scene: weather, food, lifestyle, atmosphere, living conditions, the overall variety, according to Maria.

> I enjoy meeting new people and going new places. ... Well, it's not just the people, it's the whole thing. I also knew that I'd enjoy the weather in Spain... eh, I was going to the South of Spain, it's freezing in Ireland, I hate the weather here during the winter... I know their lifestyle, the food, I adore the food! It's everything about travelling, everything is different, it's not just the people, it's your whole atmosphere, your daily living conditions are different... yes, variety, it's variety.

For Iris, this attraction to difference goes with the desire to understand why people think and act differently.

> Hm... let's see... I am very open, that's my personality... regarding people... But also, I was always very interested in other people and how they experience things and well... like to hear what they're doing and what they really have in mind... and... so that way, if you meet other people, and especially other cultures, it's really very interesting why they think in a different way or why they do things in a different way and... like you start asking questions about yourself as well: 'why?... why do I want to do it this way? I could do it some other way as well'... and... yes, that's interesting... to discover why people do differently and why people think differently.

Reflecting on others invariably leads to questioning one's world, which Suzanne refers when mentioning her role as mediator for foreign students staying in her family home. As the youngest and most easily available, she was invited to show them 'where the shops and the bus stop are' and had to answer their questions about her society. She quickly realises that she does not 'know much, but you throw back the questions and you ask them questions and... people love talking about themselves!' Having to understand or explain difference encourages one to question one's way of thinking.

Sociability or the aptitude to connect easily with individuals one encounters goes together with the need to communicate. This specific disposition of travellers must be related to their reasons for going abroad since 'meeting new people' is often stated as one of the main objectives of the project. According to Lucy, the social attribute is paramount.

> I think it's because I like meeting new people a lot… like my mother's always said that about me any time those students came into our house, it was always sort of me, I made friends with them more than anybody else did… ya, my other sisters would fairly much ignore them, you know, be polite or whatever, but would not take them into their lives at all, see them as part of their lives. I mean I made an awful lot of friends actually, at least three people that came in as students that I still write to and stuff, you know, I think it's just a sociable thing.

She links sociability to a certain 'flippancy' in relations, which she describes as the ability to entertain a friendship for a while without being too demanding in the long-term. Foreign relationships require a certain lightness, which may disturb those who prefer steady permanent friendships.

> Well, I think I am quite sociable, but also I mean it's, it's on the other side, it's being quite flippant, you know. My sisters would have been more into having their steady friends from years back that knew them really well, whereas I had no problem making friends for two weeks and writing to them for the rest of…, you know. It's probably quite flippant, going over to visit them for two weeks, not knowing them actually terribly well, maybe eventually, not being too demanding…

The ability to open up one's world even for a short time to others prepared her to accept more readily the precariousness inherent in social relationships with foreigners.[12] She understood that travellers lose some friends, gain others and 'that friends come and go'.

Maria, whose appetite for social novelty appears on a par with the circle of acquaintances she possesses, is specific about the dual advantage of going abroad: leaving a social scene which has become too crowded, too well known and too 'restricted', and starting from scratch in 'a whole new city' getting to know 'another thousand people'.

> Because I know Dublin very well, I am very well known in Dublin… and I often feel restricted… I know, let's say, every one in my year in College, a lot of people from other faculties in my year… I knew that when I went to Spain I wouldn't know anyone. It was great: I had another thousand people to work with, I could get to know new people… I know all the night clubs, pubs in Dublin that there are to know. I knew here was a whole new city that I did not know. I, I find that enjoyable. I enjoy meeting and going new places.

As a real social chameleon, she adds that her appetite for foreignness has no end. Each time she goes to a different country, she would like to stay in order to discover more about it.

A new social stage implies the competence to communicate with strangers.

This competence often starts at home when you willingly engage in communication with passing strangers in town, on the campus or in public places. Maria does not hesitate to invite them to 'join our gang'.

> Oh, now, I know foreign people. I talk to foreign people all the time. Like I made friends with Erasmus people in College. And, even in a bar, if someone's foreign, I normally say: '*Where are you from? You're enjoying Dublin? Do you know where to go at night? Ok, well, if you want to join our gang, we are going out, we are going to a club. Do you want to join with us?*' or something... you know...

However, communicating with strangers is not as simple as that for most people. A personal experience of life abroad is usually a requirement before this social practice becomes relatively straightforward. In particular, the returned traveller will appreciate the significance of communication with the natives in such circumstances more fully than the sedentary student. Quite a few students comment on the conscious effort they now make to go to other travellers and engage in conversation with them, after their return home.

These different facets of the travelling personality focus attention on the predominance of features which dispose to an openness to others, whether it be intellectual openness with curiosity, affective openness with attraction to difference, or social and relational openness with the desire to engage in new relationships. The individual who would be denied one or the other of these attributes runs the risk of being put to the test harshly, and the process of adaptation will be all the more distressing. On the contrary, the individual who already possesses some of these may be naturally inclined to accept the invitation to travel. Indeed, these qualities come back frequently in the students' comments when they talk about advice for potential travellers, about requirements for a successful adaptation, or about the personal outcomes of the year abroad.[13]

The mobility capital

The mobility capital, which is the hallmark of this migratory elite, is not quite evenly distributed among the three groups in our study. Variations may be observed in relation to their stock of experience not only in terms of the nature and the number of their various sojourns abroad, but also in terms of their country of origin, as already mentioned.

An attempt was made at classifying students so that the major characteristics by which their mobility capital before a year abroad could be assessed would become apparent. The three criteria used are, first, family connections with foreignness, secondly, the number, duration and diversity of contacts and stays abroad, and finally, previous experience of adaptation. Other criteria could have been included such as language competence, familiarity with several cultures, or personal connections with foreignness. As with most classifications, Table 2, below, must be read as a rather crude summary of complex features and the

Table 2 The mobility capital: a classification

	Proficient students	*Experienced students*	*Expert students*
Erasmus	Louis, Ava, Ania	Hélène, John, Amin?, Julie, Maria?, Daniel, Marco	Caroline, Birgitta, Hugo, Régine, Lucy
Assistants	Aoife, Cecilia, Fiona, Emily, Siobhan, Edwige, Collette	Valérie, Christine, Jannick, Sophie, Mathilde	Nicolas, Sylvie, Karine?
EAP	Josef?, Suzanne?, Bruno	Elena, Iris, Franz, Christian?	Tom, Damien, Viktor, Christophe, Thomas, Jürgen, Philip, Kurt, Marina, Eric, Matthew, Juan, Jose

categories are far from water-tight. The question marks over some names signal the uncertainty which presides over these choices. Besides, two other categories of potential student travellers could be added, the 'neophytes' at one end, who would have no experience of travelling, and the 'professional' at the other end whose profile could be close to that of Daniel's sister: 'always ready to go', who studied several languages, spent long periods of time abroad, worked as a tourist guide, and has a natural ease for adopting the role of linguistic or cultural mediator.

The three degrees selected – proficient, experienced and expert – are assumed to represent different levels of achievement regarding mobility competence. The difference between the three positions is more quantitative, related to amount of time spent abroad, than qualitative. Mobility here is primarily construed as a physical experience involving actual residence abroad rather than as the mental or virtual mobility obtained from studying foreign languages and cultures from a home base.

Proficient students are those who have stayed regularly in neighbouring countries, during their secondary schooling. Their experiences were for short periods of time, a couple of weeks at a time. They represent a total amount of time abroad of less than five months. They have limited experience of adaptation to a different milieu. Their families do not have direct foreign connections. Experienced students are those who have stayed several times, often at a young age, in more diverse foreign places, sometimes for work experience. Their sojourns were for short to medium periods of time, the total amounting to more than six months. Experienced students have not yet stayed abroad for a year and have only limited experience of adaptation to a different milieu. Expert students are those who already possess one or several of these characteristics as assets. They have accumulated trips and stays abroad, often in far away destinations. In total, they may have spent more than twelve months abroad. They have also already been on one medium- to long-term stay abroad. Some of them have gone through one major experience of adaptation, notably to a different linguistic milieu. The three groups of students are spread across the three categories, but one particular group appears to be more prominent at each level.

Students from the EAP have spent more time than the others abroad. The total number of their contacts and stays is quite impressive, particularly regarding medium-term stays of a couple of months. Elena worked two consecutive summers in France and in England; Tom worked one summer in Paris; Damien benefited from three stays of a few months outside home, one as a schoolboy; Josef went far away for two lengthy spells; Kurt worked in France at the age of 15; Caroline went on work placements to England; Suzanne worked two summers in France and in the USA; Thomas was employed by the Club Med for five months; Jose spent several months in different countries for international development projects; Iris spent one summer in a kibbutz. It is worth outlining that these stays take place in a summer work context. The student adopts a new role: from mere visitor, s/he becomes a temporary participant on the economic stage (Schild, 1962), a qualitative advance in status which is significant. Another characteristic of the EAP group is that many of them have spent one academic year abroad. Tom studied in Dublin for two years, though in his native language, Viktor spent eight months in Italy, Thomas went on a year-long language course in Aix-en-Provence, as did Kurt in Paris. Jürgen and Juan both spent a year in an American high school. Matthew spent one year in France as a language assistant. The EAP students who did not spend a year abroad before entering their international course of study are often those whose familiarity with foreignness is to be found in their family context, as is the case for the six bicultural students in that group, accustomed to holidaying in the other 'foreign' family. In short, the students who chose to enter the professional route offered by the EAP had in common an advanced initial position regarding experience abroad. As such, the majority of them are to be found in the category of expert student travellers.

The Erasmus students in our study, four of whom are from mixed alliances, benefit from a significant mobility capital as well because of the regularity of their contacts and stays abroad, but usually for shorter periods of time and in the shape of language courses, exchanges or student travels such as inter-railing. Outside the Irish students in that group, only three students have worked abroad for a summer. Longer-term stays are also less frequent in that group, with only three students having spent one year away: Lucy in Paris at the age of 18 as an au pair, Birgitta in London at the age of 17, and Régine who spent most of her childhood in Hawaii. However, these Erasmus students are those who most frequently mention and analyse their experiences of culture shock and adaptation. Overall, these characteristics would suggest that the majority of them belong to the categories of expert or experienced student travellers.

The group of assistants, the only 'professional' linguists in our study, appears at first as the less seasoned if one is to judge by the number, duration, nature and diversity of the periods of time spent abroad, the age of their first contacts with foreignness, and their family background. Only two of them, out of fifteen, come from culturally mixed families, Valérie and Nicolas. He is the only one of the whole group to have worked several summers abroad, together with Emily who worked as an au pair in the same Parisian family over three successive summers and whose sister is resident in France. The only student in our study who has not spent time abroad before entering higher education is also to be found in the assistants' group. The types of stays practised by these students are institutional rather than private: school trips or European student exchange programmes such as Erasmus or Tempus. It may be assumed that the lesser role played by personal initiative in their case, for example looking for a job abroad, prompts them to follow the traditional route for students with an interest for foreignness: they study languages at university and then opt for a career as language teachers.

On the other hand, if they give the impression superficially of being less adventurous and less cosmopolitan than their non-linguist peers, their knowledge and above all their attention to the foreign language have already disposed them to a more thorough study of linguistic and cultural distances. Indeed, they may be assumed to be more aware and more accomplished than those who have gone through a foreign experience without being equipped with reflective skills or the ability to interpret and explain a cultural event. Their professional training and knowledge in otherness may be the reason why they rarely mention going through culture shock or a difficult adaptation period.[14] The curve of their experiences of mobility reveals a steady, uninterrupted progression through short and regular periods abroad. They do not jump into adventure, but rather manage their efforts efficiently. Their university studies lead them to a continuous path explicitly focused on foreignness. This special position, alternating formal and experiential learning, makes it difficult to classify them along with the others. Even though, in the strict terms of mobility capital as identified above, the majority of assistants belong to the category of proficient travellers, their university discipline and training puts them ahead of the other more seasoned travellers in relation to experiencing strangeness.

The differences between the three groups reflect to a certain extent economic, cultural, family and national differences. Altogether, these factors are one of the reasons why we define student travellers as a migratory elite. They usually benefit, before their year abroad, from a significant mobility capital. However, they are a migratory elite in other ways as well. In the first place, they responded to the call to travel by taking control of the project as their own gamble, part of their personal history, not only their family's. In the second place, they understood before others that the itinerary they have opted for should bear fruit in the future and allow them to increase the professional, cultural, linguistic and personal capital they initially started with.

Conclusion: the potential wanderer – 'a flavour for living abroad' (John)

In what ways can previous experiences, mobility and adaptation taken together, prepare young people for the future venture? Undoubtedly, they produce a kind of background, a mental or imaginary landscape regarding the countries visited,[15] but also regarding language immersion, the experience of living abroad and the process of adaptation. 'Impressions', understood literally as imprints or feelings left in one's mind by some external event, associated with these first contacts, however immediate or superficial they may be, play a crucial role. Whether they are positive or negative, impressions will influence the young person's attitude towards foreignness and entice her/him to renew or not the first experiences. John's words sum up the general judgement on this topic: these experiences give you 'a flavour for living abroad', and he adds for living not only abroad, but in a country whose language one does not necessarily know well.

Specifically, young travellers have acquired certain skills and attitudes which will facilitate the route ahead. Caroline refers to two of these: attitude towards the foreign language and self-sufficiency.

> ...to start with because I like, I like expressing myself in another language and I am not afraid even if I know that I make loads of mistakes, I am not afraid because when I was young, I was forced to... that, that was a positive point because I have friends who are very good at a foreign language, but precisely they dare not speak it because they know that they make mistakes... well, I speak even though... I jump in the water... that's the first thing (our trans.).

Not being afraid of speaking in the foreign language represents the first step into adventure, the language jump. The second step, self-sufficiency, which stems from living outside one's home, represents a mental or material jump,[16] which Caroline details: 'I learnt how to cope... euh... not to think too much about home, well to... yes, to live independently nevertheless'. Autonomy is defined here as a twofold competence: the ability to live without material aid as well as without a mental clamp attached to the home environment. Amin adds another important outcome of his Irish boarding-school experience: 'just getting through tough times by yourself', particularly through language difficulties. Consequently, his advice to potential wanderers is to 'be prepared that it's not going to be a rose garden, 'cause that's what I expected, I thought it would be a whale of a time, brilliant, and I was so surprised'. When potential travellers acquire these attitudes at an early age, this head start smoothes the way for more experiences. The capital acquired is bound to grow in the shape of a longer period of residence abroad, bringing its spontaneous rewards.

Young travellers, temporary visitors in foreignness, epitomise a special case of potential wanderers. The attribute of youth makes them different from others. For them, the game is only starting. They are in a state of personal, economic and social absence of gravity (Mauger, 1995). Partly liberated from family constraints, they nevertheless usually enjoy some form of economic support which somewhat curtails their financial autonomy. Socially, they are often free from constraining responsibilities such as mortgage repayments or children, as Maria points out. Young people are thus in a position to 'take full advantage' of this privileged moment in a life, a moment of considerable freedom.

> Yeh… well no I like coming back. It's not that I dislike Ireland… I just enjoy going away as well and… heu I am young enough to do it, I've no responsibilities to keep me in Ireland, I've no… mortgage or children or anything like that that's keeping me here, so I can afford to do it at the moment and I realise that in the future maybe I won't be able to do that. So I take full advantage of it now.

Indeed, if one accepts that youth may be defined as a double insertion, in the job market and in the marriage market (ibid.), the student travellers who have already achieved this twin passage into adulthood and nevertheless set forth for the adventure run the risk of experiencing this parenthesis in their life in a negative way. It was the case for Josef who worked for two years and was involved in a stable relationship. Because of his 'former experience', he has the unpalatable feeling of being socially devalued, not fitting in at all. Does this mean that, once the sociological threshold of youth is crossed, potential wanderers will find the travel more arduous? This would tend to confirm the 'critical age' hypothesis regarding mobility competence.

Student travellers in Europe constitute an elite because they show the way towards the future. Even though their number is small, they are the 'yeast', which will facilitate European mobility. Their itinerary might inspire others. Their specific experience of mobility makes them aware that, like the potential wanderer, they can go as they please, as Amin discovers: 'I can go as I please […] I felt I could assimilate myself into my home environment very easily, leave, and come back. So I felt more…' Above all, they do not experience the coming-and-going as a mutilation, but as a conquest: they feel 'more'. They know they can always go back. Contrary to sedentary individuals whose possessions are heavy, these potential nomads learn to travel light and with ease. This is the kind of freedom gained. The future is open to them, just unfolding…

4 An adventure into another time-space

Introduction: an invitation to travel

The students' stories are not presided over by chance. Rather, like life stories, they are set in a personal chain of events, a temporal continuity which we try to reconstruct with them. The attempt to recall fragments of their past implies trying to retrieve some coherence from diverse scraps of life. As we saw in the previous chapter, the students' narratives start well before the stay abroad in the form of family history, school orientations and accumulated experience. But previous history offers merely a sketch of an itinerary which awaits confirmation. In this chapter, we are still looking at the construction over time of a traveller's story, but in the more immediate context which just precedes departure. We go one step further in the genesis of the taste for travelling and examine the motivations which prompt individuals to take on the challenge of spending a year abroad. In this respect, contextual factors related to the past combine with personal factors to shape the choices individuals make in response to outside stimulations. Here the focus is mainly on the part individuals play.

Researching motives implies trying to identify, and to justify, some of the many causes which determine a given course of action. But the maze of elements which rules social actors' behaviours and actions is complex. What really sets someone moving and triggers a decision? The motives disclosed by the actors themselves are but one level of representation of reality, that of verbal logic and personal history. Other motives, buried deeper or calling for a sociological explanation, may only appear at the level of consciousness in more reflective individuals. If trying to discern and differentiate in this intricate web one reason or another is such a delicate operation, is it not because the whole person – heredity, past, personal history and all – lives, acts and expresses her/himself at every moment? Isolating one attitude or cause among many does not restore the full process in train. Besides, if trying to disentangle the maze of a person's motivations is at the very heart of therapeutic interviewing, it is not the point of a research interview. The account of the motivations the students expressed must be considered as a likely sample of reasons which draw their value from the more or less rationalised meaning actors assign to this aspect of their life story.

What moves a minority to mobility when such a large majority of individuals are satisfied with staying put? Park underlines that motivations of migratory individuals are multifold, but that the one unifying element in all these individual trajectories which reiterate the same pattern is that everywhere individuals change location 'seeking more favourable life conditions'. How can we interpret the term 'more favourable life conditions' in the case of our students? What are they looking for in their temporary migration? Political or economic imperatives, the main driving forces for the vast majority of migrants, are hardly relevant in the student experience or at least need to be redefined so as to extend the traditional range of reasons and include the motivations which activate occasional transnationals such as our students.

Specifically, what are the components of the students' response to the invitation extended to them? What are the forces which inspire their choice? In many cases, travelling imposes itself as an imperative which features in their mental landscape early in their history. Subsequently, a year abroad may be seen as a value added to a formative period in a young person's life. As a result, the principal motivations mentioned by students are conventional ones – language learning and work-study experience – followed by a more private motive – desire for novelty, difference, foreignness. These three basic ingredients dominate the data,[1] but their weighting varies with each student group. However, exploring new life conditions is also an opportunity for self-discovery of another kind. In the end, travel may be construed as an adventure into another time–space.

Living abroad as an imperative

The significance of the choice has to do with desire. Travel is constructed in the potential wanderer's imagination before its actualisation. Desire is fed through indirect or direct contacts with destinations which are fantasised, so that the traveller already holds a certain representation of the object as content (country, culture, people, studies or work) and as process (adapting to a different life, going, leaving). For example, Suzanne speaks of a 'vision' in her head: 'I always thought I'd like to go... around the world, it was a kind of vision in my head'. Yet, retrieving the chronological thread, explaining why and how this desire for elsewhere emerges in you and not necessarily in others who are near you, is not easy.

Many students express their intention to travel as a long-term orientation in their life, using temporal adverbs such as 'always' or 'never'. Christine says that she '*always* liked it and it did not disturb (her) to go far away'. Valérie has '*always* had the idea' since she was small even though her sister and brother who '*never* wanted to move, even for holidays' did not manifest the same travel bug. As a child, Sylvie was '*always* ready to go, rucksack on, ready to camp, to stay here and there'. As the youngest of five, she always liked visiting relatives in Paris when her sisters 'would immediately get sick and want to go home'. Aoife talks of an urge: 'I absolutely had to do it'. Back in her childhood, at the age of five, she remembers imaginary travels triggered by returning neighbours who had migrated. She heard about different languages and cultures, those of Malaysia and Africa, and these narratives fascinated her in the absence of real contacts abroad.

> It was just kind of like something, an injection of something from the outside world! It's hard to explain, but it's only now that I want to make these stories become realisations; now that I've come back from France, a lot of people have said to me: '*So, you've done your travelling now*'. I say to them: '*It's just a beginning and I want to see what's going on in the rest of the world now*'. From that point of view, it's been a starting point. I want to travel around more.

Stories from elsewhere are like 'an injection of something from the outside world' which instil seeds of strangeness in her mind, where they are dormant as dreams and germinate to be transformed later on into 'realisations' at an opportune time. The first real experience is for her just 'a beginning', 'a starting-point', a springboard for other travelling fantasies. When the opportunity arises, the response comes as an imperative, Amin points out, and the decision to leave is not considered as 'a big decision'.

> I was never worried about going, I was never... it was something I always felt I could do quite easily... It was just something, just I presumed I'd do it. It wasn't a... it wasn't a big decision, I just saw that I could go there, so I said: '*Oh, I'll go there*'... like it seemed like a straightforward decision.

The decision is 'straightforward' when it was always assumed possible. It can indeed have been made even before the opportunity arises. As Ania explains, after several shorter periods, the year abroad is seen as imperative: 'I don't know, I really wanted to do it, and some of my friends went also to the United States for a year... I was like "*I have to do this, I don't know how, but I have to do it...*". Aoife thought: 'in the long term, this is really what I want to do and, if I can't do it this year, I'll do it next year'. Distant dream, inevitable decision: when the time comes, accepting the invitation appears as a spontaneous, obvious, instinctive choice.

Motivations: residence abroad as an added value

The notion of value added is frequently used to describe the *raison d'être* of student stays abroad, described by Régine as a 'bonus': 'coming here was a bonus, otherwise I wouldn't have gone'. What does this general term refer to? What are the elements of the value added to a student route by the year abroad? Examining motivations prior to departure provides initial answers to this question, which must be capped of course by an assessment of the final outcomes.[2] Motivations must be seen as one segment of a larger set shown in Table 3, comprising latent, active and resulting components. If motivations appear under active components and are defined as the set of forces presiding over a decision or a course of action, the other elements represented, which are semantically or

Table 3 Motivations

Latent components:
Dreams, initial representations, images: mental landscape
Desires and needs: psychological landscape
Personality, predispositions to action: personal landscape

Active components:
Influences on decision making
Motivations: set of forces presiding over a decision or a course of action
Expectations, speculation or hopes regarding a reality which gets closer
Objectives: specific directions of a course of action
Anxiety, fears and preparation as action gets closer

Resulting components:
Evaluation of outcomes, advice to candidates
Further wishes arising from action
Ambitions for the future

---

chronologically connected, frequently come forth in clusters during interviews. For example, it may be the case that students, when asked about motivations, will try and retrace back in time distant dreams, personal desires or personality predispositions in an attempt to outline the temporal continuity in their biographical itinerary.

The main migratory motivation of sojourners is usually what Siu calls 'the job'. Whatever the nature of their mission, the explicit aim is always to carry out a task within a certain time limit. In the case of student travellers, the duration of the stay is fixed beforehand, while for migrant sojourners the end of the stay is suspended in time. Secondly, migrant sojourners make their choice under duress, 'fighting for their social status', and 'the job is related to all sorts of personal needs for new experience, security, prestige, etc.' (Siu, 1952: 35). In contrast, the stay is not an obligation for students, but an option. Their desire to 'fight' for a different social status is toned down and becomes encapsulated in the idea of added value. To what extent will the stay abroad represent an experience on which they can capitalise in the future so as to improve their socio-professional status?[3] The answer to this question varies with the kind of programme abroad. As mentioned earlier,[4] the official status of the stay abroad is not the same in the three study programmes, the weakest link existing for Erasmus students, while the other two training programmes reveal a more continuous and integrated line between past, present and future experience. The relationship which the students nurture with the language-culture they are in close proximity to varies accordingly, as the analysis of their motivations unveils.

Our main finding in this area is that three types of clusters dominate the data, each prevailing in one of the three groups studied. The first cluster organised around language refers to what Jannick calls 'the exultation of being able to express oneself in someone else's language', and is at the heart of the 'professional' linguist's experience. The second cluster revolves around attraction to difference or the desire 'to live strangeness' on a daily basis as an experience which breaks up routine, and this is the preserve of Erasmus students. The third cluster, more typical of EAP students, has to do with a yearning for international openness and diversity. We could sum up the three ranges of motives as wanting to 'speak foreignness', to 'live foreignness', and to open up to foreign relations. The transitive verb indicates the direct nature of the relationship being constructed between actors and outside reality as language, culture or relationships, which for once they experience without any form of mediation.

These three dominant clusters cover the principal ingredients which recur on a regular basis when their project is broached: language, work (studying and professional experience together) and personal enrichment, often the wish for something other than routine, whether meeting new people or experiencing something new.[5] The language-learning motive subsumes the cultural discovery motive related to knowledge of the host country. The academic or professional motive includes themes such as the desire to study elsewhere, to gain professional training or to discover new studying methods. The personal motive covers a large area related to desire for travel, for personal adventure, for new experiences or for self-development The first two categories of motivations, language and study/work, may be considered as instrumental,[6] reflecting institutional objectives presiding over European study and work programmes.[7] However, these may hide ulterior motives, less overt, kindred to the 'personal needs' and the internal motivation mentioned by Siu.

In any event, motivations which we dissociate for the purpose of analysis are experienced by the actors as interlaced and branching out in a multiplicity of directions.[8] Generally speaking, the official motives, linguistic or academic, are mentioned first, particularly in the students' written answers, probably because they seem the most visible, easy to articulate, and may also be considered as expected by researchers. But explicit motives are not necessarily the most significant ones, those that matter most beforehand and afterwards. Some state that you may go for language, but you come back with more. The difficulty of assessing the relative weight of motivations, asserted or undisclosed, comes from their cohabiting rather than competing. Since they are interconnected, trying to dissociate some from others seems artificial and each traveller is part in a specific way of this whole set of motivations. Marina, for example, writes that 'the experience of three different countries' was her first objective, followed by 'working with people from different cultures' and by 'obtaining a degree in a European programme', thereby linking three elements. Similarly, Christine juxtaposes four elements: her wish to acquire greater linguistic fluency, but in a country which would fulfil her personal needs for music and horse riding (she refused an offer in the United States because of this), and which would allow her to pause in her academic career, 'while experimenting with teaching'. The assortment of motives defined by Sophie on her questionnaire, and the repetition of terms such as 'new', 'other', 'more-greater', 'gain-improve', communicate clearly the 'bonus', the value added, which life abroad means for the aspiring candidate.

Sophie's answer:

1) to improve my English, 2) to be separated from my family, 3) to enjoy 'a new space of freedom', 4) to try out new experiences I cherished (drama, film-making, etc), 5) to form new relationships, 6) to seize other opportunities on the academic and professional front, 7) to gain greater self-confidence and more certainties about my professional future (teacher or not?).

(our trans.)

This example brings to light the interweaving of motivations both official (language, academic opportunity, professional uncertainty) and private (separation from family, new freedom, new experiences, new relationships). It also reveals the extent to which departure is laden with expectations and hopes.

Motives also evolve and fluctuate with time, both within a specific stay and from one stay to another. Regarding the first point, Marina identified, more broadly in her interview than in her questionnaire, three kinds of motivation for her year in Paris: living in a large city, pursuing an interesting course of study, and meeting people from different countries. But she underlined that even though *in the beginning* the most enriching experience revolved around encountering a multicultural array of individuals, one got used to it. As a result, *in the end*, what became *retrospectively* the most striking aspect of her stay was having lived in Paris. Regarding the second point, those students who are on their second stay abroad point to different motives for each stay. Sylvie explained that her first Erasmus stay was motivated by a desire for immersion in the foreign language as well as for independence from her parents and university (she was no longer 'motivated' in her home environment). Her second stay as an assistant was inspired by more specific concerns, both professional ('what am I going to do with my life?' and 'being a language assistant is a bit like having a foot into teaching') and financial, her job providing her with greater autonomy. The professional project is sharpened with the second stay and with growing maturity; it moves the student closer to entry into adult life.

The study of motivations should be understood not only as the elements which precede a given decision and course of action, but as the engine driving actions in a continuous motion and marking each individual trajectory in a different way. One goes with some ideas and comes back with something else in one's luggage and, as Aoife stated, 'I realised in the end that beside language, French, there are lots of valuable things I had acquired at the end of the year'. Jürgen also makes the point that when the objectives initially assigned to the year are fulfilled, it may not entirely be 'thanks to the experience'. Indeed, the discrepancies which students point out between original motives and end-of-course results could be deemed to indicate that life overflows the best prepared route and that some of its most treasured effects may be situated in the cracks and crevices along the road.

The exultation of language: 'speaking foreignness'

If 'speaking foreignness' gives such jubilant pleasure, it may be because language allows for an expansion or dilatation of self comparable to a second birth. Speaking a language other than that in which one grew up sometimes imparts the deep joy of being twofold, of having at one's disposal an unusually wide range of possibilities for self-expression, of refuge into another linguistic territory which may sometimes become a new country, potentially more intimate than the first, as for Kristeva: 'French is from now on my only territory and I claim the right to be able to say more carnal, more intimate things in this language which is my shelter as an exile' (1997, our trans.). Sometimes, the opposite is true and the difficulty of living in a new language, of being 'lost in translation' provokes the painful feeling of a split between two different personalities, the intense suffering of being deprived of the ability to express oneself fully and as a consequence of being reduced to a talkative mask, a masquerade: 'My speech, I sense, sounds monotonous, deliberate, heavy – an aural mask that doesn't become me or express me at all' (Hoffman, 1989: 118). The inner language has disappeared and the feeling of dispossession is total. In between these two extremes related to experience of an indefinite migration, how do student strangers position themselves regarding language motivations?

Practically all the students quote language as the uppermost motivation for their stay abroad. Aware of the linguistic stakes inherent to the contemporary world scene, they fully grasp the efficacy of linguistic immersion as a radical way to force and give a final polish to language learning in a natural milieu. They are also quick to realise that language is the key which opens doors to relationships with natives and that without the necessary linguistic tools, one is left behind, isolated, marginalised. Communicative difficulties, experienced as intense by some at the beginning of the stay,[9] impart a feeling of alienation. Language-wise, one of the values added by the stay is precisely that it promotes context-rich communication, social contacts in real time, often crowned by personal relationships. Language and social relations are inextricably linked and progress equally to the extent that in the end students tend to evaluate language progress and social learning together in the same discovery process.[10] However, the place afforded the language experience and the degree of detail with which it is described differentiates students.

Attraction to foreignness is crystallised on language for those who have already an intimate practice and knowledge of it, mostly language students, assistants or else Erasmus exchangees like Hélène, Régine or Julie. The desire to be immersed in the foreign language is the distinctive sign of our 'professional' linguists. The image of the linguistic bath one dives into, the metaphor of linguistic breathing culminating in a 'second nature' capture these specific ambitions which Hélène expresses.

> I was really keen to, eh, to dive completely for a very, very long time into English, really... I wanted to breathe English, really, so that it would come,

that it'd be like a second nature because it's a language I like a lot and one month or one month and a half... it's not enough to acquire a certain ease. So then, that was really my first goal (our trans.).

Staying for a year allows immersion 'for a very, very long time', ordinarily frustrated by short stays. Length of stay is a factor which modifies language learning since it is only by staying for a sufficiently lengthy period of time that travellers may expect to acquire the kind of automatism whereby one does not go through the native language any more. Jannick speaks of the 'enormous joy' she felt because, very quickly, she was able not to go through French and 'immediately to start working in the language and so... to speak with someone in real time if you want'. When you stay longer, you can 'learn something every day', Mathilde specifies. The process of language learning in a long-term immersion situation is cumulative, and the second language becomes 'a second nature'.

Language is also regarded as the location where many pursuits dear to language students are integrated, particularly cultural and intercultural discoveries. Assistants often take advantage of their stay to engage in research in a specific cultural area related to the host country. Their MA dissertations focus on what motivates Irish people to learn the Irish language (Hélène), the media in Ireland (Nicolas), Irish literature (Jannick). Once again, one discovery leads to another: cultural knowledge entices students to find out more about the members who participate in this culture. This is Hélène's second motive: 'the second thing is precisely that because of all these cultural aspects, I wanted to know Irish people better'. Mathilde confirms when she explains that her two 'cultural' outings, swimming and cookery classes, always had a linguistic aim: 'there was always the linguistic aspect in everything I was doing, necessarily, and then there was also the discovery aspect of... what people read, what they look at everyday'. A ubiquitous language becomes the medium for accessing the other's world. Language is crucial, but its presence is somewhat in the background, she explains, because at that point it is considered as 'acquired of course', and students can achieve a higher degree of understanding: penetrating the other's social world.

Language students have this advantage over their non-language fellow-students whose access to an understanding of that kind may well be deferred if their language competence is less advanced. Indeed, if the language objective comes first in the Erasmus group's list of motives, these students sometimes acknowledge a certain frustration in its actualisation. Both Daniel and Louis write about their disappointment at the level they achieved at the end of their nine months' immersion. Were their expectations unrealistic given their prior knowledge? What kind of linguistic support or preparation do non-language students benefit from before their departure? What kind of awareness do they possess regarding the intricate process of foreign language learning? Their disappointment may also be related to the quality of the social contacts they manage to establish during their stay.[11] It must undoubtedly be the case that deeper knowledge, not just of the language, but of the language learning process and its multifarious vicissitudes, would contribute enormously to the overall degree of satisfaction expressed in the end. However, language preparation for non-specialist students suffers from the same uncertainties as orientation courses for the actual period abroad and it could be suggested that many students leave ill-prepared for what lies ahead of them.

For language students, the snowball effect or circularity in the area of motivations dominates. Mathilde points out that her taste for languages led her initially to go abroad, and then 'when you meet people, you always want to go further'. Potential travellers start with one country, then they come back, and realise that there are many other potential discoveries: 'it's rather contagious... a kind of thirst, you always want to leave again...'. The genesis of a taste for travelling may follow the following course: knowing a language initially motivates cultural pursuits, then a desire to encounter the people who speak that language, which opens up more and more doors, motivations embracing one another like Russian dolls. Mathilde goes on to say that once you have mastered basic apprehensions regarding language and distance from friends and family, a new balance is generated between the person and the environment, producing in its turn an openness to what is going on around in an ever more spacious perimeter.

> It's as if you always had more room to receive and welcome what's outside... while before when I was in France, I had the feeling that I was limited to my small familiar world, student or other... and when you start going away, you open up, you get the feeling that you can fill quite a lot of... not necessarily empty spaces, but some... some places which are... you see? (our trans.).

From a yearning for language, travellers progressively manage to feel 'somehow as if life is expanding... a certain curiosity which livens up, which grows gradually by looking at people, simply by living!', Mathilde adds. The live dimension of the discovery, through language and its accompanying 'secondary effects', puts pressure on the boundaries of a world experienced as too 'small' and which thus extends considerably.[12]

Bilingual or trilingual students: the deepening process

The live relation with language is special in the case of bilingual or trilingual students. The language motive appears in their comments in finer detail, an intimate part of their biography.[13] Régine traces her school career and explains that her wish to come to Ireland was born out of the fact that the variety of English she knows is of American origin since she learnt it in Hawaii. As a student in Paris, her relation to the language changed to that of studying rather than practising it, from a French perspective and with British lecturers. She observes an 'incongruity' between 'her' English and the English she is studying. Her decision to leave is motivated by 'relativism with the language'.

> Hum… often with British lecturers, well with British English, but even with Irish English… I found myself incongruous because my English was not necessarily… etc. And, well… I don't know, maybe it's relativism with the language in a way and with the Anglo-Saxon world, since in France, people are quick to generalise: *'Ah, you are going in the Anglo-Saxon world!'* as if it was one complete entity… Well! also, yes, I always wanted to come to Ireland, I'd never been, even as a tourist. I had been once to London, but otherwise the whole British Isles thing and Ireland, I had never… and so I wanted to come… first, to see the difference in language because I am already interested… (our trans.).

However, if her first objective consists in a better appreciation of sociolinguistic diversity, she is also in search of a stronger language identity, in order to enable '… to speak with my own personal accent' and to take responsibility for her personal variety of language, particularly in relation to her lecturers.

> Because, since I am aware that I haven't got at the moment a 'pure' in inverted commas American of *you know the West coast* because it's influenced by French, by my friends who come from either Lebanon, or… *East USA*, etc. I know there isn't one accent and that there isn't one good and one bad *per se*. But I wanted to be able to draw a line, well me, to speak with my own personal accent… well because even though there's no problem with all accents, nevertheless it's bizarre, it's when you have an accent and then *hints* or… traces of other accents which are… [added on?], yes added on… well I wanted to know enough… because I had this course in sociolinguistics… and I didn't get on with the professor because he was British… and he was telling me to shut up… so precisely I was against, he was saying: *'All accents are equal'*, but on the other hand he was very rigid: *'Ah, are you sure this is how it is said? Really…'*. So I wanted to know enough to relativise but knowing what I was talking about (our trans.).[14]

There is a strong link, in Régine's case, between language motivation and identity: she wants to assert her language identity in one of the two languages she possesses.

For Christophe as well, the language stake is combined with identity issues. What really motivates him is the linguistic challenge, particularly the game of hide-and-seek he plays between his various language identities. As a Francophone from Flanders, he is trilingual through his English mother and for him, the experience of foreignness takes on a complex significance where languages, cultures and identities are meshed. He describes the level of his three languages as varying according to the moment and to his exposure to them, in a kind of dance in between three language figures who come and go in his life.

> I am more at ease in French since I started studying in French, that is since the age of 5–6 because... it's the language I practised most, I suppose, but... eh... I really hope that my English will come back to a... the same level.[15] In fact I feel the levels going up and down because I had... when I was at boarding-school in Flemish, my French was even easier, but Flemish overshadowed my English... while now, my practice of Flemish has gone down, my practice of English has... which had remained at a stable level is going up and now, English... overshadows Flemish. I hope my English is going to come back and I don't see why not since it is my first language, so I try... (our trans.).

In these circumstances, Christophe's main objective in Paris is to try and acquire a less Belgian and more French accent so that he could 'pass for' French, in the sense Stonequist uses when mentioning racial hybrids who due to the colour of their skin manage to 'pass for' what they are not. For Christophe as for many others, the distinctive mark, the stigma of the stranger being language, he tries 'unconsciously', according to him, 'to pass for a Parisian, well not for a Parisian, but to pass for someone who is not Belgian'. As a true linguistic chameleon, he naturally picks up traces of accents and his Belgian friends tell him that he has taken up a Dutch accent, rather than Flemish or Belgian, from speaking with Dutch students. He claims that individuals who are accustomed to several languages, even if they have to go through the experience of foreignness, will have no 'difficulty in adapting or changing cultures'.

> Potentially, without, without, without any effort... I wouldn't say the experience of foreignness, because you acquire that by yourself by living, by having to go to the doctor, by going to sign contracts, by opening bank accounts... But, the... the lack of difficulty in adapting and in... changing cultures (our trans.).

He also draws a line between external aspects of the adaptation process and intimate ones which have to do with internal flexibility. Indeed, if language is at the heart of the adaptation process, since 'many, many things go through that, many... all the difficulties are because of that', for those who have gained the psychological power to pass for a native thanks to their linguistic competence, 'the rest follows'.

> ... I didn't experience difficulty adapting to Dutch culture... well to Flemish culture in Belgium since I could pass for a Flemish person and that helps a lot, because psychologically if you can pass for someone who

is judged as a native... I think that the rest follows. You don't have the problem of people who think you are a foreigner (our trans.).

The stranger's stigma fades away, at least in the eyes of the natives, a most crucial parameter in cultural identity. Indeed, Christophe uses languages so as not to be recognised by others as a foreigner, in other words to confuse monolinguals. But in France in spite of the language community, he did not feel 'one of them', which leads him to differentiate between linguistic proximity and cultural proximity.

Exultation for those who succeed in opening many doors through their expanding linguistic mastery or language relativism for those who play with linguistic border crossing, the language motivation is manifold. Yearning for the language is the basis or the springboard which gives rise to other stimulations or impulses. Certainly, the more advanced the language competence, the more natural it seems to 'change worlds' and 'to pursue an heterogeneous itinerary', as Marina says when she quotes students from Luxembourg for whom the programme 'is an ideal option because we have an extraordinary asset compared to people from other countries': they already possess the three languages used in the programme. Language is the over-arching key allowing access to other worlds where the second range of motivations may be fulfilled, that is to say attraction to difference or the wish to 'live foreignness' as an experience.

Attraction to difference: 'living foreignness'

The desire to 'live foreignness', not just to speak it, has two faces, implicit in the two meanings of the term 'experience'. Experience refers first of all to novelty, to a 'first', i.e. the fact of experimenting with something considered as an extension or an addition to one's knowledge and aptitude. In this sense, it implies a process of exploration defined in time. Experience is also the result of this investigative process or the specific practice and knowledge acquired. It also points to knowledge acquired through trial and practice. The various levels of meaning appear in the motivations expressed by the students, separating them into two distinct categories: those who focus on the testing dimension of the stay abroad because this is their first long stay and those who, due to previous experiences, define their objectives in finer detail.

The students expect the stay to be an experience, and they repeat the same words over and over again in their statement of objectives: 'to experiment', 'experience', 'new' or 'other' (system, people, culture, country), 'discovery', 'to discover', 'different', as evidenced in John's response.

Hum, new experiences, enjoyment, adventure. I consider that when you're travelling, especially abroad, you're going to encounter new people, new things, very much new experiences. It's going to be totally new. It's not going to be the same streets, the same people and maybe not the same language. So excitement, ya, I think excitement and adventure of experiencing a whole new culture, new language. I think very much the key word would be 'new', I think very much new experience.

This semantic sequence in the narratives signifies the desire to change worlds and to break with a familiarity sometimes apprehended as restrictive or ponderous, when it no longer 'motivates' and does not function as a generator for action. Amin wanted to do something different because he thought that four years in the same university would be too long. Mathilde felt the need 'to pause in academic life'. This perceived deficiency takes shape as the need for a break. The temporary break becomes a pause in an itinerary, a stop to refuel one's energy. It may also take on a more radical meaning and end up as a total life change, as will be the case for Valérie and Nicolas who decide to stay and live in Ireland.

Motivations around that theme are particularly recurrent in Erasmus students' responses,[16] with echoes of the same ingredients in a different order: experience (personal dimension), language and study (academic dimension), people (social dimension). For example, Ava lists (1) learning the language, (2) having new experiences, and (3) meeting Irish people and seeing their way of life, as her three major reasons for spending a year abroad. Similar ingredients are listed in a different order by Louis who writes: '(1) an original experience (100 per cent), (2) to encounter a new culture (50 per cent), (3) to meet different people (70 per cent)'. Beyond common components, individual variations are perceptible and inform on a particular personal concern or on a more advanced knowledge of the experience itself. Some students, interestingly, specify the degree of realisation of their objectives, Louis in percentages, Hugo globally (he writes, 'all largely achieved'), and so naturally link the issue of objectives to that of outcomes.

Overall, they expect the experience to be as comprehensive as possible and to include academic and professional, social and intercultural, and finally personal enrichment. Suzanne sums it up in her own hierarchical order: 'I think what would sum up why I did EAP... was my own personal development and... learning about people, more than the academic things'. For her, 'personal development' comes before the social and the academic dimensions. But what precisely do the students mean by this general wish expressed as wanting 'to live abroad', which is at the heart of their preoccupations? This wish is polarised around the main area of their life, the official justification for their period abroad, 'studying' for Erasmus students together with professional experience for the two other groups. At the level of explicit motivations though, this area remains rather indistinct. It is only later, as the experience develops, that its many facets are more clearly detailed: teaching content, study methods, lecturing style, relations between students and staff, examinations, whatever leads to a contrast between their national academic practice and the new one. Marco, for example, explains at great length the differences between being a student in Rome and in Dublin.[17]

As a result, in the Erasmus experience, the verbs 'to live' and 'to study' are nearly interchangeable. One specific example will illustrate the point. Lucy, who had already spent a year as an au pair in Paris, uncovers the specificity of the study abroad experience compared to other forms of residence abroad. For her second stay, her generic desire 'to study in a foreign university' is broken down into two specific intentions: language development and discovery of student life in another country. This new aspiration proceeds from her first experience since her purpose is to move beyond the linguistic level achieved previously in the context of conversations with her host family or friends, to see if she can achieve the linguistic level required in an academic context, thereby extending her language repertoire.

> Hum, I was interested in studying, in being in a university, not sort of… meeting other au pairs or whatever it is, other students. Actually, classes and whatever, how difficult it was going to be. I was almost like a child because, I mean, I knew my French was OK, but wanted to see exactly how good it was because I could speak French in a conversation, after the year abroad, but I mean technically my French wasn't all that good, you know… academically. So, I was… that was one point… [one expectation…]… ya, for French.

Her objective of discovering student life in another country originates partly from her observing that her sister did not really 'get involved in French university life' because she stayed within her 'own little social circle, full of Irish girls'.

> Hum, just the life, student life, you know, because I know my sister had been to Paris and she hadn't really… student life there. I don't know why, I think it was, I mean, you get sort of lost… She was living with my cousin and her friend, and they made up their own little social circle, full of Irish girls and whatever. So she didn't really get involved in French university life. So I wanted to see… so just to see what it was like, just the student life… and also living alone. I was just basically moving out, you know…

Finally her objective 'to live alone' highlights the fact that the au pair experience, while it confers a certain autonomy, does not include this element of total independence. Overall, it is noticeable that the place assigned to the academic dimension in the Erasmus descriptions reflects the context of their programme and distinguishes their experience from that of the other two groups.

The other two groups, half-way between student and professional life, are also generally speaking more experienced in their foreign knowledge through their language competence in the case of assistants and through their familiarity with life abroad for many EAP students. Their period abroad contains work experience which is a powerful motivation. Valérie, who changed from Germanic studies over to English studies in order to come back to Ireland, explains that it is the opportunity of going to live for a year with a job, 'without undertaking too much', which allowed her dream to become reality. This professional initiation is a test for many assistants: they want to know if teaching will be their chosen career. Valérie echoes the others in underlining that the professional pursuit is coupled with 'the pleasure of living in another language'. She also 'likes the "one year..." as a parenthesis in a course'. The experience is a true one: most of them teach for the first time and the duration of the test is limited. Siobhan decided to go because it was 'a chance not to be missed' since it is so hard to get a paid job abroad. Fiona hesitated between 'the chance of a lifetime' and fear of going away, but her parents guided her choice. The assistant sojourn is a unique opportunity in a variety of ways, which Fiona lists: 'good for language, good for academic studies, good for material independence, and professional experience'. It is nevertheless a source of anxiety. Students have to teach their first language as a foreign language when they have no experience of language teaching and have not studied their own language as an academic subject for the most part. Indeed, initial orientation and training structures are crucial in their case. The EAP work placement is also experienced by the students as a considerable asset in the programme. It represents not only a coveted professional immersion, but also a rare opportunity for them to engage in direct contacts with natives as part of their social immersion. But we come back to this point later.[18] The academic or professional side of motivation is at the very heart of their desire for novelty and change from their national context. It represents a major part of the value added to their training path.

Outside the professional dimension, the second facet of this range of motivation, attraction to difference, is the desire to meet different people. All students share this desire, but express it differently. Sometimes, the students' expectations are rather vague, a fact which probably reflects the absence of preparation for the stay abroad. What are they really looking for in terms of social experience? Do they want to meet other students, whether natives of the host country or other student travellers like them? Or are they interested in a broader discovery of the people whose society they find themselves in temporarily? Some students display a more advanced awareness in this area. Birgitta associates her language objective to the social one by reporting that she hopes to improve her oral English through socialising with Irish people. Marina relates that her objective, 'to encounter a new culture', changed in the course of the experience because she met 'not only many Irish people, but also many people from different cultures'. The occurrence of intercultural encounters modifies expectations, the international or European dimension transcending the purely national dimension. The prior degree of intercultural awareness affects the way these motivations are formulated, as Hugo's example shows. More aware than others, his expectations are somewhat more precise:[19] he wishes 'to acquire long-term friends' and to discover the language and culture 'from the inside'. Conversely, the less aware students will not relay their expectations in great detail.

Attraction to difference, novelty, foreignness, be it academic, professional or social, goes with attraction for a particular mode of learning, learning through experience, first-hand or 'in real time' in Mathilde's words. The live dimension of the experience is frequently underlined as a major asset of the sojourn. Fiona was aware from the beginning that she was going not just to improve her language competence, but also 'to learn the living aspects of French life, the language they use'. John uses the image of immersion in the new life so that you 'learn in your brain'.

> To be immersed not just on holidays, but to be living there. And I feel the only way you can really know a city or know a country is to live there [yes] you can go on holidays every single year for three weeks, but you're not learning it. You have to live there to know the streets, the people, hum, the culture. So it was a chance for me to learn a new, to learn in my brain a new country and a new language and a new culture. So that was very much the motivating factor, that I'd know something else, apart from Ireland, very, very well...

This kind of holistic participation which integrates streets, people, country, language, culture, becomes as familiar as a second nature, just as for language, and promotes in-depth learning ('I'd know something else... very, very well'). Such everyday, ordinary, private knowledge is specific to the year abroad and cannot be acquired on a three-week holiday.

Live contact with the country, language and people is necessary to contextualise communication. Then, the language experience expands into a taste for living and experiencing foreignness. Jürgen specifies: 'language is an experience' which 'comes with living on the spot' to become 'the basis for other events'. For example, Thomas describes how it can lead to a 'transformation' in the way one thinks about cultures, because if 'there was no word in French, so perhaps they don't feel this way'.

> ...for me it would be interesting also going to Spain, Italy and to do all this transformation, like to talk the language because when you talk the language, then you have to think in a different language. Like in France, I understood that there are some things you cannot say in French, because there are no words for... like, eh..., I can give you an example in German '......', '*it's comfortable*'... I couldn't, I always wanted to say: '*ya, it's very cosy here!*'. It didn't work because there was no word in French, so perhaps they don't feel this way... So I said, for me the result was to see that the culture could be completely different...

Language and cultural discovery are concomitant. Language is an experience in that it is a trial, but it produces an enrichment and a learning. Indeed, a change in language can bring about significant personal change. It becomes evident that the live dimension of both language and life abroad is the hallmark of this original learning experience. In sharp contrast with formal learning circumstances, 'living foreignness' implies two essential ingredients: lengthy and first-hand contacts with difference in all its forms.

International openness: at ease in diversity

The third kind of motivation conveys above all the idea of expansion, translated first as a fundamental principle of continuity, previous experience tracing a path which students wish to explore further, secondly as the need to open up to an international dimension so as to enlarge one's life space, to extend one's range of contacts and to spread one's wings. This range of motivations is particularly visible in the EAP students' comments.

The principle of continuity reveals the growth in a personal chronology of a travelling itinerary which gets more complex with experience. Students who have gone for a year elsewhere wish either to come back to the location of their experience like Thomas or Matthew, or to leave again towards new horizons like Juan and Jürgen. Juan, back from a year in the United States, would like to leave again immediately, but his parents advise him to wait. All his academic choices are made on the basis of his going abroad and starting an international career. Jürgen decides to complement his 'American experience' with a European experience, the three EAP locations corresponding to 'one block' in his mind. Thomas goes back into his past in order to elucidate his motives for choosing the EAP programme. He sees four stages in the evolution of his decision. First, the numerous travels to distant destinations with his parents, where they were doing 'other things than just going to the beach', his father talking about the history of the place and about 'what people were doing, what is a foreign country', made up 'one push'. The second push came from his work experience with the Club Med in Montreal where he spent six months away from home and felt so 'excited to go alone in a place where nobody knows [him]'. Then, he rounded off his academic studies very fast and, having time 'to go for an adventure and explore something different', decided to learn a foreign language and went to Aix-en-Provence for a year. The language experience transformed him, he 'changed attitudes' and, as a result, he wanted to come back 'to try and continue the French immersion… become more… more like French people'. This is when he decided to apply for the EAP programme. His experiences complement and deepen one another.

In a similar fashion, Matthew compares his motivations for his first and second sojourn. While, during his year as an assistant, he was looking for a pause in his university course to 'relax' and have time to reflect on his future, the first experience urged him to come back to France. He chose the EAP so as to have direct access to jobs in Europe rather than working in England first and waiting for a post abroad. For him, the stages are progressive: he left his native Scotland to go to university in England, then he decided to go and work as an assistant in France, and finally he chose a European course of study.

These students are accustomed to larger spaces than their national space. A European course is the most efficient way to pursue a trajectory initiated earlier on.

The accumulated experience allows them to embark on these coming-and-goings naturally, without experiencing the uncertainties and fears expressed by those with lesser experience like Elena. Before going on her Parisian sojourn, she was excited, she recalls, but also worried at the idea of 'starting something new you don't know', with all its unpredictability about courses, people, language.

> I was excited, but I was very scared... no, ... not scared, it's not the word, sort of worried and... you know... starting something new you don't know..., you see, it's just the uncertainty because you don't know... what the college course is going to be like. You don't know what the people are going to be like. You don't know how, you know, you can't judge your language ability when you are not in the country. So, you know, everyone might say: '*oh, you speak really well*', but you don't know until you're there...

By comparison, before setting off for her second year abroad in Oxford, she felt 'much more confident'.

> I feel, I feel... sort of much more confident and, you know, about going over and... you know, getting ready this year is just like getting ready, go and get your shopping, you know, and it's sort of like you have done it before, so it's not really... hm... I am not traumatised by it...

The second sojourn becomes somewhat run-of-the-mill and unexceptional, because 'you have done it before'. The value of the first experience and its propaedeutic function are clearly demonstrated here. The principle of continuity is in train: mobility is becoming a habit.

Consequently, since one experience leads to another, the choice of a European programme answers a need to enlarge one's life space. Many of the EAP travellers repeat the magic number of 'three', countries, languages, experiences, in relation to their motivations, particularly those who do not originate from the three countries on offer. Elena lists: (1) three European countries, (2) meeting students from other nationalities, (3) working in three countries. Thomas mentions (1) staying in France, (2) going to Oxford, (3) living in Berlin. Multiplicity is lessened in the case of Thomas and Jürgen who are German, but 'living in Berlin' is nevertheless regarded as a discovery when travellers come from another area. For Marina, who possesses the three languages required for the course, the main interest lies in the academic opportunity offered by a course which does not exist in her country. As for Tom, whose life space is already international, but anglophone, the objective is to diversify his knowledge of Europe and to learn languages other than English.

Multiplicity proliferates. These students are going to study in three different educational systems, unknown to the majority of the group. They are going to work in three different countries. They are going to live in three different cultures and speak different languages. Tom relays this cumulative effect, explaining that he had never lived in France, England or Germany: 'so that was three more places I could explore'.

> ...well, I had been in Dublin for two years and I spent my summers in France and the opportunity – I mean Ireland is not my home... although I enjoyed it a lot I haven't that same attraction to Ireland that a lot of Irish people have, that it's home, that's where they want to be – of moving some-where else was very attractive. I had never lived in France for more than three weeks at a time, I had never lived in England at all and I had never lived in Germany, I had never been to Germany. So that was three more places I could explore: that was an attraction.

An attendant motivation is inherent to the multicultural nature of the EAP group. Viktor from Russia finds the 'many nationalities in the group... from fourteen different places' a powerful incentive. They are also going to live in three different cities, notably Paris which is regarded as a dominant attraction by many students, communicated with great enthusiasm by Marina: 'The EAP, I chose it because there was this kind of brochure with all the *grandes écoles* in France, I leafed through and suddenly I fell upon the EAP and I saw '*Oxford... ouah! Paris, Berlin... super!*'...'. Franz is equally 'very attracted by the metropolitan character of Paris' and 'expects a wonderful year'. Multiplying their life experiences, they transform themselves step by step into potential wanderers.

Taking off is also a way of leaving behind a space experienced as narrow. The wide-ranging person may feel that the surrounding domestic space no longer acts as an incentive. Josef finds his work with IBM in Germany 'too boring' and reports that he 'wanted to engage in new experiences and to break up with this routine way of life'. Jürgen is frustrated and dislikes the small Bavarian town where he is studying. He would have gone anywhere, to Berlin or Munich, but 'Paris makes the experience even more pleasant'. Bruno explains that one of his expectations was 'negative... to get away from Italy'. As for Philip, he 'wanted to taste something else'.

> I am grateful to England for educating me, but at the same time I think I was satisfied with England, but I wanted to discover something new. Maybe I was aware that there were other things out there in the big world because of the Italian side of my family... and I felt I had spent quite enough in England and I wanted to taste something else.

Christophe feels the same urge to leave Belgium, a space he considers all the more restricted because 'there is a certain family culture, by that I mean a certain number of families in Belgium who get together all the time... *it narrows things*'[20]. The desire to taste something else is the most powerful stimulus, a major part of the invitation to travel, spurring them on, somewhat impulsively, to consider familiar spaces as confining and to nurture the desire to widen their life space.

Widening one's life space is mentioned as a motivation in terms of diversity of social contacts and roles. Sometimes, it is a question of going from national to international contacts, as Jose does when he describes this gradual widening of his social circle thanks to his involvement with AIESEC. His responsibilities led him to remain outside Portugal for ten months within a year, 'a bit everywhere', and 'all this international experience' results in his knowing people from all sorts of places: 'you broaden your mind a lot'. After such exposure, going back to a national routine is difficult.

> So you get people... to know people from all over... and you broaden your mind a lot. Then, eh... AIESEC led me to EAP because, after getting that environment, when you finish your career in AIESEC, you don't say '*now, I am going to go back to Lisbon*', because the wide majority of your friends are spread around the world. My girlfriend is Swiss, so she's nothing to do with Lisbon... A lot of friends are spread all over, so it's natural... all of a sudden, you don't feel that much difference between Paris and Lisbon and... Estonia and... Egypt.

He adds that each time he wants to phone a friend, he must dial an international number and 'that has a big impact... not only on the phone bill, but also on you!'. Meeting and working with individuals from different nationalities inevitably enlarges one's social world.

But the experience also provides the opportunity to enlarge the range of social roles available. The more foreign cultures one knows, the more different ways of being one can avail of, Thomas says. For example, 'you can behave like a French person in a restaurant and like a German person in your family and so on...'. This process, according to him, consists in understanding that 'life may be richer than it is in only one culture. There are other possibilities.' The practice of alternative social behaviours according to the context and circumstances one finds oneself in is well documented in the literature on life in between different cultures (Huston, 1999). It is often symbolised by the image of the mask, which allows for duality, even multiplicity in the parts one plays in life.[21] The main qualitative shift between the roles available on an ordinary stage and on an international stage is that they range across national and cultural repertoires. Undoubtedly, the ability to take on cultural attitudes and behaviours other than the habitual ones singularly extends the social gamut at one's disposal.

Finally, international openness fulfils the desire to spread one's wings and to take off. Damien uses this image, which contains the notions of elasticity and elongation, to describe his motivations. He was expecting to be extended and stretched. Indeed, flexibility or the absence of rigidity is constantly cited by students as one of the fundamental features of the adaptive personality.[22] Even if the EAP students will mostly deploy their professional wings, it rapidly becomes evident that the professional project is but a pretext for an ulterior motive related to a long-awaited extension of self. The two aspects are linked, Damien points out. Opting for a European course was a means for him to get down to work, to go further than what he was ready to accomplish in a familiar environment, in a word 'to wake up'.

> No, I wasn't particularly motivated or engaged in Business Studies. At the time I decided to go, it was because I picked this business option... And economics in second year is what woke me up. So, I decided to try and join the EAP. I decided that, if I got it, I would go. Once I decided to try and get in, I was definitely going to go... so that was my motivation: to see if this form of business education was anymore satisfying than what was going on.

In his usual environment, he is sleep-walking. Going abroad quickens and sharpens individuals into higher gear with the new personal demands made on them. Josef as well mentions his wish to extend his 'international or multicultural competence' and he lists the skills he expects to acquire: 'In order to get integrated, you need a practical intelligence and you need to compromise. I expect my ability to understand new situations and to prepare myself for them is going to increase.' The choice of opening up to an international dimension represents a double challenge: to spread professionally and personally. The process of adaptation which accompanies this movement is defined as the art of approaching novelty, new situations, and in particular intercultural diversity. To be at ease within diversity is one of the essential skills a programme such as the EAP fosters.

To sum up, whether it is 'speaking foreignness', 'living foreignness' as an experience, or opening up to diversity, the official motives which delineate the sojourner's 'job' during the period of time spent abroad are like so many movements, more or less dominant according to the performers, in the symphony of possible motivations. However, minor variations appear which form a kind of musical accompaniment to the principal theme.

'A kind of emptiness' (Sophie): life abroad as self-discovery

These individual intentions focus attention on the invitation to travel as a personal call, sometimes precocious, in a life story. The meaning of the project is not entirely contained in dreams of extending one's horizons or discovering other scenes and other actors. For some, the sojourn is above all an opportunity for travelling inside, 'far into oneself', a *rendez-vous* with self (Martineau, op. cit.: 55) which Régine encapsulates: 'I feel that to be myself and not to be observed, I have to be somewhere else'. Being somewhere else and being self are synonymous when being at home means being 'observed'. Leaving liberates from the familiar controlling gaze.

Travelling creates an opening, but it also creates an emptiness which travellers must fill. Clearing one's life, unloading its usual content may be felt as a blessing. Maria is seeking a vacant social space and anonymity because she knows too many people at home, just like Christophe and Jürgen, who wish to escape from a world conceived as too small. Others are looking for vacancy in their senti-mental life and weigh on the decision to go or... not to go. Iris made up her mind only after she split from her boyfriend. Josef's girlfriend wanted to go back to Paris where she had lived and contributed to his choice of the EAP programme. Valérie had 'personal problems' which prompted her to 'go to fresh pastures and to start all over again'. She wanted, she says, 'a change of life, a change of country...', which she certainly achieved since she met an Irishman to whom she is engaged and intends settling in Ireland. The change of world in her case produced a complete life change.

Several students aspire to a certain vacuum in relation to their milieu to gain some form of autonomy, first material and then mental. Those who have never left the family home before regard this aspect as substantial. They wish to gain some form of self-management, learning 'how to survive for a year far from home', as Collette says. But, most of our students had already acquired this form of autonomy, notably through studying far from home.[23] Others may wish to find their own identity away from the family cocoon or, in Hélène's case, away from 'the pull of older brothers'.

> Well... and then the second thing, heu... is as I was saying first is that there are four of us children at home, I have three brothers, I am the youngest, and we are very close in age, my eldest brother is 30... and I am 24... and so in fact I have always been cradled by this movement at home, my brothers were involved in lots of things, music, sports, there were always loads of people... in fact, I... I lived on their experience and I was like... drawn ahead by the pull of my older brothers and precisely, this first experience in the United States showed me that finally, all alone, lost in this vast world, I did not have much left in terms of my own identity, that without... outside the family cocoon, eventually, it was difficult and I realised that I did not have much of... a life belonging to me... and so, I have been fighting with this since I was 18... so, I try to leave the house because I say to myself that if I stay, it's comfortable, but it's not what's needed... precisely to try and cut the umbilical cord (our trans.).

Cutting the umbilical cord, breaking away from family warmth, facing new life conditions alone represent so many steps to engage in which test your ability to survive abroad. Collette and Sylvie comment that living alone means having your own budget to manage, making your own decisions, and above all getting used to distance from loved ones. For affective or mental independence can only be achieved if you triumph over 'the desire to go back home', which ties you to former links through telephone calls or other forms of attachment.[24]

The peculiar position of the stranger in between proximity and distance is in full view in this game of to and fro between the familiar and the unknown.

Emptiness created by displacement also provides an opportunity for reflection and sometimes meets a need for solitude and introspection which may temporarily distract from other pursuits, as was the case for Hélène.

> And then, it was a year when I wanted to think a lot about… euh about my involvements, well I really wanted to think about that and this is partly why I wanted to live alone and so, I don't know, when I arrived, meeting people just like that for the pleasure of meeting people seemed to me rather gratuitous… so I did not particularly want to… rather this time I needed time for introspection (our trans.).

The gaze directed inwards diverts from other encounters which appear 'gratuitous'. Consequently, even though she knows people in Dublin, she does not contact them. She 'retires within herself' and feels that she is becoming 'antisocial': accepting an invitation requires 'a huge effort… when it's something I would have done easily before'. The wish to travel responds to various biographical demands or aspirations and for some, the desire to travel within oneself overrides all other aims. In any case, travelling provides a perfect time for reflection, if only because language learning 'makes you reflect a lot in a positive way', as Bruno puts it. Distanciation from language induces distanciation in relation to other aspects of life.

For Sophie and Bruno, emptiness is a personal necessity, a kind of therapeutic move. New life conditions offer an opportunity to escape from your normal self. He is trying to forget something which does not work for him in Italy: 'at home, things are not too good, I am going elsewhere…' expecting that 'elsewhere, it can be better, we can change ourselves'. He goes even further by saying that 'you can change your skin'. At first, his ambition was to be either like local people or like a person who is already international. At the end of his stay in Paris, the equilibrium he had lost is somewhat restored, but more by 'assessing what I already had' and by developing himself rather than by adopting a different personality. The experience 'made [him] move in his head… unlocked' him. Sophie' s point of departure is quite similar. She too is trying to change something in her life and regards the sojourn as a therapy. She wants to get rid of her 'French identity as a not very successful girl'. If the experience is successful, it will allow her to move forward. According to her, all candidates for the year abroad 'want something else, are expectant, want to change' and staying abroad is a therapy in that it is 'a way of discovering oneself, of pushing oneself to the furthermost limit'. Leaving behind a certain social and family milieu, a period in one's life, personal habits, is the necessary condition to find oneself. In the end, Bruno assesses the experience as fostering progress in one's own itinerary, 'something to put with the rest of the luggage', he says. As for Sophie, Ireland is a starting point, a first step towards a new life. For a stay to be successful, she states, you must leave 'with questions… with objectives, even frustrations… there's a kind of emptiness waiting to be filled…'.

Whether it is to discover others, other than self, or to uncover self, other in self (Kristeva, 1991), displacement outside a familiar space heralds a void, perceived as a sweeping stage to be occupied by new players or else as a potential new character and performance one may invent since remoteness liberates from roles assigned before. Whether the discovery focuses on the outside or the inside, invitations to travel are fertile in potentialities, expectations, interrogations. That is why travelling is an adventure.

An adventure into another time–space

Indeed, asked what travelling means to them, students mention adventure, but mean different realities. Adventure consists in exposure to certain risks, to uncertainty, to surprises. Chance and newness define the area. The specific adventure which life abroad represents may range from the pleasant revelation of a different place to a more binding involvement with another time–space.

For some, adventure is like a game. It means enjoying the revelation of cultural differences. Travellers, in a way, anticipate encounters with the unexpected and the unknown. Sophie explains that the first trip that really mattered to her was her stay in Florida with a family where the 'American dream' came to her as a shock and, from then on, she made up her mind to travel. Other trips did not matter because they did not include amazing revelations apt to jolt out of routine. For Lucy, seeking adventure leads to a different time–space, but to be 'controlled'.

> It's… it's a great adventure, I love going away. I always feel like *'where am I going to go next?'*, you know, if I'm at home for a year: *'what's wrong?'*, you know. But, I've always done it, gone for a good space of time and I think it's interesting… well, as long as you know people, well I mean it can't be lonely. But, I've always sort of known people, I mean when I was going to Paris, I knew I was going to be in a family and I knew Mylène. When I was going to Belgium, I knew the other seven were coming. I mean I don't think I would go alone, sort of… where I don't know anybody. It represents an adventure, but it's got to be controlled, you know, I don't think I am that independent.

In this case, the adventure of going away which makes her ask where she is going next, is mitigated by her need for security, that is knowing people beforehand.

Adventure takes on other meanings as well. For Amin, the adventure was mitigated since travelling seemed normal to him, 'if you have the resources'. But, he found that the conventional aim of travelling, i.e. broadening your horizons, sometimes leads to the opposite result. Some travellers come back with negative opinions about the countries and people they visited. But awareness of this type of adverse reaction may lessen its impact.

I haven't really got a big philosophy, it's just something that I know I will do, I should do, I always will do it. It's something that, I think, if you're, if you..., if you can do it, if you can travel, if you've the resources [...] I think it's something you should do for... just to broaden your horizons, even though I know some people say that it can in fact narrow your horizons, but.... Hm, well some people travel and they come back saying '*Oh, I didn't like Belgium or I didn't like the Belgians*' or wherever they were... I think generally speaking if you... once you're aware that that can happen, I don't think it will.

At the other extreme, Maria alludes to travel in terms evocative of Giddens (1979), defining it above all as complete immersion into another time–space.

Hm, travelling means to me going to a new place, seeing the new place, trying as much as you possibly can in the timespace that you've been given to integrate yourself into the space even if it's only two weeks, you'd want to see as much... I only went to Italy for two weeks, I thought I was Italian when I was leaving, hm, trying to get a good grasp of what these people enjoy doing themselves, I love seeing the way they do things differently to us, what peculiarities they have, against Irish people, and I have used that myself, I suppose, when I thought it was a better way... Like eating... having your main meal in the middle of the day, I think, is far healthier than eating it at the end of the day. That's something I do now, and eat light meals now, or ... heu, just little things. I go out much later at night than my friends, I think that's great, I think you let off loads of steam and tension, great, go out and ... whereas, Irish people, pubs close at half eleven, they don't tend to go out as late. Hm... learning off other people, I suppose, as well...

Even on short two-week trips, she will try to integrate herself into the environment and to absorb new habits when they seem better than her own, the onset of what Joseph calls the 'hybridisation of life styles'[25] (1984). Indeed, the fit between her personality and the environment is so tight that she imagines herself easily as a member of the new group: 'I thought I was Italian when I left'. Above all, she outlines the specificity of staying abroad: you learn 'off other people'. The process of osmosis is dual, both with the environment and with the people.

Conclusion: continuity and discontinuity

Student travellers of today engage in a new kind of nomadism. What distinguishes them from others is the qualitative investment in their future. Aware of economic competition, they appreciate the professional stakes of an international position, while at the same time being initially scared of the card they are playing as they have not yet mastered the game fully. Suzanne suggests that it 'was not really a strategic choice', but ends up being something which was 'meant to be'. Student travellers are willing to seize opportunities with all their uncertainty.

> That was not... really a strategic choice... I mean, you say this in your interview to get into EAP, but it wasn't, it wasn't... 'a goal'... my initial reaction was '*Wow! that would be brilliant! But, I would never be able to do that!*', because I was very..., not because of any fear of going away, I mean, that was never a problem... and living in three countries, but I just thought it would be too difficult, I thought academically that it was '*oh!...*' [...] I think it was something I knew deep inside that I wanted to do, but I was really scared, and I did the interview so that if I got it, it would force me to do it... So really, when I did the interview and stuff, I wasn't 100 per cent sure of going, but then once I got it, I was like '*this is meant to be*' and then... got all excited and I was really happy and I think I would have been very unhappy had I not got it.

Outside the academic challenge often imagined as most important, Suzanne mentions other fears related to proximity of entry into adult life. Periods abroad frequently imply work experience and this new step into an approaching career path may be conceived as the end of student life.

> I thought... I think the biggest thing was actually academic. [...] I thought that everybody going would be completely career-minded and that student life would be over... and I thought that everybody going to the EAP would be very..., but I didn't know if I would find close friends like I had in Ireland like that... I thought that it would be like... an American graduate school, like a job... and this thing of working was very exciting and I thought that... I was really worried that my student life would be over...

Between two social statuses, young nomads get ready for internationalisation, inscribing it from the outset into their professional position thanks to their sojourn, so as to have at their disposal, depending on circumstances, a choice of social settings where to settle, even temporarily. Investment in the future sketches a potential position, longed for, yet undetermined and unpredictable.

Some lives seem to follow straight lines without any break between childhood and adulthood. When accidents or asperities cross them, these collisions do not succeed in breaking off continuity. A constant thread leads them in a certain chronological permanence: stable and fixed family, work, social spaces, memberships construct an uninterrupted biographical link. Other lives incorporate eclipses, marked by a rift between self and self (Huston, op. cit.). These discontinuous lives are like biographies with parentheses, absences, lost chapters, because they exchanged language or country, job or family. Their existence does not make up a continuous whole, their worlds are juxtaposed. The succession of usual events may be interrupted only momentarily, the time required for an experience, and may then retrieve its previous stability, or else the discovery of precariousness may be sufficient to destabilise earlier certainties and confer a permanent taste for potential wandering. Time and space open up and diversify. Life is conjugated in the plural and the navigator into discontinuity gets accustomed to grasping opportunities, as Tom points out.

> I think the more you travel, the less sure you are. I mean, it is quite possible that I will never directly choose where I am going to live, I will simply go where I find work… or where opportunities lie for a time and I may end up staying there, I may end up moving on, I don't know.

His choice of linguistic items marking uncertainty and lack of permanence: 'less sure', 'quite possible', 'never… choose', 'opportunities', 'for a time', 'I may', 'I don't know', highlight indetermination. Chance which offers no guarantee constantly presents new prospects, fugitive and rejectable.

The future is a question mark for student travellers. The students mention several possibilities: coming back (Cecilia, Aoife, Fiona, Christine, Régine), staying on (Nicolas, Valérie), going somewhere else (Ava, Daniel, Marco, Thomas), all containing the idea of repeating an episode which they wish to refer to cyclically so as to ensure its permanence in some way. Others talk about continuing at home the process of encounters with different people or maintaining contacts initiated abroad (Birgitta, Hugo). Their pursuit of some form of continuity is a sign of the desire to renew or lengthen an experience unanimously identified as enriching. What weight will this stage have in their life as a whole and in their personal history? How many of them will conquer the freedom of the potential wanderer? Only a longitudinal study could bring some light to this aspect. The balance between permanence and precariousness is fragile, yet necessary for the construction of an identity which refers both to what is identical, everlasting, and what is singular, ever changing (Kundera, 1997). A period of residence abroad is the very event which places individuals in that dilemma.

The time of the experience abroad juxtaposes several temporalities. The moment of inception remains somewhat an enigma, but the past relative to the sojourn is the time associated with family and personal antecedents, private and invisible abroad. The present of the stay refers to a specific moment, a stage in life with a distinctive place, characterised by a precise duration, beginning and end given from the start, and by successive phases.[26] The present of the interview is now gone, as is the retrospective narrative disclosed about an episode of their life which may fade like an old photograph. Consequently, time experienced by student travellers partakes of both continuity and discontinuity, another facet of the stranger's paradox. The biographical thread draws a continuous line in that travelling is intimated early, auguring a path of disconnecting oneself from one's roots so as to allow take off. Bruno reports that breaking with that initial period in one's life ends up transforming an attachment to a family history into an internal and portable attachment. Life abroad consolidates in a limited present the work of personal deliverance from the past during which individuals discover themselves.

5   The arrival: a rite of passage

Introduction: admission into a new cultural world

What is a stranger? Lucy identifies an essential characteristic, in words echoing Simmel's,[1] when she defines a stranger as 'not having grown up there from the start'. Non-membership to the group from the beginning constitutes one of the fundamental characteristics of strangers. It determines the position assigned to them, away from the centre. Newcomers usually 'wouldn't know the norms or the native domestic ways of living, they would do things differently', John points out. Confronted with otherness in usage, their behaviour is outside 'normality', at odds, easily identifiable. As a result, whether they are apprehended as intruders or welcomed as visitors, their arrival disturbs the established order and puts to the test existing norms. In other words, initially, strangers are perceived and defined negatively as non-members afflicted by a socialisation deficit. What does this negative status entail for arriving strangers?

In this chapter, students' entry into the new cultural world is compared to a rite of passage because the process involves a change in life, resulting in changes in their position in the group and in their relations to others (Wood, 1934). Indeed, the territorial passage from one culture to another constitutes for students a multiple rite of passage signalling numerous transitions: they must adjust physically, linguistically, professionally, culturally and socially to a new environment, at a time when many are already experiencing other transitions. What are the characteristics of the initiation process student travellers encounter on their arrival before being admitted into the new world?

We examine this issue from two different perspectives. From the perspective of the approached group or society, existing social borders are challenged. In this sense, arriving goes beyond merely entering. Strangers must gain entry; they do not receive it automatically. Since they introduce the unusual in the group and jeopardise native assumptions, they may be kept at bay for a while. Entry is then more like an admission in that some form of membership is to be negotiated. Host environments, the degree of receptivity and openness to members from other cultures they are prepared to grant, thus become an important element in the adjustment process.

From the perspective of arriving strangers who are staying long enough, a new socialisation process must be engaged in. This effort takes up considerable energy at the beginning and makes the arrival a trying period.[2] Initially, for individual strangers, the dominant feelings are disorientation, communication strain and solitude. These feelings are akin to those described in conventional definitions of culture shock as the 'second phase', when negative psychological reactions to the strangeness of the environment come to the fore (Furnham and Bochner, op. cit.). The personal crisis is even more acute since, at the same time, newcomers face material demands of all sorts, accommodation, bureaucratic requirements, organisation of study or work, social life. Passage into the new social context also coincides with a growing awareness of the absence of the familiar world and its attendant homesickness. All these factors contribute to the arrival acquiring particular significance in the overall learning process.

The stranger as an intruder

Assuming the central position of relationships and interactions within social groups, 'the coming of the stranger creates a dynamic situation' (Wood, op. cit.: 17) which calls for adjustments on both sides. The stranger is initially outside existing social boundaries which draw the lines for inclusion and exclusion. These boundaries naturally produce social distance and create a major hurdle between strangers and members. What kind of changes in the social fabric are necessary for social relationships to be extended to arriving student strangers? Two general features of social cohesion stand out in this discussion: the issue of recognition and the prominence of feelings.

The socialisation process whereby social cohesion is achieved implies mutual recognition among members belonging to a group. The need for recognition corresponds to a primary need for inclusion, vital in relationships between individuals and their entourage. It manifests itself through a craving for communication and contact, an effort to attract other people's attention, or through concerns with affiliation, consideration and esteem. But recognition in the case of strangers is somewhat double-edged, a token of their dual position. On the negative side, newcomers are identified and labelled as strangers. This maintains them at a distance, away from the centre, at least for a while. For example, Sylvie explains that being recognised as 'the' French girl made her feel like the extra-terrestrial ET on her arrival in the town where she was to spend a year.[3] On the more constructive side, strangers may actively seek some form of recognition as members of the group by trying to cross existing borders. Between these two poles, recognition as a distinctive other and recognition as a member, several intermediary positions are likely. However, on arrival, the predominant feeling is frequently one of exclusion: exclusion from the language community, from communication situations, from media and public discourse, from social interactions, and above all exclusion from the feeling of belonging to a group whose cohesion is based on a past in which the newcomers have no part. Indeed, shared feelings, memories, implicit knowledge, as Park underlined, are the very cement of cultural groups. Consequently, their collective memory sets mutual strangers apart.

The second feature highlighted by Wood is that feelings take on a prominent part in the foundation of social relations. The feelings acquired about rightful behaviours for members and for others become an 'attitude' or a 'sentiment' with an emotional content.[4] Simmel, discussing relations between members and strangers and the common features they share, refers to the coolness or warmth of relations and mentions the 'centripetal character' of forces connecting individuals (op. cit.: 406). In other words, the sense of commonality, of shared experience is by nature affective, largely because it is rooted in early socialisation, a period of life when social representations are given rather than reflected upon. The prominence of emotions partly explains the cohesive force of our systems of representations, the cognitive misjudgements (stereotypes, prejudices) they give rise to (Murphy-Lejeune, 1996), as well as the depth of the sense of membership. As a result, unwritten cultural rules and behaviours are implicitly acknowledged and understood. Strangers, however, are excluded from this kind of tacit complicity and from the sentiments which form unifying social bonds.

As stable relationships are assumed to be a key attribute of the group, mobile strangers disturb the establishment and appear in excess, 'as a supernumerary', Simmel writes. Newcomers are easy to identify: they do not fit into the environment. Their appearance, the sounds they produce, their behaviour are odd: 'another mouth to feed, an incomprehensible speech, an unorthodox behaviour' (Kristeva, 1991, our trans.: 15). Their awkwardness and gaucherie underlines their difference, Maria says: 'Definitely, awkward, they feel awkward, because they know they don't look, sound or behave as the people that are all around them and they stick out like sore thumbs'. Arriving strangers are social weights, clumsy and inelegant. Their language betrays them. In the new environment, they have no recognised status. They find themselves in a position of numerical inequality, although the relation of strangeness is by definition mutual. This asymmetry, highlighted by Stonequist and others, and the resulting tension precipitate the feeling of marginality. Strangers feel socially retrograde and lose the sense of security which goes with the familiar. Their initial visibility may recede, in their eyes at least, as they progressively make the environment their own. But the profound embarrassment generated by the absence of intuitive linguistic and social knowledge may endure much longer.

Mobility has a price and newcomers have to pay for their social anonymity and eccentricity: 'being new in the group makes you the outsider', says Maria, at least until you know the rules. Whether they are foreigners or natives from somewhere else, newcomers 'don't receive the respect they are due'.

> Simply because they don't know anything about you... hum, not 'cause you're a foreigner, the same as if you'd come from a Spanish village and you were new in the class, it's nothing to do with your race, the fact is that you are new. People always have to pay the price for being new, even if they are from the place.

Newcomers 'have to pay the price' for intruding from the outside or from some-where unknown. But this position also grants newcomers the pleasure which some may cherish of not being recognised.

What factors affect the students' passage into the new social environment? From the point of view of individuals, at the beginning of the stay, the outside position is experienced more as a disadvantage than as a benefit. As newcomers, face-to-face with members of a new group, feelings of loss, communication strain, social isolation and strangeness predominate. Intimate relationships which cement group members have not been extended to them yet and contacts are exacting. The issue of inclusion is pressing. This is why the period of the first contacts may be likened to an initiation.

Arrival as a rite of passage

Rites of passage accompany all major life changes or events of a biological, professional, family or social nature, the ritual helping to strengthen the new relationships. They signal a transition from one world to another and constrain the individual concerned to establish a new way of being in society, in confor-mity with the new position.

The concept of the rite of passage is used by Wood to describe the changes in the system of relationships which the stranger's arrival institutes. In this instance, she adds, 'it is not so much the presence of the stranger as an individual, but as the representative of a class which makes reorganiza-tion necessary' (op. cit.: 34). It would be difficult to argue that the presence of 'foreign' students in a European country makes social reorganisation necessary. The concept of the rite of passage is used here more to account for the personal experience of the traveller at the beginning of the stay abroad, mainly in relation to the arrival. It is used to refer to those aspects of entry into the new culture which are experienced as a gradual initiation, with its social rituals. It is mostly used as a metaphor since some dimensions of initiation rites may be lacking, such as profound transformation of the individual or deep bonding to the new community. For the majority of students, the feeling of going through a rite of passage may be confined to the initial period of the stay. For some, the changes will be more radical and enduring.

Rites of passage imply a certain duration. Time is necessary for changes to take place in the social order. Though their meaning is largely symbolic, they usually involve some form of hardship, often emotional, which the initiate must learn to control. The purpose is to cause changes in individuals on a par with the changes attained in their position in the group. For, 'it is primarily the social order and not the individual which is sacred and it is the change in this that is the real object of the ritual attitude' (ibid.:37). For newcomers, the ritual consists in trying to break through already formed groups. Their integration depends largely on their initiative, their personality and whatever interest they manage to arouse in others.

Rites of passage also demonstrate the power of connections to past relationships and to the physical environment associated with them. Any change in the environment, as indicated previously,[5] brings about other changes. Departure from one's country may induce homesickness because of the separation not only from cherished members of familiar groups, but also from familiar scenes that have become dear through association. The stronger the attachment to the physical world, the more poignant the separation. 'It is not strange then that leaving one's own country, even though temporarily, should be regarded as a ritual occasion' (ibid.: 42). The rite of passage creates an emotional state which will bridge the gap between the old order and the new.

Van Gennep (1960/1909) defines three types of rites corresponding to three different stages: preliminal rites which separate individuals from their previous associations; liminal rites or rites of transition, which prepare them during the marginal period before crossing the threshold; and post-liminal rites or rites of incorporation, where they become aggregated to the new world. This distinction calls to mind the chronological stages inherent to the adaptation process: breaking away, experience of transition, and adjustment. Strangers approaching a group were subjected to purification rites: 'the object is to remove from the stranger anything adhering to him from his former associations' (Wood, op. cit.: 40). Before being 'eligible' for admission into the new community, strangers must demonstrate that they are separated from their old one. What forms will this separation take in the case of temporary strangers? What is the length of time necessary for the separation to be effective? The stranger coming home may also undergo similar purification rites before re-entry: 'his absence and his return are events which have a bearing on the organized group life and the changes produced must therefore be marked by some form of ritual ceremony' (ibid.: 41). Returning home for travellers is no ordinary event and implies a new entry to negotiate, whose difficulties are often ignored.

The concept highlights the fact that the age group is subjected to more than one rite of passage. Each threshold confronts individuals with a status dilemma, since each phase of life offers its own status definitions, rewards and punishments. For example, student life is typified by a 'conventional relaxation of convention' (Hughes, 1949: 64). Besides the physical, linguistic, social and symbolic passage from one world to another, the student stay abroad also implies professional mobility, another rite of passage where students must acquire new skills. Indeed, this period sanctions passing from adolescence to adulthood, from dependence to autonomy, from school culture to university or professional culture and, in the case of student travellers, from one national culture to another.

However, Thomas explains that the statutory freedom students enjoy predisposes them to questioning their identity, a search which the stay abroad with its many opportunities enhances:

> … also because now is the time in life, like twenty to twenty five, when you learn a lot about values, who you are, what you want, identity, where you come from… And you're free as a student to ask a lot, though when you're

working, you cannot spend so much energy, mental energy on questions like this... [...] I would say it's the most important experience because you open your mind and you have an overview. You get more good things to see, just only one thing is good whereas... also decisions... like what you would do, like family, you know, when you want to marry, perhaps... a German girl, German girls are like this, perhaps that's not so good, perhaps... why not a French girl? ... You can compare and make major decisions.

Youth is an age of uncertainty regarding status, but it also offers numerous possibilities. It is a period of intense negotiation when personal dispositions and future positions are put to the test. The young traveller opens up the range of possible positions beyond the limits traditionally imposed since s/he 'can compare' before making important decisions, as Thomas says. The initiation then consists in confronting their desires with reality, in assessing the various options which could help them to find a new social position, in adopting uncharted roles, in deciding whether or not a change in status is beneficial. All these represent so many aspects of the adaptation process, itself a replica of the first socialisation process under different terms.

Host environments and approaching strangers: perceived openness

At first, before interpersonal relations are established, encounters between members of different national groups provoke reactions involving not only approaching strangers, their personal dispositions, origin, personality and aptitude to change, but also the host environment (Kim, 1988). Group boundaries will be perceived by visitors as more or less open according to these many factors. As well as this, potential visitors feel more or less attracted to some countries. These two features of the cross-cultural experience constitute the collective and individual facets of the same phenomenon – perceived openness to outside factors.

In their answers concerning the degree of openness or receptivity which they perceived in their host environment, students did state that it was an important factor in the overall adaptation process. However, the signs by which this dimension of cross-cultural contacts might be assessed remain more difficult to pin down. What do students mean when they refer to the host environment as being open or closed? Judging by the subjective and often contradictory nature of the answers, it would be difficult to draw profiles of countries as more or less welcoming to foreign students.[6]

To start with, it is important to remember that the most common attitude is natural group closure. Individuals from established groups 'don't have to make an effort' to extend their social relations, Maria explains. In their secure social position, they have their own friends and it does not occur to them that other people may not enjoy such comfort and may need friends.

I think when you come from a secure kind of social position, from where you're from, you don't have to tolerate other walks of people, heu, like I would… this sounds terrible, I am just being as honest as I possibly can… euh… that you don't have to make an effort, you have your friends, you know who your friends are, and it didn't really occur to me that there could be people, let's say from the country, who'd moved up from Cork in Trinity, who needed friends.

To include newcomers, groups of all kinds must somehow open up, but openness does not come naturally to the majority of people. As mentioned earlier, among the natives, those who approach foreigners are usually those who have gone through a similar experience themselves.

The degree of openness to foreigners might be related to a country's size and geographical position, small countries rejecting outside influences as potentially dangerous because they threaten their sense of identity (Raphael, 1986). But larger countries are often reported to be indifferent to others in a kind of self-contained ignorance. Openness might also be linked with the country's history of relations to the outside world, particularly its colonial past or lack of it and its historical relations with other nations. Damien contrasts French and Irish traditions from this perspective. For him, the fact that there is a large Irish diaspora all over the English-speaking world makes it easier for Irish people to see themselves from another point of view. Recalling an episode about some French students who behaved in Oxford as if they were on their home territory, he says that the Irish 'are more aware of this type of prejudice'. He also mentions history: 'we don't have any history of invading anyone or starting wars, we have no colonial past the way the French and the English do… so I think that makes us quite open'.

Being accustomed to the presence of foreigners on one's territory, as tourists or as migrants, could be construed as another sign of potential openness. Maria thinks that in Spain, particularly in the South, they are 'wary because they're not used to very many foreigners'.

They're wary because they're not used to very many foreigners and they look at them differently. Let's say they are very traditional in the South of Spain and they'd think that German girls, French girls were certainly a threat to them, they thought they were sexually more easy. Spanish girls would live at home until they're married, still in the South of Spain and this was an object of curiosity and often, maybe, kind of coldness towards, let's say, the other foreign girls.

On the other hand, the behaviour of those who 'go wild… very out of control' because they are abroad reinforces negative reactions to some visitors.

Traditions of hospitality are equally ambiguous. While superficially some societies are supposed to be more hospitable than others, it is always hard for a foreigner to break into a native group, Maria thinks.

> We have a name of... such open people, but they're so cliquey, Irish people are very cliquey, they want to know where you were in school, who your friends are, what you're up to before they decide to make friends with you, hum, and yet they're very open on a very superficial level... it would be very difficult, I would imagine, for a foreigner to break into an Irish group... superficially they might, but to integrate well with Irish people, you'd have to make a big, big effort.

The effort required of the individual stranger must not be underestimated. Successful adaptors will be those who possess personal qualities facilitating their contacts with others[7] since openness is required not only from the hosts, but from the individual travellers. However, the host environment is a prominent factor at times, for example when one is making the initial choice of where to go or at the beginning of the stay, and less so at other times. Julie thinks that after a while, when social relationships gain strength, the environment is no longer a major preoccupation. In time, contextual features are relegated to the background while the experience becomes more personal.

The choice of host country: selective affinities

The encounter between individual strangers and their host environment is extremely complex. In a way, it is fortuitous: it may work and it may not, 'so you can never predict, it is absolutely random', says Hugo. He could not 'go over the dissimilarities' between his world and the American world he discovered. Consequently, he could not adapt because he 'gave up after a while' and was 'not interested': he did not fit. Marco thinks that one adapts in different ways depending on the chosen country and that what matters is the degree of correspondence between each person's aspirations and what the selected place has to offer.

Host countries do not seem to be so much selected through reflection as imposed irrationally and inexplicably through what the students call 'falling in love' with a country, as is the case for Nicolas, Maria, Aoife and others. This sudden attraction may be polarised around what is different in the other place compared to one's own context. For Aoife, the fact that France is both so close and so different from Ireland is appealing: time-keeping, social gatherings, food, a different culture fascinate her. The very first contacts are crucial in this encounter between a traveller and her/his destination. So are preconceptions. Amin explained that he fell in love with Italy: 'just everything, people, food, just the climate, the architecture, the whole Italian culture thing is so... rich'. By contrast, his 'preconception about Belgium was that it was not a terribly interesting country' and that it was not 'worth getting to know'. When he arrived, this idea was reinforced 'because (preconceptions) are self-perpetuating' and he just 'kind of switched off'. Personal attraction has an impact on students' attitude, interest or lack of it, about their stay.

Initial reactions may be largely emotional, but rationalised later. Proximity is expressed primarily as a 'correspondence' between an individual and a place. Christine, Valérie and Mathilde, who preferred Ireland over England as a language destination, list all the advantages they see in the country they love. Travellers 'feel' something is going on between them and their environment: they 'feel on the same wavelength' (Christine) or 'like it immediately on arrival' (Mathilde). This kind of natural affinity creates an affective terrain which facilitates the adaptation process to come. Students who mention this favourable predisposition, with one exception, assess their stay as very satisfying and did not experience any difficulties in adapting. The impact of emotions in the choice of a foreign country highlights the fact that cross-cultural boundaries are more perceived than given.

However, the selection of a host country is usually limited, even compelling, since most destinations are language-based. Assistants may only choose among the languages they are studying; for EAP students, three countries and languages are already chosen; Erasmus students may benefit from a slightly larger selection, but their language competence acts as a serious barrier. Countries with lesser-taught languages suffer from a real disadvantage in terms of European exchanges.[8] In a way, the dice are thrown very early on. Young Europeans' linguistic horizons being constrained to the languages taught in their schools, their discovery of other European countries is also constrained, as already mentioned in relation to the cautious progress of their earlier mobility experiences. Consequently, the two English-speaking countries in Europe receive more students than they send. Conversely, whilst a Danish or a Portuguese student may have the opportunity of a study period in England or Germany, an English or a German student is unlikely to go and study in Denmark or Portugal. European programmes based on university studies give prominence to the language dimension, but hardly facilitate openness to linguistic and cultural diversity.

Arriving in a foreign country and feeling lost

The initial impressions which accompany arrival in a foreign place sometimes obtain disproportionate significance in the overall assessment of the stay. These early moments are lived through with great intensity because they are infused with a strong emotional charge as if the senses, particularly the visual sense, were suddenly endowed with unusual sharpness. Recollections and images of the very first moments on foreign land often remain etched out in memory as symbols of the passage into a new space and filter perceptions to come.

The materiality of being a stranger manifests itself as a feeling of loss, loss of orientation, loss of security, loss of language, loss of confidence: 'the first thing to acknowledge is the loss of home and language in the new setting... irredeemable, relentlessly anguished, raw, untreatable, always acute' (Said, 1999a: 93). The word is repeated across the students' narratives, highlighting the impact of dislocation, of separation from the past: 'you feel very lost in the environment'. Hugo goes on collecting negative terms to describe this feeling: 'I had no contacts with my culture, I had no, no, nothing to build on to, to hold on to'.

If you go to America, you get kind of lost in there, it's very different. At that time, I was 18, 19. And I made a lot of mistakes, I think I made mistakes... [like what?] being in a kind of way arrogant from your culture point of view. I think you get very defensive when you are abroad... I had no contacts with my culture, I had no, no, nothing to build on to, to hold on to, I would say. And then you get more and more arrogant, you get more and more defensive on your culture. If it comes to the comparisons, it always comes to comparisons '*How is it in your country? and how is it in...?*'. And then I got very defensive because my country wasn't there, just disappeared. You feel very lost in that environment.

The feeling that his 'country wasn't there, just disappeared' led him to a defensive strategy based on what he calls arrogance about his culture, which expresses itself through hyperbole and excessive defence of one's own territory as if to verbally deny the presence of the other country. Aggressive reactions of this kind are usually concomitant with the feeling of loss (Zajonc, 1952).

Loss or disorientation is triggered by the change in spatial, social and cognitive position. Originally, 'any scheme of orientation presupposes that everyone who uses it looks at the surrounding world as grouped around himself who stands at the centre' (Schütz, 1971a: 99). Strangers, having no status as members in the new group, find themselves outside the centre of the social world in which they arrive: 'a border case outside the territory covered by the group's scheme of orientation' (ibid.), deprived of the comfort of centrisms. They are no longer at the centre of their familiar social environment either. This situation causes a dislocation or a 'disintegration' which Schütz describes as a violent displacement. Disorientation is manifold, spatial, material, linguistic, affective, cognitive, symbolical, cultural.

The first difficulties are common to every traveller who settles for a while in a new place. But added difficulties arise in the case of student travellers, who leave their familiar setting and have to study in a foreign language (Furnham and Bochner, 1986). On arrival, students are faced with the material organisation of their life, for some for the first time, in a cultural context whose rules are different. Accommodation is the most urgent problem to be dealt with, since having one's own place forms the basis of spatial appropriation. However, this imperative must be added to other professional and social demands. They must structure their presence in a given social space just when they feel vulnerable and fragile. This is why the kind of welcome extended to them on their arrival is crucial.[9]

The traveller may feel overwhelmed by the many 'small technical problems'. Régine felt these prevented her from having 'a grand view' of her stay initially.

When we arrived, there was the problem of accommodation, the problem of admissions, we had to get a... in Paris, we had to undertake so many..., all these small technical problems which really... you didn't have a grand view, not at all... with luggage, I didn't know anyone in Dublin, really no one... hum... I didn't know the city at all. So I went to the accommodation office, really submerged... so that, that was difficult and all these small problems, when you get the apartment, all these chores, all this... which makes you say '*pouh!*' ... during the first month and it was really difficult to get back on your feet to see a bit further (our trans.).

These first steps represent the first obstacles students must overcome. Even when travellers imagine they know the place because they have been there on holiday, settling for a year has nothing to do with a holiday trip, according to Hélène.

It is not at all the same thing when you arrive for a long time... while usually, I am looking forward to my departure to Ireland, I leave with my back already turned to everyone and saying '*here we go!*', my rucksack on, my own little trip and I'm always sad to go home. And over there, I realised that a year, it's a long time, leaving your friends, leaving your family, it wasn't easy and I remember when... my parents and my eldest brother came to the airport... and I remember it was really hard to say good-bye without crying a little... (our trans.).

Expected familiarity with a world visited in 'holiday mode' becomes inoperative under the impact of duration and turns into strangeness. All these difficulties contribute to make the arrival in a foreign place a period of stress in many ways.

The arrival is also the time when the experience of uprootedness is strongest and when the familiar world is most missed. The sudden discovery of all sorts of discrepancies between the new and the old worlds, sometimes unexpected, shakes individuals. 'Culture shock is the result of a sudden change from a predictable ordinary environment to an unpredictable strange environment' (Kracke, 1987: 79). The disparity between expectations of an imagined reality and reality is particularly disconcerting, even for experienced travellers such as Maria or Valérie. The former summed up her initial difficulties: the university did not match her expectations, the accommodation she was offered did not correspond to what she wanted, she found herself alone without any friends from home, she thought that her Spanish had suddenly vanished. She experienced 'a big shock' on her arrival.

Moreover, the discrepancy between one's habitual behaviour and that which is expected of you by your new entourage presents strangers with a feeling of socio-cultural dissonance. Valérie thought that 'the first weeks were abominable'. She found herself in a protestant seminary, without enough money to move elsewhere. Coming from a family of 'atheists like everybody', she was faced with very ordered rituals, including grace before meals, 'a practice nobody had explained' to her. She did not understand her new milieu, could not decipher what was expected of her, did not know whether or not she should do like the others. Arriving in the refectory with a short skirt, she immediately felt herself surrounded by horrified glances: 'I felt everyone freeze'. It was 'the first experience where I had difficulty adapting', she added. Her reaction was to refuse this new world and to shut herself up in solitude.

There was the phase '*I am going home*'... from that place, not from Ireland... it was really a nightmare, total refusal: I was feeling bad, I didn't want to talk to anyone... meals with everyone in the refectory were an ordeal, people would force themselves to converse, with the difficulty of the language... (our trans.).

In her case, the shock originates from the fact that normal set behaviours, valid in her own system, no longer match the environment (Torbiörn, 1982). The shared system of meanings, recipes or norms which culture represents is ineffectual: the refuge becomes a labyrinth. The discrepancies noted by students manifest their loss of meaning and underwrite the impact of cultural distance.

Individuals, shaken in the 'confidence of their thinking-as-usual', react. One defence mechanism to disorientation and loss of control is rigidity. Hugo explains that the shock emerges from the fact that, one's personality being static, the new environment 'switches you around because it is stronger than you'. The feeling is like falling, 'losing the ground under your feet'.

Shock is a situation where you have a... like from medicine,[10] oh, no, not from medicine, but I think the situation happens when you have a strong perspective on something and you think you are really static and then the environment changes you, just switches you around because it is stronger than you. And as soon as you realise that, you suddenly feel you're not under control any more, that's kind of a shock. [...] You fall, you have feelings of losing the ground under your feet, the ground, the culture and the base, you understand... But, the shock is only if it's done suddenly to you, if you're turned around slowly... it doesn't appear to you as a shock.

Two aspects stand out. First, the situation demands personal changes from the individual exposed. As soon as flexibility to the environment is restored and 'you no longer resist', the shock disappears. Rigidity or stiffness is an instinctive reaction, but it proves unproductive. Flexibility appears as the solution: one must bend without breaking, as Damien says. The capacity to bend with a changing environment depends on the personal resources of each traveller. Some, such as those with 'authoritarian' personalities (Adorno *et al.*, 1950; Nash, 1963), might find it more difficult than others. Secondly, Hugo mentions that this encounter between individuals and a new environment will only result in shock if the process is sudden. But, 'if you're turned around slowly... it doesn't appear to you as a shock'. The force of the impact varies with the evolution of the process.

The arrival is not necessarily an initiation, with its irritation and discomfort, for all students. Quite a number of them acknowledged that they did not go through a crisis at all: Christine, Mathilde, Cecilia, Fiona, Emily, Nicolas, Karine, Jannick, Edwige, among the assistants. Edwige indicates that on the contrary, at the beginning, she felt very enthusiastic and that if she compares realities, it is not so much to say 'in France, things are better', but rather to say 'well, here it is like this', to try and understand. Her positive experience is duplicated in several stories of her fellow group. Assistants have the enormous advantage of language competence, which obviously softens the blow. They also benefit from early assistance from locals who advise them and take them 'under their wing', as Edwige says. In particular, Irish teachers frequently took students in their homes at the start, with the result that the newcomers 'did not feel alone at all'. Among Erasmus students, entry is more often characterised by a negative initial period, especially for those whose language competence is inadequate. The same is true of EAP students. Their main problems are brought about by language difficulties, as was the case for Josef and Tom.

The magnitude of the adaptation process, the hardship of the road to travel and the dexterity with which travellers journey depend on many factors. Park and Burgess (1921), then Schütz (op. cit.), before others (Klineberg and Hull, 1979), draw attention to two factors which are assumed to influence the speed and degree achieved in adapting: communicative ease and intimacy of social contacts. These two related concerns are omnipresent in the first phase, the period of linguistic settling in and early contacts. Iris underlines that the first major difficulty to solve is language because it is the key to social interactions. Julie concludes that these two factors are what maintains the stranger 'outside the culture, a total outsider'. As a result, going from the outside to the inside implies that travellers learn to overcome communicative and social barriers.

Communication strain or 'culture fatigue'

Feeling lost and disoriented goes along with the discrepancy between the schemes of interpretation and expression which Schütz identified. Strangers' natural use of their native model to interpret the new produces dissonances which initially block mutual understanding. Practice of the new interpretive system and a certain communicative ease are required before strangers feel free to use the system of expression, going from mere absorption to active use of the language. When they are temporarily maintained in a situation of language assimilation and deprived of their means of expression, strangers may feel as if in a kind of pragmatic infancy.[11] They assume that the natives think they are stupid because of their ponderous language, as John observes.

> And I think at the start, when everything is going badly, you think '*this can't get better, I mean, it's going to be the same all the time...*', you'll be struggling with the language and you'll be struggling with making friends, no one speaks English, I mean they must think I'm a Wally 'cause I can't speak Italian well, I can't converse, I can't tell jokes, I can't laugh, because I don't understand what they're saying to me and I'm trying to be funny back and it doesn't work... very difficult period [unpleasant, frustrating], frustrating and unpleasant. So that was really...

At that time, John is on the phone home constantly and is thinking of cutting his stay short. Perceived language deficiency is gauged by the inability to crack jokes and to be casual in conversation. Initial communication difficulties result in other people being bored in your company. Guthrie (1975) called this frustration, which emerges when strangers discover the extent to which language and cultural differences obstruct social interactions, 'culture fatigue'.

For approaching strangers, the pattern of the approached group and that of the distant group interfere, producing difficulties with issues of relevance, intimacy and typicality: 'hence the stranger's lack of feeling for distance, his oscillating between remoteness and intimacy, his hesitation and uncertainty, and his distrust in every matter which seems to be so simple and uncomplicated' (Schütz, 1971a.: 103). Initial social encounters are crucial in this regard. Even the most basic forms of contact, i.e. elementary manners and civilities, may cause discomfort when one is on the starting line of the social race. Both Elena and Régine speak of their embarrassment in early social relations with members from the cultural majority. Initially, Elena found the French she met cold and explained that, by contrast, her Irish friend and herself were considered 'over-friendly', even 'strange', by their French friends.

> I think one thing that I would have liked to have known before was... I think French people that we met in France were sort of colder, not colder, yes colder than an Irish person in a typical situation, because when you meet someone Irish in the pub and just talk to them and whatever, within say any length they launch into conversations about anything and everything whereas I think with some of the French people that we met... I remember meeting this girl, she is French and we are living with her in Oxford... When we met Cécile in the beginning myself and Suzanne were sort of over... as she perceived, over-friendly, and you could visibly see her going *'what do they want? why?'*... As far as we were concerned, that was normal and I think we may have insulted people that way, not insult them, but they thought we were strange or *'why are they being?'* or *'what do they think they are doing?'*.

On the other hand, Régine interpreted the initial communicative cordiality she encountered in Ireland as a sign which should lead to further developments and was disappointed when the relationship did not progress: 'you can talk for two, three, four hours in a café with someone, then you start feeling that you're getting to know the person, then he gets up and then *'bye bye!'*. So, it's very open, but there is a blockage after a while'. The initial warmth or coldness of communicative exchanges among mutual strangers, the rules regulating social proximity or distance and the expectations they generate, form a locus for cultural differences to which arriving strangers are particularly sensitive.[12]

Language limitations isolate socially, but also sever individuals from a part of their personality, as if they were 'only half a person'. 'The filter of language', Hugo notes, makes you feel that your personality does not adequately come through the simplified language you use.

> First of all, language, language is a major problem. If you can make jokes, as soon as you can make jokes in another language, this problem dissolves... hum, as soon as you can keep up with the conversation, so it's fun for the others to talk to you. If you meet anybody, you want to tell them something, but there is this filter of language and you think your personality is not getting through. The first experience as a foreigner is that you feel awfully stupid, because you hear people about you talking and you know what the theme is about and you could say lots of things about it. But, you can't express it in the language, so you feel... isolated, first of all... A kind of... your character is not coming out, you feel '*Oh, I'm only half a person here*', but this is actually not really true.

The signs which denote difficult language boundaries are well documented. Schütz mentions the inability to write love letters, to pray or to swear in a foreign language. Geertz (1973) analyses the limits experienced in understanding a poem, a proverb or a hint. Hugo, John, Iris, Jose and Christophe mentioned the difficulty of understanding or cracking jokes as the sign of their language limitation, which restrained their capacity to penetrate inside a cultural group. But, 'as soon as you can make jokes in another language', because others can have fun in your company, conversation regains its lightness, and strangers are no longer perceived as cumbersome. Christophe concludes that sure signs of adaptation are not only the ability to joke, but also to get angry in the other language. Humour or emotions are two essential language registers where linguistic and pragmatic proximity or distance are tested.

Crossing the language threshold is a requirement for embarking on the integration process. But language is also the stranger's stigma which signifies her/his irretrievable difference. Bruno for example adopts a position of withdrawal at the beginning for linguistic reasons. He pulls back from contacts because he feels that 'other' foreign students speak more fluently and understand faster than he does. Even when, by June, he is able to express himself with greater ease, has 'lots of things to say', wants to take part in conversations and is starting to feel integrated, he still regards language as an indelible stigma: one feels a stranger as long as one is identified as such through language. A foreign accent betrays and marks the boundary between strangers and natives. By contrast, the ease with which natives possess their own linguistic and cultural territory, and which non-natives severely miss, may be interpreted as a carefree 'lack of cultural awareness', says Damien about the EAP French students in Paris.

Language isolation increases difficulties in the case of students who are the sole representative of their language or national community. Jose describes this as never having 'the possibility to communicate in my own language' or to comment on TV or politics. The opportunity to share cultural references disappears. If you want to mention a politician from your country, cultural explanations are required. The resulting cultural solitude induces him to listen to Portuguese music and to read more Portuguese books than before. His need to sing 'a different song' and to write 'a different book' represents a vital necessity to express a social world left behind.

> It's a weird feeling, because I never have the possibility to communicate in my own language. I never had the possibility to tell jokes about TV series, politics, references that belong to my own development… So, if I want to tell a joke about a political person in Portugal, I have to explain it, and I have to explain in each language, so it's… I realise for instance since I am in Oxford that I am listening much more to Portuguese music, and I am reading much more Portuguese books than I read before or than I listened before, because you need… eh… there's a need to… it's a need to … when eh…. take for instance a song, when an Irish friend sings a song, they talk about their reality. So I need to be talked about my reality instead of talking about the troubles with the IRA in Northern Ireland, I need to talk about the problems related to… joining the EEC!… and that makes a different song, it makes a different book, it makes a different perspective radically.

Physical distance from a familiar world, and trying to maintain some proximity with it, is primarily experienced through language. Consequently, one must not underestimate the relative advantage of students who share a language with others and may on occasion relieve the tension of having to express yourself in other people's languages. We will see later[13] that language isolation and fatigue are strongly related to the highs and lows which characterise progress abroad. For example, Jose experiences more turbulence in his second year abroad in Oxford than he did in Paris, where he could obtain language rest and affective support from an uncle married in France.

Iris, a Dutch student in Paris, also seeks refuge and rest in her native language in the evening. For these students, this period of tension is even more wearing since they are constantly in between three foreign languages: German which they study, and French and English which are used in the EAP year in Paris.

> So at night I was sitting there and I would want Dutch radio, Dutch newspaper, everything Dutch. It was really tiring because I had to concentrate all the time and after four months… I started thinking in French myself and then I think that once you think in French, then you are comfortable with it and you become a lot more at ease.

Kurt too describes his first term in Paris during his first stay in similar terms. Language fatigue comes from having to concentrate on what the natives are saying, so as to reduce linguistic distance, as well as from the mental gymnastics of trying not to think in your own language. But, once you think in the foreign language, the problem is resolved.

Other efforts to integrate, to appear 'more confident' than you really are, to go up to people, to acknowledge that you did not understand something and ask for help, are added to the language stress. The whole period is one of struggle with linguistic and social obstacles, vital because, as Julie says, 'you know that it's by being with natives that you'll learn the language'. It forms what Maria calls 'the first round'. During that initial round, the opportunity to speak one's own language comes as an enormous relief. Maria goes to her American friend at night to laugh and to relax, all things she is deprived of during the day.

> The effort to integrate, to become superficially more confident than I actually was. And I knew I'd never make friends unless I did. I mean, I am quite open, but I can also be, you know, shy, embarrassed, feeling awkward, and you'd really have to go: '*I don't care, I'm going to do this!*', and you'd have to go do it, you'd have to go up to somebody and say: '*Sorry, could I have the notes?*' in your heavily accented accent and wondering whether they would even give them to you. And I found that quite testing. And sometimes, I'd go home and I couldn't get a word of Spanish out. I was too tired to even think in Spanish and I'd call into my English friend in the evening. And I did that quite often... So when I was tired of speaking Spanish, I always reverted back to her and we'd have a good few laughs together...

Adaptation follows the progress of language competence. After a few months, students feel at ease in their study or work, they are able to take notes, they can follow conversations, and are in a position to make friends. Each stage is like a stepping-stone allowing students to take stock, gain confidence and feel better integrated. Patience is vital to travel the road successfully.

Language fatigue is not the only symptom of distress. Even students who state that they did not experience a 'shock' remember nevertheless going through a kind of malaise, which revealed itself through minor complaints.[14] Sophie was unwell for the first two months of her stay and recalled that she 'really suffered... worn out, truly drained'. Christine found the change of rhythm, of food, of timetable, of climate precipitated 'a huge acne crisis' which 'was psychosomatic'. She felt the cold as well in the beginning, acclimatisation being the first level of physical accommodation. Sylvie mentioned that culture shock during her first Erasmus experience abroad took the form of numerous mishaps. She had the feeling of being 'numb, totally unstable and unbalanced': she would fall on the stairs, misstep, fail to understand what was happening. Then, quickly, she found herself in the role of having to guide and orient another French newcomer. The change of role, from a wobbly person to that of linguistic and cultural guide, restored her balance and stability.

Alienation, which sometimes marks the early stages of the experience, feeds on communication difficulties and the frustration felt by individuals whose personality is perceived as diminished for want of being fully expressed. Language is described by Julie and Lucy as a safety belt for those who have a sufficient level of competence not to undergo the initial trying period of linguistic fatigue. Language competence enables strangers to survive language immersion, to swim and to get out of trouble on safe ground.

Solitude, alienation, anomie

Solitude, alienation, anomie refer to three states which characterise the position of individuals in society. These states differ in the degree of disorganisation between individuals and the social structure which they denote. Solitude applies to the situation of people finding themselves physically alone in a depopulated social setting, here caused by territorial mobility. Alienation denotes the estrangement of individuals from themselves and others. Described as a negative social condition by Marx,[15] it calls for transformation of the social world so that individuals may recognise themselves in their environment. Durkheim's concept of anomie, which in Greek means disorder, is a condition characterised by the breakdown of norms governing social interaction. The situation of people in between cultures was described as an anomic state associated with feelings of powerlessness, uncertainty and social isolation (Torbiörn, op. cit.). The experience of strangers is likely to inspire one or the other of these states in that it represents, from the perspective of individuals, a disorganisation in their relationship with society and a discontinuation of their subjective and social landscape.

Isolation is not only linguistic and cultural. For some, solitude is a physical test. Erasmus students may find themselves more on their own, isolated among many students, than the assistants or EAP students. Régine analyses the loneliness of her early stay when she was particularly off balance since it was the first time that she was alone.

> Yes, it was weird because when I arrived here in mid-September and I was home the first two weeks without her (other student) being here and it was the first time... I didn't know anybody in Dublin and I had no idea how to... well *how to get around to knowing people*,[16] because I had always done that through lectures or sports or this or that and here, really, there I was in this city, I had nothing to do 'cause I wasn't going to start studying two weeks before the beginning of term and all that... and really, I didn't know how to meet people... it's sad, isn't it? So in the evening, I'd play patience games, and for the first time in my life, I felt alone, *lonely*... while, well usually at home, there's the family and I have to try and be on my own... and really all my life, it was more looking for a bit of time for myself rather than: *'well! I must try and find people! I am really bored all on my own!'*... it had never happened to me before (our trans.).

Lacking the tools necessary for social learning, she does not know 'how to get around to knowing people' because she never had to take charge of her social contacts at home. She has not had time yet to organise her activities and social contacts.

Matthew whose arrival in France as an assistant took place in particularly poor conditions[17] resorts to a specific strategy to remedy his initial situation which was 'a real nightmare!'. To start with, regular phone calls to his girlfriend help him to hold his own: 'that's what matters, to hold on and to get better because you get used to it'. He stands firm until Christmas, buys a television and ends up savouring his time alone. He even refuses retrospectively to say that he was depressed: 'not really depressed, it's too strong, I was rather down'. As a result, he does not associate his 'down' period with culture shock because in the end he enjoyed the whole stay enormously.

> Well, I didn't really see it as a culture shock because I loved it even though it was quite a bad experience at the beginning. I was still quite happy that I was there in a way and I didn't think that French people, French culture…, I can't cope with this. It was very much the situation that is in this school.

Interestingly, he is aware that the experience is not negative, but just the specific situation in which he temporarily finds himself. The solution then lies in changing the situation. He talks to the headmaster of his school about his loneliness and looks for accommodation with a local family. This strategy allows him to feel integrated in a family first and then in the local environment, and to spend a most enjoyable year. Quite a few students acknowledge that even though at first there are difficulties of that kind, they are nevertheless temporary and may be solved.

Alienation in the case of the newly arrived stranger is mostly due to the fact that feelings of strangeness predominate at first, when one is confronted by a different climate, an unusual landscape, a foreign language, strange people. This is what John feels on his arrival in Rome. How can it be hot in October? The ground is brown, scorched when he is used to seeing green. Disconcerted, he is suddenly lost for words: he has forgotten his Italian and the accent which he discovers is quite dissimilar to his teacher's accent. His apartment seems strange and its occupants even more so. Above all, he realises that he is the only Irish person there! So 'the first month was pretty much dreadful'.

> Well, the first month was pretty much dreadful… As I said to you earlier on, arriving at the airport, when I arrived, it was about 37–38° outside, roasting! I mean it was October! How can you reach those temperatures in October?… Ten minutes in the car, my landlady collected me from the airport, I was sweating… and to see these palm trees which you don't see in Ireland on the sides of the road, and the scorched earth, everything was

brown where I'm used to seeing green. And this lady besides me in the car, where the heat didn't seem to bother her, the windows are up and I'm trying to open up every window I can reach and speaking a language which... apart from '*I am*' and '*Yes, please*', the only words I could understand... My mind just went blank... an accent... the accent was something I had to deal with because the only Italian I'd heard was from my teacher in school and the accent of my teacher – she was Irish... So it was quite a daunting experience... And then arriving in my apartment, hum, was again not very nice as it was an apartment with... there was an *autostrada* literally right below our window... again it seemed so foreign! They had these big steel girders and they close them during the day. So, I remember arriving and the apartment was very dark and dingy and the people I was living with were very, very different... but it was just so alien! And I knew I was the only Irish person there...

The word 'alien' sums up the first impressions, and the feeling of alienation may linger for a while. The attribute 'daunting' suggests a blow which knocks you down and makes you fall, albeit temporarily. Discovering strangeness in so many forms does contain a potent destabilising power. If alienation implies that individuals no longer recognise their place in the environment, then surely arriving in a foreign land is potentially alienating.

The word 'daunting' comes back in Julie's narrative as well when she mentions how 'vulnerable' the stranger is when s/he does not know anyone. This is the time when a good welcoming organisation is vital, she says. In Trier where the Erasmus students' arrival is well organised, she quickly met other foreign students. Nevertheless, in the beginning when students do not dare go out and are alone in their new environment, there is a tendency to think: 'I'm so far from home and I'm here for such a long time...'. Travellers momentarily find themselves defenceless, clueless in an alien territory. The temptation is strong to go back home at that time: 'I missed my family, I missed my girlfriend, I missed my friends', says John. Frequent phone calls, a feature of this period, demonstrate that connections with the past have not loosened. John understood after the event that his return home after the first three weeks was 'irrational, a mistake due to youth' and that he would have been better off holding on, as Matthew did.

Sophie's feeling of alienation comes from another source. It originates from the disparity between her own beliefs and those held in her new environment. She explains that 'the feeling of alienation is compelling' since adapting to the milieu implies that one must 'more or less adhere to certain values, certain rituals, certain... for example with religion, it's very difficult'. She had not received a religious education ('there is a void there on the religious front') and found herself in a Catholic family where she felt she had to hide the truth from her entourage. As a result, she was 'taking on another body, another personality even'. She illustrates this change in her personality and the need for taking on different roles by a hand gesture suggesting a mask in front of her face, as in Greek tragedies. Individuals who undergo this kind of transformation and no longer recognise themselves in their environment run the risk of 'not recovering' from the conflict between the old self and the role forced upon them. Such a case of personal conflict represents an exception in the student population we observed however.

Conclusion: jumping from the stalls to the stage

The stranger is a member of the social body whose position is uncertain and ambivalent. Between proximity and distance, inclusion and exclusion, socialisation and lack of socialisation, belonging and uprootedness, the stranger represents a social constellation where opposites coexist. The experience inevitably involves complexity and disorder. Arriving in a foreign socio-cultural territory implies loss and disorganisation between individuals and their social environment. It constitutes a rite of passage because what is offered to students is an introduction to a new world, which implies discontinuities from the past. The arrival is the period for breaking away from the past before crossing the threshold and trying to become part of the new social setting. Its potential side-effects, homesickness, communicative strain, sense of loss, physical loneliness, social isolation and feelings of alienation, result from the loss of one's psychic home. As Hoffman stresses, the first lesson of uprooting is the 'enormous importance of language and culture' (1999: 48) as the media through which we live. It makes one understand retrospectively 'how much of our inner existence, our sense of self, depends on having a living speech within us. To lose an internal language is to subside into an inarticulate darkness in which we become alien to ourselves' (ibid.). The second lesson of uprooting is that it is not all pain. There are prospective gains. When travellers eventually detach themselves from their past and open themselves fully to the lived experience, the prospect for learning is considerable.

For many, the stressful period is short-lived. The difficulties which the students face usually do not last. Julie suggests that the situation is resolved 'quite naturally after a certain time'. The transitional period of discomfort corresponds to the first phase of the adaptation process, the phase of 'accommodation' to the environment (Park and Burgess, 1921). Its length varies with each individual case and the circumstances of the stay. Those who found the shock non-existent or less intense were students who had two significant assets: language and social contacts. Indeed, students put an end to the initiation period by working on those two major obstacles, frequently mentioned, which are the real bridges to intercultural communication

The period of initiation is followed by a period of development, which includes what Maria calls the 'cultural experiment', during which strangers get to know each other, through observation as well as through language exchanges.

> People make this great experience and this is like a cultural experiment, I would say... you feel people can tell more about you without the language, without talking to you... they see you behave, they see you, what you're

doing… and so people have a very good idea about you, you're surprised how much people know about you without you actually telling them about it… and so you make this experience…

Through the experience, strangers gradually modify their status. They find ways to break through existing social boundaries. 'Jumping from the stalls to the stage', 'the former onlooker becomes a member of the cast, enters as a partner into social relations with his co-actors, and participates in the action in progress' (Schütz, 1971a: 97). Newcomers learn to find their way spatially through geographical explorations, as well as socially by organising their territory and their daily activities, and finally by establishing social contacts, as we will see. Strangers learn how to participate in the new world. In the end, strangers remain strangers, but with time the feeling of strangeness decreases for themselves and for others.

6 Redefining culture shock in a European context

Introduction: the personal crisis questioned

During the process of adaptation to a new culture and environment, it is generally assumed that culture travellers will experience some form of culture shock. Conventional definitions of culture shock, arising from research on migrants' adaptation, presume that adaptation is a predominantly psychological process and that the sojourner will experience unpleasantness before adapting. As Furnham and Bochner pointed out (1986), the first wave of empirical research is marked by a strong clinical flavour. The term 'culture shock', coined by Oberg (1960), is in itself an indication of the negative slant taken: living in a foreign environment for a period of time is considered traumatic and stressful. The temporal concept attendant to the notion of culture shock is that of the U-curve (Lysgaard, 1955), whereby adaptation follows a descending and then ascending movement in a three-phase cycle: elation–depression–satisfaction. This notion that normal healthy functioning is suddenly disrupted was dominant in American literature for a long time and only later replaced by a social learning perspective.

In this chapter, we question these assumptions in the light of the interview data obtained from European students and we investigate the conditions which may lead to varying degrees and forms of culture shock. More particularly, we look at how students define culture shock, its content and the terms appropriate to describe what they felt, in relation to evaluations which preceded Oberg's use of the term. We also examine the U-curve hypothesis and the various stages of the sojourn in the case of European students spending about nine months in another European country. Finally, we discuss the movement back and forth between the new and the old environments and the characteristics of home-coming (Schütz, 1971b).

During the time preceding the formation of new links, Wood stresses, there may be a period of unease or 'mal-adjustment' associated with painful consequences for the individual concerned, discussed in the previous chapter, but which resolves itself during the process of adaptation. Both Park and Stonequist also postulate that the tension between proximity and distance is echoed in the mind of strangers and causes the 'conflict of the divided self'. The conflict results from the internal confrontation between the two cultures to which the individual now belongs. It manifests itself in the form of a movement back and forth, the traveller oscillating between two worlds, the secure warmth of the past and the anonymous coldness of the new. Do the in between experience and its attendant hesitation manifest themselves in the situation of European students in the form of a 'culture shock'? A small proportion of our students seems to have experienced a test of that magnitude. So what happens to the notion of culture shock in a European context?

Our student travellers are not for the most part neophytes since most of them already possess a certain mobility capital, distributed unevenly among 'proficient', 'experienced' and 'expert' students. In the case of 'expert' students, who have already experienced a medium-length stay abroad, the first experience of adaptation was frequently accompanied by an initial period of turbulence, which now is for them a learning outcome from the past. Generally speaking, it seems that the first major shock is linked with the first lengthy stay abroad. This is how Hugo describes his summer stay in the United States, Lucy her year as an au pair in Paris, Sylvie her year as an Erasmus student in Dublin, Thomas his study year in Aix, Kurt his language course in Paris, Matthew his assistantship in Vernon, Juan his summer in an American family and Jürgen his year in an American college. As a result, these students do not mention culture shock in relation to what is their second lasting stay abroad. Indeed, their previous experience of culture shock is one of the main characteristics of the 'experts'. For Juan, the ensuing adaptability results in travellers acquiring strength, confidence and independence. They learn not to be afraid of going away.

> I think I was all by myself... many times and I had to... to do a lot of things by myself: go get buses and... I was nine or ten years old and in Spain, there were children who wouldn't even do that in their own home-towns and they would go out with their mothers always... And for me, it was very important because I felt independent and I think when I got lost for example, you know [in a foreign environment! difficult!]... difficult, but ah... So, all those experiences, they help me... build strength... and I am not scared to go to another country and talk to people and I feel like I could go anywhere.

By contrast, more students belonging to the intermediary category of 'experienced' travellers spoke of experiencing some sort of shock during their stay, often short-lived, but which nevertheless destabilised them temporarily. The category of 'proficient' students, those with the least travelling experience, is mixed in relation to this dimension of the experience because it includes a majority of assistants who had assets other than their mobility capital to assist them. So how can culture shock be defined in a European context?

The narratives on culture shock

Findings from our data suggest that we redefine the term 'culture shock'. To start with, answers vary with the data collection instrument used. Responses to the written questionnaire refer to a content, to specific traits. Responses gathered during the interviews, by contrast, tend to focus on culture shock as a moment in a dynamic process. In other words, culture shock may be understood at various levels of reality, for example as a fossilised product or as a process in time. Moreover, the very word implies a kind of violence not quite applicable to the student experience in Europe. The first terms used to describe the experience of relocation to a foreign environment – 'conflict' with Park and Stonequist or 'crisis' with Schütz – emerged in the specific context of American migrations where circumstances seemed to emphasise rather than reduce socio-cultural differences. In an inter-European context, our students reject the term because they consider it excessive and inappropriate to account for a situation they seek and value. Variables preceding the experience play a crucial role here. Motives for going away, personal project, age, previous experiences, duration of the stay, task, membership orienta-tion, all these factors differentiate the traditional migrants' experience from that of the student traveller, young, motivated, educated, adaptable.

The diversity in the answers to the question on culture shock, figured in the questionnaire as 'What is the biggest culture shock you experienced?' and in the interview as 'Did you experience any kind of culture shock?', draws attention to multiple possible levels in understanding of the term. The two main characteris-tics emerging from this catalogue are on the one hand, the fact that culture shock is described as the meeting between two elements which are foreign to one another, and on the other hand, the extremely diverse forms which underpin the description as Table 4 illustrates.

Table 4	Descriptions of culture shock
Elena	Absence of student culture in France compared to Ireland. The coldness of the French.
Damien	How quiet French people are at a party compared to Ireland.
Marina	The way French people behave, for example, when renting accommodation, compared with a similar situation in Luxembourg. How difficult it is to obtain information in France.
Jose	Three previous culture shocks: life in an African society; Switzerland because he perceives the country as closed to foreigners; meetings involving people from many different nationalities.
Thomas	French administration. The preparatory system for *grandes écoles* in France.
Josef	Being considered as an outsider when one lives in a foreign country and having to start from scratch in terms of social recognition and social position. The French notion of 'intellectual superiority'. The strong memory left by the Second World War and the Occupation, even among young French people. The *grandes écoles* system to educate a national elite.

continued

Kurt	Did not experience culture shock, but rather surprise.
Philip	Lack of trust between French and British people. The way the French shop for food, smell and sometimes taste before buying as if in a bazaar.
Matthew	The different sense of humour for each nationality. Discovering differences in attitudes in relation to objectives or timekeeping when working in a pluricultural group.
Franz	French formality. The 'EAP shock', i.e. discovering so many different nationalities.
Viktor	No shock in Paris, but in Oxford the shock of having to adapt to a small town.
Daniel	The ease of initial contacts in Ireland as opposed to Belgium.
Caroline	Sharing a house with people from such diverse origins (Africa, Jordan, etc.). Having a drink with Irish students and speaking with them as if she had studied all her life in Trinity.
Régine	Finding out how nice people are, even if relationships remain rather superficial. Her first experience of material independence, having to live outside her family home. Having to adapt to the new roles of an adult and a foreigner in a different context came as a shock. Tutorials with seventeen students.
Hugo	No culture shock, rather a slow process.
Marco	No culture shock in a social context, but in an academic context the shock of discovering how freely students in Ireland can express themselves, choose their work and readings. Less standardised lectures than in Italy.
Valérie	The impact of religion and sectarianism in Ireland compared to her own atheist background. Finding a conservative mentality even among young people. Differences in terms of cultural pursuits such as art, politics, interest in foreign cultures compared to France.
Collette	Food and wine in France. The *maternelle** system of schooling: she is shocked to see three-year-olds in school.
Christine	Discovering through her pupils a disadvantaged social milieu unknown to her in France. The impact of unemployment and a 'television-hamburger' culture on young people.
Siobhan	Her disappointment with French hospitality: the visitor must make a real effort since people do not naturally come to you.
Sylvie	Irish students' way of life (the way they eat).
Edwige	Difficulty in understanding how a town can function without a municipal system similar to the French.
Mathilde	Being introduced as 'the French girl', in the role of ambassador for her country, makes her realise the extent to which her French roots make up an important part of her identity.
Suzanne	The shock of living away from home.

Note: * The *maternelle* refers to the pre-school education system in France.

Culture shock is the process emerging from the confrontation and implicit comparison between two different cultural realities. The home culture element of the comparison resulting from this confrontation lurks strongly in the background when students are examining the foreign culture. For example, Elena remarks on the paucity of French student life in comparison with what she perceives as its fullness in the Irish context. Several students note differences in the area of initial social contacts as opposed to their own native context. The contrasts under scrutiny are not necessarily expressed as value judgements, either positive or negative. The discrepancy observed between two cultural contexts generates a kind of shock, but the difference is contextualised in that students are generally aware that what they are expressing is nothing more than the relative distance – proximity between their world and the new. In that sense, culture shock corresponds to a loss of meaning or rather to the loss of a single system of meaning since another system erupts suddenly. What provokes a temporary loss of balance comes from the cognitive breakdown between the traveller's system of thinking and the external environment.

Expectations play an important role in the appearance or otherwise of culture shock. Jürgen mentions that he did not experience culture shock precisely because he had very few preconceptions.[1]

> Not so much culture shock, because I had very few preconceptions. When I go to a new country, I have very few preconceptions... I rarely even try to imagine what it's going to be like. I suppose I must imagine a little bit what it's going to be like... but I actually go with a very, very open mind... without any preconceptions, so that I'm ready really for anything. And that was the case in France.

In other words, the traveller who holds few preconceptions or expectations before the experience will have the advantage of going with an open mind and being less unbalanced.

Secondly, the realities which sustain what the students identify as culture shock are extremely diverse in nature and often more personal than cultural, as is the case for Suzanne whose personal shock of living away from home is the most important. They range from external traits such as wine and food to collective behaviour either observed or attributed such as the French notion of intellectual superiority, or to specific incidents such as administrative difficulties, or to a general feeling about a specific country as in the case of Jose with Switzerland or Africa, or to more personal feelings like Josef's, who finds his social loss of value as a student painful. Such a diverse range signals the personal origin of culture shock and its arbitrary content which is dependent on travellers' individual experience. What is reported as a 'shock' more often than not is what has not been previously experienced, autonomy for some, cohabiting with multi-cultural people (Franz), living in a small town (Viktor), discovering an unknown social milieu (Christine) or the importance of religion for others (Valérie). As a result, each case of culture shock varies according to the individual, notably the travellers' relative position of strangeness, their attitude and expectations. Nevertheless, the signs on which culture shock rests are often linked to a given cultural context or reality. For example, the same comments are repeated about French bureaucracy or the system of *grandes écoles*. So if culture shock comes under many guises, what about its nature?

Culture shock is not always cultural, or at least not exclusively cultural. On the one hand, shock may arise when an individual is placed in an unfamiliar situation other than living abroad. On the other hand, living abroad represents more than just a cultural experience. This is why experience of previous shocks caused by other situations are propaedeutic. Viktor does not experience culture shock in Paris because he has already been exposed to three preparatory separations from his familiar world: military service, university studies and his first ten-month-long European stay in Italy. This is also why foreign experience may be likened, as Park, Stonequist and Schütz do, to experiencing other life transitions.

So what is the specificity of the kind of shock one experiences when confronted with a different culture? The difference is assumed to be in the duration and the intensity of the crisis. The uncertainties associated with other life transitions may not be as acute or as profound as the conflicts which centre about race or nationality because 'the sense of racial and nationality identity is one of the very deeply lodged elements in an individual's self' (Stonequist, 1937: 7). The degree of conflict as well as the level of adjustment varies with each concrete and individual situation 'from the acute and prolonged conflicts of many mixed bloods' to 'those groups whose degree of exclusion is small and transitory' (ibid.: 8). Temporary travellers such as European students generally consider that the specificity of their culture shock lies in the new roles they have to adopt. Two new roles stand out: the role of adults responsible for their daily life (Régine) and the role of foreigners, 'ambassadors of their own country' (Mathilde), this latter role highlighting their national identity and their being perceived as belonging to a 'type' or a category rather than as individuals. Discovering that 'foreigners are easily exploited', as Marco explains when talking about the theft of his bicycle or Marina when describing her difficulties with the estate agent, has something to do with this new role. Awareness of one's social role as a foreigner, in other words being able to see oneself at the distance at which one is perceived by others, softens the shock since distanciation helps to gauge the situation in relative terms, not in absolute ones: 'it is exactly the same thing in other countries' (Marco). However, as we know, host members tend to keep foreigners at a distance. This strategy causes Jose's culture shock in Switzerland: he finds that 'they are only interested in themselves'. The ethocentric attitude of ignoring newcomers exacerbates the strangers' awareness of their new role.

The awareness of the interplay between proximity and distance, which underlines individual reactions to or interpretations of the new reality, calls attention to the cognitive dimension of the experience. Schütz is the first to explain that culture shock results in a twofold loss which questions 'not only the picture of the approached group but the whole hitherto unquestioned scheme of interpretation current in the home group' (1971a: 99). These two ready-made interpretive schemes become invalidated when perceived *in situ*, so that 'the discovery that things in his new surroundings look quite different from what he expected them to be at home is frequently the first shock to the stranger's confidence in the validity of his habitual "thinking-as-usual"' (ibid.). It seems that initially distance predominates and differences come to the fore, most notably, as Table 4 illustrates, external differences. Yet, as knowledge progresses, proximity surreptitiously gains the upper hand. Indeed, Caroline's shock comes from discovering that at the end of the year she was speaking with native students as if she was a member of their group. The interplay between proximity and distance challenges cultural naivety and the illusion of proximity. Suzanne explains that her 'biggest surprise' came from realising that 'everybody is not like you'.

> You always expect people to be like... to talk about the same type of things and your friendships to be on the same level, but just in different languages... but, it doesn't work like that and that was a difference. That was the biggest surprise for me. You realise that everybody is not like you, speaking different languages. But people have different sets of values, different sets of beliefs and it is very interesting to discover that they are just different and you really learn to understand them from their point of view and that is really interesting.

The various phases she mentions are worth noting. Surprise leads to discovery ('interesting to discover'), then to learning about difference from the inside ('you learn to understand them from their point of view'). Knowledge, from being insular, anonymous and 'typified', is gradually transformed into a more realistic, complex and personal inquiry.

Conflict, crisis, shock, surprise or discovery?

The major distinction between previous descriptions of culture shock and our students' descriptions comes from the very understanding of the experience itself. The majority of students reject the term 'shock' as being too negative. Jürgen felt that it is the type of term that one would use if witnessing a fatal accident, but not an experience which prompts one to change position. Others like Sophie find it hard to define the term and wonder whether it refers to the uneasiness caused by the feeling that one does not belong to the new culture or the difficulty of having to question one's own culture, stressing the dual aspect of the process. Culture shock does not originate solely from coming face to face with a new environment, but mainly from seeing the old one disappear.

What then can we call the crisis which results from a change in one's environment and which, according to our authors, establishes the distinctive sign of the experience abroad? If all of them dwell on the existence of a period of difficulties varying in degree and extent, the names they use change with the social conditions analysed. 'Conflict' is the term used by sociologists following Park's tradition when they describe social change (Lynd and Merrell Lynd, 1937). Stonequist opts for 'crisis' to name the personal process in the mind of the marginal which reflects the social situation s/he is in. Schütz as well takes up the word 'crisis'[2] to refer to the 'interruption in the flow of habit' which gives rise to changed conditions of consciousness and practice, and mentions this discovery as the first 'shock to the stranger's confidence'. His description may be conceived as a precursor of the term 'culture shock' generally attributed to Oberg (op.cit.) and subsequently divided into numerous adjacent denominations: 'language shock' (Smalley, 1963), 'role shock' (Byrnes, 1966), 'deep ambiguity' (Ball-Rokeach, 1973) or 'culture fatigue' (Guthrie, 1975). Kim's choice of the term 'adaptive stress' (1988) reflects the medical conception of the phenomenon.

Why do our respondents challenge the term 'shock' as too severe to represent what they experienced? The notions of conflict, crisis or shock depict a negative psychological state, a gloomy uneasiness, characterised by 'spiritual instability, intensified self-consciousness, restlessness and *malaise*' (Park, 1928: 893) or by 'double consciousness' (Stonequist, 1937: 145). These pathological traits born out of the migrant experience are not relevant to the average student experience, and this may be the major difference between migration and mobility. The circumstances which surround the experience of mobility induce a different approach to the individual project. The duration and severity of the personal crisis is lessened as a result. In the young traveller's situation, the discomfort is usually short-lived and circumscribed to a specific phase in the adaptation process, generally corresponding to the arrival and the settling-in period.

This is why our students prefer replacing the word 'shock' by the adjacent and more positive terms of 'surprise' or 'discovery'. Surprise refers to what strikes one's mind and alerts it to what was so far hidden and indistinct. Discovery infers a more advanced level of penetration into the unknown. Thomas indicates that he was surprised, but not 'uncomfortable', because he takes the task of understanding others as a challenge.

> I was surprised, but I took it as a challenge… I was not feeling uncomfortable. I was feeling perhaps uncomfortable in the way that I knew I had to work a lot, but not in the way I would not do it, I would not pass, saying '*Oh, my God! I don't understand the words! what am I here for?*', but keep smiling and asking your neighbour…

Similarly, Caroline finds that she is only 'amazed', because 'meeting people from all sorts of cultures is a very positive thing'. Mathilde suggests that the right word is 'discovery', which she places in between 'shock' considered as 'too private' and 'difference' deemed 'too external, too neutral'. She thinks 'discovery' should replace 'shock' because 'it can be positive, but it can also be negative…'. Eric specifies that in order for a surprise to take place, one must find 'the right cultural distance'. According to him, European countries have a limited potential of surprise for someone from Luxembourg where proximity between cultures is great.[3] As a result, he quickly feels at home in Paris and looks for cultural difference elsewhere among the English-speaking group to extend his 'range of knowledge' there. Damien also finds that 'culture shock' is an inappropriate term because he 'learnt a lot from French people, from French students, real natural teachers of how to behave in France'.

In this context, the 'shock' is not conceived as an enduring destabilising process, but on the contrary as the mechanism which opens up 'another perspective... a new life', according to Franz.

> What I experience as eh... the French people... they shared their experiences and told their stories, which was very interesting as well what... inspired me... and... it made me actually discover... one could say, at first I restricted myself in my outlooks towards... towards the future... and then after, after having heard, after seeing, seeing what I and other people can do... so this is another perspective... it was a new life...

The experience of the student traveller 'inspires', brings about revelations, new perspectives on a future which could have been limited. In that light, the 'shock' is the necessary lever which prises open individuals in their search for shared meaning. Culture in this process becomes a personal reality, dynamic, evolving, to be negotiated in the immediacy of shared discourse.[4] A more positive conception would shed light on the fact that as the foreign culture becomes more and more part and parcel of one's personal 'kit', distance and proximity evolve as well (Torbiörn, 1982). The experience of culture shock is what provokes and stimulates the cultural learning process.

The term of 'culture shock' appears inadequate to describe the experience of European students who, due to personal factors such as language competence or previous experiences, or contextual factors such as cultural distance–proximity or the duration of their stay, tend to view the process of adjustment to their new environment in a positive light as a life-enhancing venture. The initial phase of turbulence which they encounter seems to fade retrospectively while the learning outcomes become prominent. But the term of 'culture shock' is ambiguous. We have analysed it so far to refer to the destabilising phenomenon which some have called 'the culture disease' and to its symptoms. Numerous researchers use the expression in reference to moments in the adaptation process, sometimes the specific phase at the bottom of the U-curve, sometimes the overall curve and all its phases (Furnham and Bochner, 1986; Adler, 1975).

The U- and W-curve hypothesis revisited

Staying abroad may be regarded as a journey which follows a typical evolution or cycle as most of our authors show.[5] Two main hypotheses must be tested against the students' testimony. First, the evolution of the stay is supposed to take the shape of a U-curve, the first peak representing the initial period of euphoria followed by a period of difficulties and the second peak representing the problem-solving recovery phase (Furnham and Bochner, op. cit.), or the shape of a W-curve if one adds on the phase of re-entry shock (Gullahorn and Gullahorn, 1963). Secondly, the progression is supposed to include a certain number of stages (three, four or five) in the course of a stay lasting from a couple of months to a few years. What kind of evidence do we find to support or not these hypotheses in the case of European students' year abroad?

Regarding the first hypothesis, our data suggest that rather than one single U-curve, what most students describe is the movement back and forth of a wave, certain moments recurring at times under the pressure of singular events. In other words, the shape of the curve is slightly different, more irregular than is usually inferred. In reference to the three adjustment experience profiles of culture learners outlined in Furnham and Bochner (op. cit.: 135), students' journeys rarely follow the flat line of 'experienced culture-travellers' whose course is unruffled. Their route looks more like the normal U- or W-curve typical of 'successful culture-learners', but with a difference: the U-curve may reoccur several times during the year and consequently take the form of a gentle wave.

Jose for instance describes the overall cycle as made up of several mini-cycles triggered by key events. The initial excitement of going on an adventure is rapidly replaced by the unpleasantness of having to 'fight' over material complications.

> I would describe it more as several consecutive cycles like those. Yes, you are right, you are totally excited: adventure, and then, and then... when you have to fight for three weeks to get your *carte de séjour*, you start to question... I think that those cycles exist, but I would put them more as several mini-cycles... that might have a lot to do with euh... there's a... there's a lot of moments that are especially important in the different cultures... (...) ya, it gives you a lot of ups and downs.

The ups and downs are a function of outside events or incidents and demonstrate the fluctuation, the ebb and flow between strangeness and familiarity. Jose explains that, at 'certain specific times which are particularly important in some cultures', such as Christmas or birthdays, or during trying periods such as group work when one is in a minority position,[6] the feeling of strangeness seems to predominate. Maria endorses this analysis and refers to a failed exam or an incident at a party as events which 'would trigger the up and down rather than the actual stay itself'.

> The ups and downs were more events that happened. I'd failed an exam in Spanish and I'd be very nervous about how I was going to manage to do this. And that might keep me down for maybe a week. [She describes an incident at a party] ... and this made me very insecure. This was one of my big, big down things that happened to me. I was going: '*oh, why did I come to this place at all?*'. Hum, it was more events would trigger the up and down

than the actual stay itself... I think it's kind of more like a small currenty wave that constantly goes like that (hand going up and down) and whether you decide to settle in the country will depend on whether it's doing that (hand ascending regularly) and if you decide you're never going to live there, it will do that (descending hand)...

These 'currenty waves', which also mark the long-term resident experience according to Maria who quotes an American friend's story, originate when travellers feel that they do not really belong to the foreign country, and one is inclined to say '*if only I was at home!*'... This feeling occurs when strangers do not receive the respect they are due[7] because natives take advantage of their assumed social superiority.

Another difference emerging from our data concerns the first 'honeymoon' phase during which students are expected to be like spectators observing the novelty of their environment with trepidation and enchantment (Torbiörn, op. cit.). Our students are not beginners in terms of travel abroad. They might have behaved in this fashion during their first lengthy stay, but have accumulated some experience since. This is precisely where the greatest contrast between a beginner's stay and an experienced traveller's sojourn might be pinned down. Jürgen corroborates this evidence when he tells about his American study period as a teenager, and the initial three-months period of 'complete happiness' followed by the typical stages of the W-curve.

It is a common experience if you talk to other exchange students who have gone through a similar programme... The first three months are complete happiness, you are extremely excited, everything is new. After three months, nothing is really that new any more and that is when you start getting annoyed with some things... and then start missing things from home. It was after three months that I got a bit homesick, and exactly the same way after nine months when all of a sudden it became clear to me that I only had another two months to go... I got really sad and didn't want to go back home. I think it was harder to re-adapt in Germany afterwards.

Christine's experience also substantiates this theory. She belongs to the category of 'proficient' students who have travelled quite often, but for short periods of time not exceeding five months in total and who have no previous experience of adaptation to a different milieu. Consequently, she describes herself as being excited and impatient during the first two to three weeks, then less at ease and not very happy during the first term, and dying to go home at Christmas. But, after Christmas, she starts her two social activities, horse-riding and choral singing, and 'everything gets under way...'. By the end of March, she was wondering how she could possibly extend her stay in Ireland.

One possible conclusion would be to correlate the students' mobility capital and the presence or otherwise of this first phase of excitement. The more substantial the mobility capital, the less likely the initial stage of euphoria. The majority of our students have travelled, have already stayed in the country where they are now studying and have studied its language. As a result, their journey starts off directly with the second phase, that of difficulties to solve and tasks to fulfil at the beginning of the stay,[8] which might be conceived as the hallmark of a longer stay.

The year abroad: the different stages

Regarding the second hypothesis related to the number of stages, not just their order, students in our group generally identify two main stages rather than four (Oberg, 1960) or five (Adler, op. cit.), though a third phase of reflection may be added. Their stay usually starts off with a period of stress due to the disorientation and unrest (described as a rite of passage in the previous chapter), followed by a phase of construction during which students build up their social territory both as physical environment and as personal entourage.[9] During the third and last stage, students assess the benefits accrued from their new position and can take in the full measure of their learning experience in terms of their personal 'growth', their new social position and the 'qualities' acquired.[10]

Within that cycle, travellers may experience several highs and lows according to their individual experience and context of entry. Adler's five-stage theory of culture shock development, where two negative stages, disintegration and reintegration, are followed by two positive stages, autonomy and independence, would not quite correspond to the stories we heard. Our students mention a negative stage followed by a positive stage and so on. As a result, their stay develops in a more cyclical manner: 'two steps forward, three steps backwards' (Sophie). Their progress consists of a series of steps, since the same fears or negative moments come back regularly.

Nevertheless, it is possible to chart a certain chronology of the broad course of action over the year. The most difficult period at the beginning leads to the 'bottom of the wave' around Christmas time, in November for Sylvie and John, just before Christmas for Maria, Franz and Amin, when they return home for Christmas in the case of Siobhan or Elena, or immediately after Christmas when they return for Sophie, Julie, Edwige and Régine. The latter explains that returning home for Christmas 'breaks off the experience and then when you come back, you feel... wow! ... and it also corresponds to the bad months of the year...'. We remember that Maria called this first stage the 'first round', the second round starting after Christmas. As Sophie specified, 'the end of the trial is around January, February'.

> That's when integration started to take place because I was able to get involved, I was able to join in the drama club, I was able to take part in a literature course,... which was very difficult at the beginning because I arrived on the 27th of September and everything had started before... So I found myself cast aside during the first three months... but, then, from then on I really felt that... that my life was going through something, something... unique and fascinating (our trans.).

However, some students mention a negative phase recurring in spring, either in February (John), at Easter (Sylvie) or in April (Sophie). What then are the dominant characteristics of the two broad phases during which the adaptation process manifests itself fully?

As we saw in the previous chapter, the first phase starts off with a feeling of being thrown about, shaken up, jolted. The newcomers' position lacks stability and assurance, as if the ground under their feet were wobbly. The numerous tasks they have to undertake lead to continuous stress: 'at the beginning, it was very stressful, you always felt under pressure and you had to be nice all day and missing home and the circle of friends who have known you for ever and with whom one can joke' (Elena). The temptation to shelter in the comfort of your own language group is strong at that very moment: 'that's why I was always with the English-speaking group then', she explains. Added to material chores, and the initial feeling of alienation and the language and social difficulties detailed earlier loom large. Integration demands a continuous effort: everything must happen quickly. We know that phone calls home are a sign of this early turbulence, indicating the need to maintain existing affective links as long as new ones have not been established: 'you try to keep all these contacts going at the same time', says Lucy. However, if home links are too tight during the first couple of months, adaptation will be delayed, as if the stranger were kept attached by an umbilical cord to the old world. Régine talks about being 'not surrounded or enclosed…, but constantly called back' to her family by a succession of visits.

The first phase varies in length with each individual according to their personality and the context of their stay. Maria has only two to three difficult weeks before she feels comfortable, 'integrated', yet 'things had not reached a peak'. Within a month, Fiona has a place to live in, starts her job and makes contact with some French people. It takes Lucy two months to settle down in the same way. These are rather fast learners, quick to adapt. Most students spend the first term until Christmas finding their way. Sophie says that the first two months are difficult because 'there are hardly any contacts, but between January and March, there were lots of opportunities to go out'. The remedies are obvious: accommodation, work, contacts. The feeling of 'uncomfortableness', of 'not fitting in' is then replaced by a feeling of being 'comfortable' or 'at ease', two words which students use constantly to identify the process of integration.

> Yeh, up to Christmas, it was like quite difficult because… college only starts at the beginning of November and then there was sort of in the first month meeting people and then I went home in the middle of December. And then when I came back after Christmas, sort of… the friends I'd met were still there, so I mean there was a friendship already found. That was when I felt most at ease.
>
> (Julie)

Julie goes on to describe the period from January to July as 'brilliant'. Fiona explains that 'you start relaxing then and thinking that everything is going well…

you feel at home'. The natural development of the year abroad indicates that Christmas marks a crucial moment in students' progress and integration.

Indeed, after Christmas, things start falling into place quickly, as if naturally. When you come back, according to Lucy, the second stage of the stay is the best time because students begin to have a life of their own in the new environment. Pressure gives way to confidence. They can reassess the experience and start 'having a good time'. Amin recalls that one realises then that things are better than if one had stayed at home, which is exactly the opposite to what the students may have felt initially.

> I sort of felt, when I went back and things... when I felt I was getting the better of..., then my kind of view of the whole thing improved... well because I hadn't got on well in Belgium, that's what I felt, and your confidence is quite at a low ebb... and, you know, you're feeling just not very good about anything really and then, when you go back and things improve and you're having a good time, you realise you're probably having more fun than you would at home... the reverse...

The two main outcomes associated with this stage of culture learning may be understood in terms of proximity and distance between the stranger's two membership worlds.

As travellers get closer to the new world around them, they get away from the old world and start considering their old culture with 'a new gaze'. The sense of proximity with the local milieu gains in strength gradually with the sense of 'togetherness' (Suzanne). Distance between self and others progressively decreases. At this stage, travellers regain confidence in themselves as they fulfil their professional role and as they conquer their fear of communicating with local people. Increased communication leads to transformations in the way others are perceived and initial stereotypes are put to the test of personal knowledge. This stage of 'getting to know people' (Valérie) facilitates a certain liberation from old emotional ties, like 'breaking away... you no longer cling to them' (Lucy). The signs which manifest this growing distance with the old world may be that loved ones are less and less 'interested', parents appear rather aloof on the phone, and travellers themselves begin to feel that they do not really need their support as much: 'I did not really need them' (Lucy). The old world gets further away, students gain in autonomy. The testing phase is replaced by a constructive phase.

In brief, the two main findings in relation to the culture shock hypotheses for European student travellers are in the first place that the shape of the curve is not one single U, but rather several mini U-curves which reoccur for a while as a gentle wave. In the second place, when proficient or experienced, European student travellers miss out on the first stage of elation and identify two main stages in their journey: a trying phase during which they have a number of difficulties to resolve, and a constructive phase when they can enjoy the benefits of discovering a new culture and people as well as a new dimension to their own life.

Sojourners and home ties: the sanctuary of the past

The interplay between distance and proximity at the heart of the experience implies that, before reaching the final stage of autonomy, travellers have to endure a certain number of movements back and forth which intersperse their period of residence abroad. As Siu (1952) underlined, the story of the sojourner is in a way a story of failed dates with the home culture. Sojourners believe their experience is only temporary and, as a consequence, they do not consider themselves detached from their own culture. They are *in* the group, but not *of* the group. They never totally abandon their mental links with home: 'The essential characteristic of the sojourner is that he clings to the culture of his own ethnic group as in contrast to the bicultural complex of the marginal man. Psychologically he is unwilling to organize himself as a permanent resident in the country of his sojourn. When he does, he becomes the marginal man' (op. cit.: 34). Both types are 'products of the cultural frontier' (ibid.), but mentally, sojourners distance themselves from the new country by looking towards the past. Siu includes in the sojourners the 'colonist, the foreign trader, the diplomat, the foreign student, the international journalist, the foreign missionary, the research anthropologist abroad, and all sorts of migrant groups' (ibid.). This category of travellers seems to correspond to the expatriates of today, temporary strangers whose stay is programmed to be limited in time. Similarly, international students usually have no desire to settle indefinitely in the country where they spend a year studying, even though some of them choose to come back for another stay and the destiny of others may eventually mean permanent residence in the new culture.

What may be the impact of the fact that individuals know from the beginning that their stay is of limited duration? One of the first consequences may be that individuals do not consider themselves cut off from their native culture. To what extent do European students detach themselves from their home culture and cut off mental links with home? In the student experience, this swing backwards and forwards between the old and the new worlds is materialised by concrete links maintained with one's group either at home, in the form of correspondence or trips back home, or abroad through the medium of the 'ethnic' social network. However, this fluctuation is also visible in the symbolic or mental trip which makes individuals look back on their native culture and assess their home attachment in a different fashion (Fiona). Generally, this movement leads to distanciation with one's first culture, which in turn brings on what students perceive as greater autonomy.

The movement back and forth is a sign of oscillation between primary attachment and potential emancipation. It means moving from the sanctuary of the past.[11] Returns home come in two principal forms: short trips in the course of the stay, mainly at Christmas, and the final trip home in the summer. It could be assumed that the more frequent these trips back home, the greater the difficulty the traveller has in cutting off links with the past. Eric suggests that going home in the early stages is often prompted by the cultural or linguistic fatigue inherent to the beginning. Others like Iris think that, if they opted for a year abroad, it is not to spend 'half the year' in their home country. Most students only went home for the Christmas holidays. Maria remembered the feeling of relief, 'because it was very tiring having to make this huge effort one is not used to'. The need for home links varies in strength with the traveller's age, experience and personal character. For example, Lucy needed to go back regularly to the comfort and warmth of her family cocoon. During her first long stay as an au pair in Paris, she maintained strong links with her family: her mother visited her in October, she went back home at Christmas, her sisters visited Paris at Easter. During her second Erasmus sojourn in Belgium, she went to her sister's in Germany every weekend where 'it was really like going back home'. However, going home operates in two ways. It means relaxation and shelter after a difficult period. But, returning home also produces uneasiness because the stream of experience is interrupted and discontinued.

This is why returning home for Christmas is laden with ambivalence. John remembers 'dying to go back home at Christmas in the comfort of the house' and at the same time feeling at odds with those who had stayed behind. Amin and Hugo felt like strangers at home where nothing had changed, while things had changed for them. Régine said that 'one felt like a tourist at home'. Sylvie found that 'you feel that you have missed a lot at home, the trip is short-lived, and as you cannot see everybody, you feel torn between opposites'. As Elena summed up, the traveller must re-adapt to life back home. Nevertheless, Christmas is a physical and psychological break necessary for recharging one's batteries in the warmth of the past before going back refreshed into the world of adventure. Maria explained the process.

> By Christmas, I was definitely well integrated, I mean, 'well integrated' came after Christmas, but feeling very secure with my friends and then just wait for it to become better [...] I was anxious to get back and to see how everyone was and what they were doing and tell them all about how my first half of the year had been. So Christmas was kind of like a necessary break for round 1. I called it 'recharging my batteries' and I went back, I found my batteries had been completely recharged and I was dying to get into the second term... I was looking forward to the going back with a new... I knew where I was going, I had friends, I was bringing them back little things from Ireland, you know, Christmas pudding, this kind of stuff, Irish sausages, Irish tea, I mean the fact that I even had people to bring things back to, I was really happy about that you know [...]. So I was more comfortable then the second time.

Christmas implies two separate periods of re-adaptation. After re-adapting to the home environment, returning to the foreign context is like a repeat, albeit weakened, of the first arrival. A short period of re-adaptation is often necessary. Students, who know where they are going and have friends to go to, are sometimes surprised to have to readjust to what is becoming their second home.

After Christmas, home links are more sparse and two-way mobility becomes possible. Instead of going home for Easter, Aoife asked various members of her family to visit her so that they could visualise her life, because at Christmas she had found it rather sad that she 'had all these extraordinary stories to tell them', but they were far away, inattentive. Indeed, distance is more mental than physical. Schütz in his analysis of the homecomer describes how those 'left at home have no immediate experience' of how the absent one lives (1971b: 113) and when the returnee starts to speak about his experiences, 'he is bewildered to see that his listeners, even the sympathetic ones, do not understand the uniqueness of these individual experiences which have rendered him a different man' (ibid.: 114). So the strategy of bringing one's family into the new environment is often used by students to try and restore the fullness of their inner life in its continuity. Sharing with them what has been her life for a year means that Aoife's family 'no longer feel like tourists' and thanks to her contacts, they see things 'from the inside'. Their world becomes inhabited by her new people and social distance between the two social worlds is lessened.

Leaving early may be seen as a sign of failed integration. Maria quotes the case of two English girls who went back home at Easter, when generally students realise that they only have a couple of months left and try to make the most of their stay.

> So they left early, I stayed till September, hum... I stayed in Spain up until the very last minute. The English girls just left early, they went home at Easter, they... clearly didn't integrate as well. That's what I would consider 'not integrating', if you were rushing home at every given opportunity.

By contrast, she prolonged her stay in Spain until September, like other well-integrated students. Indeed, quite a few students did not want to leave their new life and tended to delay their homecoming.

Re-entry shock

The final return home at the end of the year is like another U-curve, producing a W-curve. Some students consider that re-entry shock, which more often than not they do not expect, is potentially more disturbing than the first shock. It is anticlimactic (Sorti, 1997). Julie is reluctant to qualify the whole experience as 'brilliant' purely because of the re-entry shock she had to weather.

> The whole experience of coming back and having to re-adapt, I didn't consider that very good. Like... the whole year, my Erasmus year from October to July was amazing in Trier, was brilliant... But my time between Stuttgart, from my work experience, wasn't brilliant. Neither was coming back to Trinity having to re-adapt. I found that very difficult, having to re-adapt to Trinity because I only came back the week before College started and then I was sort of quite tired after having worked... Then it was just so

different, the whole experience was different, getting all these courses, that I think... maybe people should come back a few weeks beforehand to go back into their own culture and go back to getting used to things.

Similarly, Maria went through 'serious return culture shock', she said, and solved it by travelling back abroad immediately. If coming home is difficult for most students, those who have to go back to university courses which were interrupted for a year find it even more so. The main difficulty is that they must adapt to an entirely new social group of friends. Indeed, this difficulty which students are generally aware of before deciding to go away is perceived as a major obstacle to studying abroad by those students for whom the social circle plays an important role. Their friends from the first and second years are a year ahead and they find themselves isolated in a new group, often younger and relatively more inexperienced. One student described this period of trying to reintegrate the home environment as 'being homesick at home'. The homecomer is no longer the same person as the one who left: 'each homecomer has tasted the magic fruit of strangeness, be it sweet or bitter' (Schütz, op. cit.: 116).

Re-adapting requires time. At Christmas, travellers may stay outside, as if they were tourists. But, on returning at the end of the sojourn, they have to find ways of integrating their personal history into the collective history of the group. While the traveller may partake in the history of the group from afar, the reverse is not possible. As a result, the 'discrepancy between the uniqueness and decisive importance that the absent one attributes to his experiences and their pseudo-typification by people at home, who impute to them a pseudo-relevance, is one of the biggest obstacles to mutual re-establishment of the disrupted we-relations' (ibid.). The success or failure of homecoming rests largely on the foreigner's experience being understood and integrated into home history and relations. Unfortunately, the most common homecoming experience reveals that there are no attentive listeners to hear the traveller's story: 'they don't want to hear about it' (Hugo). The personal story must remain silent, confidential, only shared by those with a similar experience,[12] as Hugo explains.

> And then I came back and hum... it was a nice experience and on the other hand a very difficult experience because I was talking about this change, you have the feeling that you have changed, all this experience, but then you realise you cannot tell anybody about the experience and they listen about five minutes and then, they say '*ok, come back, you are in Germany now*' and they don't want to hear about it... and if you're not a writer of some kind or a really good story teller, you can't attract this interest in the other country. So it is something very personal, you have to keep it for yourself.

The break in historical continuity and shared intimacy is twofold. Homecomers were absent from the group's life and their own foreign experience is inaccessible to them: 'the homecomer appears equally strange to those who expect him, and the thick air about him will keep him unknown' (ibid.: 119).

The homecomer appears strange, but familiar things appear strange to her/him also. Indeed, the most striking experience for travellers is probably the distance which emerges in their representation of their country. This mental move constitutes in Hugo's view the most important learning outcome of being abroad: 'I think that what one learns most in a foreign country concerns our own society'. In another national context, one's origin comes to the fore while it seemed to have been invisible at home. This sudden prominence goes both ways. Travellers become aware of it and at the same time, they are perceived by others as unwitting 'ambassadors' of their own country. Mathilde[13] describes this dual process: 'Before, I, I did not know I was French, but... you become even more French when you are abroad... because you arrive with your identity,... in the eyes of the Irish, you are *the* French girl...'. Travellers are then forcefully aware of the national part of their identity, which becomes inflated. Consequently, Valérie explained, the feeling of being French changed from an oblivious to a conscious sense of membership.

Mathilde's words describing this to-and-fro between distance and proximity are singularly evocative of Simmel's paradox of the stranger.

> Even far away, when there is the distance between France and Ireland, you feel closer to your own culture in a sense because you are constantly asked to talk about it and hum... and then you feel closer to it, well... you get the impression that you belong to a... a country... while when you are in France, it is acquired, you are French, and you never talk about it really because you live through it and people around you live it too... when you are abroad, hum... you are a bit like ambassadors of your country, people... ask you all sorts of questions and you are there thinking: '*well, I have to be able to answer because I am French, so I must be able to answer*'... So in terms of your country, your culture and your... relationships with France, in terms of your family, your friends... they appear closer while they are far away (our trans.).

Those who are distant appear closer and those who are close by appear distant.

However, distance is necessary for strangers to acquire a new perspective on their culture. It is only when far away that individuals start seeing things which were unnoticed before, as Edwige points out.

> When you are at home, you don't question things. When you go away, you look from a distance and you discover loads of things which you hadn't discovered before. In the beginning, it can hurt: you are no longer on the same wavelength. But afterwards, you think that it's very good because you wouldn't have been aware if you hadn't gone and... you have a totally different way of looking... that's, that's quite clear (our trans.).

The distant gaze one applies to familiar realities includes reactions to world events and she goes on to mention French nuclear testing in the Pacific. Being introduced to a different interpretation of political events through reading foreign news gives you a different outlook because 'when you are inside, you don't see all of this'. The stranger goes from an internal implicit understanding to a less organic external perspective. This capacity is indeed one of the attributes of strangers, which Simmel described as their objectivity, applicable to the old world as it is to the new. In this sense, life abroad implies going from a restricted to an increased cultural awareness (Adler, 1977). Individuals liberated from conventional perspectives are freer and their individuality gains in strength since they are in a better position to take stock of their own identity and to master the social construction of their life.

Conclusion: redefining culture shock – 'you bend, but you don't break' (Damien)

The concept of 'culture shock' is a complex generic term which refers to many different realities. It may be understood as a moment in time, either the specific phase when travellers are at the bottom of the curve or the overall U-curve; it may also be defined as a psychological event characterised by cognitive disorientation and usually restricted to the beginning of the experience abroad; it may also be identified by its symptoms – rejection of the foreign culture, frustration, anxiety, loneliness and general dissatisfaction. This is why it is necessary to redefine culture shock in Europe relative to the conventional literature in the area. The term itself appears to be inappropriate to describe the European experience. Whether because of their relative past experience, their language competence, the cultural proximity within European countries, the fact that mobility is a cherished dream and desire for most students and not imposed from the outside, or because of other personal factors, 'shock' is perceived as too negative a word by our students. They generally view their year abroad as an added value and an exciting period of their life. It could be proffered almost as an axiom that the greater the difficulties encountered, the more meaningful the learning outcomes gained. As one student said, 'it is the toughest experience of my life, but the most fantastic'. In other words, the benefits accrued surpass the difficulties encountered. In that light, the 'shock', whether it refers to the bottom of the wave or to the whole experience abroad, takes on a positive connotation which Damien's image exemplifies: 'you bend, but you don't break'. As a reed in a storm, the secret for student travellers hurled in the wind of foreign experience lies in acquiring flexibility, a dual-faced quality which consists in bending with the pressure of difficulties without breaking under the strain endured.

It also seems that the culture shock hypotheses are slightly modified in a European context. The stages which were cogent in other contexts are not mandatory, particularly if students have acquired some mobility capital beforehand. They do not necessarily go through the first stage of euphoria, nor through the second stage of depression. The overall curve representing highs and lows seems, in the case of European students, to be of lesser magnitude and more in the shape of a gentle wave than a deep curve. If the general progress of their stay appears rather similar to the U- or W-curve, it seems to be the case that the European student experience follows the chronological development of the academic year, with the Christmas period representing an important juncture in time. Finally, the stages deemed to be difficult are conditioned by students' activities and social life and depend largely on their personal involvement. As their social contacts and degree of participation in the local culture increase, as the boundaries of the established group are forced back, as they progress in their task of social seduction, their satisfaction intensifies, and they feel more and more 'at home' in their new milieu.

In the perspective of the European year abroad, culture shock may be conceived as the necessary jolt which leads students to opening up their world, to understanding other fellow Europeans, which many of them identify as one of the main benefits of the experience. As such, 'culture shock' is a step in the process of cultural discovery.

7 New spaces, new places

Introduction: a strange environment

At first, strangeness presents itself as a strange environment. Student mobility implies the discovery of new spatial conditions, organising a familiar territory for themselves, and choosing a place to live which can become their own. Space and its corollary, mobility, are multifold. Whether physical, personal, professional, cultural, social or mental, it is redefined in the stranger's experience.

In this chapter, we examine various dimensions of the students' discovery of their new spatial conditions and some of the options available to them to try and 'fit' in the new environment. The different settings in which students find themselves, city, town or rural community, create the territorial conditions in which to settle. They play an important role in the students' integration, validating Simmel's proposal that space is the condition and the symbol of human relations. To establish a place for themselves, students must familiarise themselves with their surroundings staking out their habitat. In this respect, the choice of accommodation represents a crucial step, the significance of which usually escapes students initially. In the end, each of these dimensions, together with the way they enter their new professional setting and participate in the new social scene,[1] constitutes learning steps.

Change in spatial position is the most immediate aspect of strangers' situation. Strangers, like all social individuals, must adapt to their surroundings and non-adaptation leads to dysfunctional behaviour. The way they integrate into the new geographical milieu and the strategies they use to appropriate new spaces, so as to transform non-affiliation to places into a feeling of belonging, physical at first and then social, may be construed as the first visible sign in the adaptation process. How do students approach the new spaces and in what terms do they perceive them? How will they overcome the strangeness in their new milieu?

New spatial conditions: the geographical territory

The spatial context is apprehended at first as a geographical entity of variable size, the local territory. Three types of spatial entities represent the context in which our students had to integrate: cities, sometimes the capital city, towns and rural communities. These geographical contexts are not necessarily chosen by the foreign student. The EAP experience takes place in cities – Paris, Berlin or Madrid – and in a university town – Oxford. Erasmus students find themselves necessarily in a university town. The greatest variety presides over language assistants' appointments, since the determining factor in their case is the school to which they are assigned. Overall, most of our students lived in cities or large towns: Paris or Dublin for the majority of them, but also Brussels with the Louvain-la-Neuve campus, Rome, Trier, Cadix and Bordeaux. A minority lived in towns such as Newbridge in Ireland (5,000 inhabitants) or Arcachon in France (11,700 inhabitants). Only three assistants found themselves in rural communities with a population of a few thousand. What is the specificity of each of these spatial contexts in the student experience?

The students in their comments unsurprisingly identify the main differences between the three contexts as being size and population density. More importantly, they reaffirm the link between space as a physical quantity and space as a social milieu inducing certain human relations. Their comments reflect Wood's theme that each community organisation produces a certain type of social relations that conditions reactions to strangers.

Spatial density and interactional possibilities appear inversely related to some individuals, who find it easier to make contact in a smaller, more personal environment, whereas others prefer large cities. Because of the constant flow of strangers into the city, social space may appear dilated and hospitality lessened (Le Bras, 1997). Those students, sometimes from a rural background, think that larger, more populated places entail loose relationships. Fiona establishes a causal link between geographical size and social distance along those lines. She contrasts three places of different size: Arcachon, Bordeaux and Paris.

> Arcachon is a very rich little town, beautiful little town and then Bordeaux is more... it's bigger, it's just... it's not as friendly as Arcachon, but more friendly than Paris. The more people that are there, the less communication there is between people.

For her, the anonymity of a big city gives rise to communication difficulties and increases the feeling of strangeness. Other students relish the city precisely for its anonymity and the air of freedom. The city is described as the place where 'nobody cares about you' by Viktor who contrasts Moscow and Paris with Oxford. For him, being lost is not a negative state because with it comes independence and individuation.

> Before... Moscow is a big city... Paris... nobody cares about you. You... sometimes you are lost in a big city, but at the same time, you feel more

comfortable[2] because you feel a bit more independent. You feel like a...
individual, and in a small town, you really have to care, sometimes it's
annoying... .

He perceives a small town like Oxford as a place which compresses and lessens
individuality. 'Not used to seeing neighbours' or indeed to others caring about
him, he feels uncomfortable in it. Physical and social proximity in the small town
are experienced as stifling. By contrast, he describes the city, where physical
accessibility and impersonal relations are combined, as the natural habitat of the
stranger. The newcomer in a city is a stranger as much as anybody else. Personal
affairs are of no interest to those one has contacts with and individualism is the
norm. Consequently, social relations are seen as more symmetrical.

Exposure to constant observation, a form of social control which contrasts with
the anonymous freedom of the city dweller, may irritate newcomers. Sylvie, as we
know, feels like 'ET flying to a different planet' on her arrival in the rural community where she is appointed. She finds her new place very small and until Christmas
is embarrassed by the novelty her presence generates, particularly by the fact that
she is recognised in the street or that her movements are watched. Her first strategy
to cope with physical proximity is to 'keep her distance': she takes her car whenever
she is free and goes exploring further areas, creating a physical distance between her
and the community. On the other hand, Edwige, in a rural community of a similar
size, finds it 'fabulous that people say hello to you all the time in the street'! These
varying judgements about recognition,[3] whether irritating or gratifying, draw attention to the delicate balance between proximity and distance which obtains in new
spatial conditions.

Consequently, diverse reactions tend to show that there does not seem to be
an ideal place for foreign students in which to adapt. It all depends on individual
travellers, where they come from, how they perceive their native milieu and what
they expect from their foreign experience. Jose for example finds adapting to life
in Paris easy, because it is a large city: 'there are so many people that nobody
pays any attention to who you are [...]. If you are open, Paris is a perfect city to
be independent, whatever your nationality.' Smaller cities like his native Lisbon,
or Dublin for Maria, generate family-type relationships, refereed by local conversation and gossip: '[Lisbon] tends to be a society and a city that is much more...
gossip. Everyone knows what everybody does on a certain level... It is a very...,
eh, you know, it's family' (Jose). For others, a medium-sized city is the perfect
place where to reach a balance between recognition and anonymity. Régine who
comes from Paris finds that Dublin, like Amsterdam, is 'cosy' without being
anonymous. As such, she thinks that Dublin is ideal to adapt to because its size is
reassuring.

> And that attracted me the fact that it's a small city because I've often been to
> Amsterdam to see friends who live there and it's about the same size... it's
> both '*cosy*'[4] and... it's not anonymous, but at the same time if you don't want
> to be recognised, well... that's why I was very tempted by Dublin (our trans.).

Sylvie concurs, saying that a stranger is not afraid in Dublin 'because it's only a million people, it's not like being lost in something massive'. The volume of space is related to a certain vision of the way one is to appropriate this space in a movement between two contradictory needs, recognition and anonymity.

Different social relations

Apart from size, population density in big cities can be a critical factor in the adaptation process. Elena, accustomed to Dublin, finds Paris and London inhospitable. In the city, with its mobility and traffic (Hannerz, 1983), daily indirect and impersonal contacts, too varied to allow for personal relations, are increased. Urban contacts appear cold, distant, indifferent: 'they will walk by'. However, as Elena talks and reflects, she wonders whether this interpretation of others as unconcerned and aloof is not the general impression any stranger arriving in a new city, large or medium-size, will encounter.

> I think the first thing that hits you when you arrive in Paris is that it's just so big... and there are so many people and I think that's the feeling in every big city because I felt that in London as well... It's sort of, it's like people don't care and they will walk by. And I think that's normal... If you walk out in Dublin and if you arrive in Dublin as a foreigner and you don't know where to go, I'd imagine you'd get the same feeling. That people just walk by, it's a big city. Whereas, we don't get that feeling here, we say: '*Oh, Dublin is wonderful!*', that's because we know exactly where to go when we are here.

Familiarity with a place generates a sense of attention to others which may not truly be there. Elena's comments underline again the correspondence between the city dweller's experience and the stranger's, faced with the same feeling of estrangement in their environment.

This is why a place with an international flavour may facilitate foreign students' integration. They are not the only strangers. For example, Julie views the geographical location of Trier as a border town in a 'Euroregion', an hour away from Luxembourg or France, 'not in the heart of Bavaria',[5] as a factor which eased her adaptation process. Hélène, by contrast, when she discovers that Dublin is a cosmopolitan capital, is 'enormously disappointed' because the Ireland she was dreaming of is associated with the rural West, not with a capital city like so many others. Since the matching of individual expectations and reality has been found to be an important factor in the adaptation process[6] and since lifestyles vary so much between country and city, Sophie points out that 'personality', by which she means individual wishes, must be considered. She chose Dublin because she wanted to meet a variety of people and had specific desiderata with respect to her stay abroad, i.e. drama and literature study groups. But Christine who wanted to do a lot of horse riding, explicitly wrote 'country' on her teaching application. In other words, potential student travellers would benefit from an understanding of the properties attached to different locations, as well as from an explicit awareness of their personal objectives for their stay.

Evidently, social relations vary from one context to the other. In an urban context, they are assumed to be founded on 'intellect' rather than on sentiment (Wood, 1934: 223). In a city, strangers must learn how to respond quickly to multiple, fragmented contacts, acquiring a certain relational ease in the process. City residents seem to possess more freedom because they can choose from among the multitude the kind of personal relationships they wish to engage in. However, the city also has in store for residents and strangers alike a potential stock of solitude. 'Specialised' relations, contractual or professional, arise more frequently in an urban context, each individual belonging to several social groups, separate from one another. Such fragmentation contrasts with the apparent cohesion that prevails in smaller places.

In smaller towns and communities, family and neighbourhood relationships are assumed to be more prevalent and contacts are liable to become personal more rapidly. Strangers arriving in such places are usually in a minority position and have no other choice but to try and become members. In a way, complete isolation from one's own social milieu may stimulate integration since attachment to the original nucleus is no longer nurtured. In this case, strangers are really immersed into the local society in a 'sink or swim' situation, as Aoife puts it. Integration may be facilitated if potential members are ready for integration and possess an invaluable asset, an intermediary in the local community.

Aoife analyses this phenomenon when she recalls the extraordinary chain of friendliness she experienced on her arrival in Arcachon. One social group seemed to lead to another as if naturally. Her initial contact, the local school inspector, provided her with free accommodation. His wife, herself from a distant land, and teaching colleagues organised furniture for her. Her neighbours frequently invited her to dinner and guided her around.

> Then after the month, they provided me with accommodation free of charge upstairs in one of the schools where teachers' families and the inspector live. So I moved in there: it was in the centre of the town and I was moving into a new neighbourhood and getting to know people. So, the first evening I arrived there and everything was totally new again and starting off again in a sense. After about an hour, a knock came on the door and this lady presented herself as the inspector's wife and said she was living two doors down and she heard I was Irish and she'd never met an Irish person and she wanted to meet one! So she came in and said if there was anything she could do to help me, she'd love to help me. And I said '*fine*'. Naturally enough, I wanted a lot of help as there was hardly anything in the flat, but I was modest as I didn't want to say '*I want this and I want that*'. Then she looked around and she said: '*it's strange in here. Maybe it's because there are no curtains. Would you like curtains?*' I said: '*it doesn't really matter, it's OK*'. She said: '*fine*'. And then she came back about half an hour later with a measuring tape and she measured around the window, and she came back the next day

with curtains for the room which she had made for me overnight and then she brought over an iron and so many things: saucepans, everything that wasn't there, cutlery... She was amazing... as well as that, she mentioned to the teachers in the school that I had just moved in and that there was nothing in the flat. So all of the teachers provided me with tables and furniture and a family gave me a TV for the year. It was unbelievable! Then the principal of the school arranged for a cooker, chairs and fridge. So it was fantastic! I cannot speak highly enough of them. She told many neighbours that I had arrived and she introduced me to the neighbours on the street and I got to know them and it was absolutely fantastic. I just can't describe it and it continued on right through the year. It wasn't just the first week. As well as that, neighbours would call and say: '*We're having dinner. I think we might have made a little too much. So if you'd like to come over now and you can join us*'. It was actually better that I moved into that area in the centre of the town because there were more people living there and more families, it was easier to get to know people and everything. Then they showed me the different things in the area.

This kind of welcome may be more compatible with a smaller community, where each member is linked to others in several ways, while in a larger society, connections between individuals might be less fluid, sealed in different categories or groupings.

Consequently, the role of the intermediary,[7] who acts as a bridge between newcomers and established community, may not be stressed enough. On the positive side, Christine who is appointed in what she calls a 'small village' is introduced to the local society by the language teacher responsible for her. This key person[8] promptly stretches her role beyond mere professional dealings. She meets Christine at the airport, puts her up in her own home for a few weeks, introduces her to her niece with whom Christine eventually shares a house. In the end, the teacher's family turns out to be 'Irish parents' for her. On the negative side, when Matthew recalls his total estrangement on arrival in the town of Vernon,[9] he draws attention indirectly to the teacher who did not fulfil her role and 'dumped' him in what he perceived as a hostile environment.

So when I was on the train, it was weird because I felt that I was alone, I was going off on this big adventure. In some ways, it was quite fun. But, when I arrived, it was quite bad because this teacher came and picked me up, drove me two minutes along the road and dropped me, she really dumped me in a *foyer*. So, this was where I was going to be staying for the year... I was standing there in this *foyer* which was awful. It was just like... hostile, it is very impersonal, it is like a prison to me, it was just awful, just this bed... it was like a cell, just a bed, a sink, a cupboard and a desk. Obviously I didn't have anything with me like posters or things that would make it mine.

Matthew's story as an assistant is interesting because it involves two discordant experiences, highlighting the fact that for assistants, entry into the community depends largely on professional contact. He is appointed to two schools. In the first one, 'the headmaster was a real tyrant. The atmosphere was echoed in the staff room... as you walked into the staff room: "*hello, everybody!*", and no response, it was awful'. He did not know who the English teachers were until late in the year because they did not communicate with him. The other school 'was the complete opposite'.

> Everyone came over and was talking to me, they gave me coffee, I was shocked!... the English teachers spoke to me, all the other teachers spoke to me... I participated in the classes whereas in the other school I had to sit quietly in a corner and observe...

The teachers invited him out. The school principal put him in touch with a family who wanted English spoken in their home and he ended up 'becoming part of the family'. He changed accommodation and is 'still in contact' with the family he stayed with. His social life expanded from there. This dual-faced experience seems to indicate that in towns, newcomers may be ignored, even rejected, or welcomed and integrated. According to Wood, there are no half-measures in this context.

In smaller communities, the sense of belonging can become very tight. Indeed, the smallness of a place seems to add to the aura of warmth and hospitality which often arises in such a context. Social relations happen unstructured, as if spontaneously. For Mathilde, this kind of serendipity where each social situation spurs on encounters and recognition is a property of life in the country. Through the teacher and her family, she started going to cookery classes: 'it was a way of meeting other people as well... she'd introduce me to other people who happened to be my pupils' parents...'. Locations are restricted, therefore encounters are facilitated. Activities with local people speed up the process of acceptance.

Edwige too, in a similar context, stresses the benefits of physical and social proximity. She quickly knew what to do and who to get in touch with. She became so integrated in the local milieu that she was even mistaken for the new solicitor. The resulting sense of 'belonging' to places and milieu is described by Mathilde in terms evocative of Lego.

> Everything seemed to fit... the people I was living with, the school, hum... the fact that it was a small town, that I'd automatically see practically the same people when I'd go out... it creates hum... a feeling of belonging to a place... in a bigger town, I wouldn't have had the same impression (our trans.).

The term 'to fit', which occurs when students want to express the process of accommodation to the physical milieu,[10] echoes Hannah Arendt's words: 'I don't fit'. It conveys the idea of a match between self and the environment which results from reaching a certain ecological balance. Individuals have found their right place. They are in agreement with the local landscape. They are no longer as conspicuous as dissonant foreigners sticking out. The verb also suggests the existence of a set in which the various parts are closely connected, not separated or dislocated, a true sign of adjustment to a territory where newness was initially experienced as strangeness, but also a sign that travellers have entered another stage in the adaptation process.

The fact that the three students located in rural communities had such a positive experience apparently contradicts the interpretation of small as socially constraining.[11] When newcomers are accepted in this fashion, the bonds which are established have the quality, warmth and strength of primary relationships. Sometimes, the very first contacts with a caring person – the teacher at the airport or the penpal's parents – are transformed into lasting affiliations, in the proper sense of the creation of filial bonding. Quite a few students mention this new locus of affection as their 'family' abroad.

Staking out a familiar habitat: from dislocations to familiarity

Considered in terms of a tangible geographical territory, the experience of strangers comes as the physical discovery of a more or less known world, source of the coveted novelty mentioned earlier. From a distance, new spaces appear blurred, vague, an uncharted territory to be mapped out. There lies one of the major attractions of travelling. One of the features of the stranger is precisely this fascination for the unknown and readiness for explorations to come. Nevertheless, individuals seek to give sense to new spaces.

Departure disturbs one's natural habitat in its most intimate aspects and requires the transformation of strange spaces into one's own. Spatial change, the simple de-location is sometimes felt as a dis-location in the sense that some part is detached somewhat painfully from the original whole and becomes separated from what was contiguous or close by. This almost physical disconnection from familiar places is anticipated and lived through by individuals in different ways. For some, leaving places which are cherished is a painful mutilation; for others, the lure of the unknown overcomes the pain of dislocation. What the period of first, radical dislocation brings home, Hoffman notes, is 'how much we are creatures of culture' (1999: 49). It is because culture and language go so deep that 'one's original home is a potent structure and force and that being uprooted from it is so painful. Real dislocation, the loss of all familiar external and internal parameters, is not glamorous' (op. cit.: 50). Eventually, the wish to secure a new place and identity may overcome the sense of dislocation. What are the key moments and what strategies are used to go from dislocations to familiarity?

The strategies students used to stake out their habitat were varied. Some were constructive, like preparation for the stay before departure, the organisation of one's 'nest' or the exploration of surrounding areas. Others were defensive, like the search for shelter in a special place, a ranch for Régine as a child in Hawaii or a friendly hostel in Donegal for Hélène, reliance on the ethnic national group or dependency on friendly houses for social contacts.[12]

One tendency consists in the organisation of places in identifiable zones, the division of large expanses into smaller discrete units centred on a specific familiar location. These are often represented as a series of concentric circles which get larger. In other words, differentiation in sub-spaces appears as a first cognitive step towards familiarisation with new spaces. The delineation of these smaller areas constitutes a safe-keeping step. Before the experience, space is structured for Régine in relatively large units, hierarchically organised: the country, the city, the university.

> There were three dislocations: there was Ireland, then there was Dublin and then after there was Trinity. And before going, they'd already been presented as three different worlds... and it's true that it's what happens... we were somewhat prepared in the sense that our lecturer had mentioned it and told us to be careful not to be stuck in Trinity or not to be stuck in Dublin... so, to be able to go further afield... so that was sort of a warning... it might be the reason why I know nobody in Trinity now! (our trans.).

The three different 'dislocations' she mentions correspond to three different worlds which became meaningful to her in her new territory. For Marina, an EAP student in Oxford, space is shaped as three different 'islands': her house, the city centre, the school. She adds that in Paris, there were only two islands for her: Paris and the school.

The terms 'dislocations' and 'islands'[13] bring forth the idea of separation and disconnection between the old and the new world. The discovery of new spaces is then conceived as crossing 'bridges' as Marina explains: 'as a matter of fact, there are bridges... what we do is to cross from one bridge to the other'. From one known space to another, the 'bridges' which are established are often represented by the specific individuals or activities associated with the place. Interestingly, students pick up quite naturally well-known metaphors to translate their experience of strangeness.

Space is not only grasped as a broad environment, but also as a territory in the ethological sense, as a place where one establishes one's presence by mapping out a reference zone inside which it is possible to feel secure (Fischer, 1981). This zone or life space is made up of a set of familiar people and objects which altogether create a personal habitat. Spatial appropriation involves the creation of a setting where travellers mark their presence through personal artefacts. A single object, seen as one's signature, may be sufficient (Goffman, 1973). Matthew regrets not having even a poster to transform his first unpleasant room so as to make it less alienating. The presence of familiar objects, a form of material intimacy, fortifies and protects, particularly initially when discovering strange conditions upsets habitual orientation schemes. Many students mention this phase of shaping one's personal habitat as a first stage towards feeling part of a place, evidently related to the issue of accommodation. The recreation of a familiar place shows that individuals are starting to leave their mark in the new scenery, unlike visitors who live out of an open suitcase.

Consequently, it is quite natural that the affectively laden array of familiar people and things left behind comes to be missed as well. Some may feel tempted to discount the importance of their familiar domain, temporarily forsaken, as if the fact that it is mostly made up of 'little things', almost impalpable in their flimsiness, is embarrassing. Valérie mentions 'silly little things' which, just before she leaves, take on excessive value. To inhabit the unfamiliar place, there are 'lots of things, posters and so on' which travellers are tempted to bring away with them. In the end, she decides to clean out her past and to wipe everything away, leaving with as little luggage as possible. Christine identifies what she misses from France, apart from her family and some friends, as wine and cheese, but also her flowering cherry in spring and some areas of her garden. Familiar food takes first place in this list and parcels sent by parents often contain their children's favourite fare. The loss of one's original domain is partly compensated by the effort to recreate a personal habitat. It might be beneficial to advise departing students in this respect.

Learning new spatial conditions also involves becoming accustomed to the climate. Customary climactic conditions may be sorely missed in a physical sense. Jose links the highs and lows he experienced during his stay to the change in climate. Away from the sun and not near the ocean for a year was particularly hard for a Portuguese student used to daily contact with both. He felt that there was not 'that much light' in Paris and even less so in Oxford. He expected Berlin to be difficult as well because he associated a cold climate with a cold society.

> It basically means since one and a half years ago that I don't live in the sun or the ocean. And in Portugal, I can walk from the beach and basically I was raised at the ocean and always with sun. And that has a big influence in all the way that you play, the way that you act, the way that you go to school, the way that you read, what you eat... and now all of a sudden, you are in an entirely different environment, and that has a very big influence. Paris was more or less... I think that Oxford is being more difficult, and I think that Oxford is being more difficult because... oh! you never see the sun... In Paris, you could see it every once in a while... Not here! It's always raining, it's always foggy, it's always dark... You don't have that much light, so it's more difficult, and Berlin, I think it will be difficult as well, eh... because not only the society is much colder, but also the weather...

Others like him find it demanding at first to get used to a different climate. Christine remembers being 'very cold' in the beginning while, at the end of the year, she thinks getting back to French 'heat' might be difficult. Maria too finds that 'the climate has so much effect on people' that 'some people actually have to go away because they get depressed because of the climate'. Climatic conditions constitute a relevant variable in the adaptation process, particularly when the contrast between home and abroad is severe. However, students also note that the climate is part of a larger concept which some delineate as 'the country' or overall external conditions which characterise the environment. But usually the environment fades into the background as the experience becomes more person-oriented, a point we will come back to.

A personal space: the issue of accommodation

The new setting remains strange as long as students do not possess a place they can call home. Choosing that place represents one of the main forms of taking root. Moreover, the issue of accommodation is one of the very first problems travellers have to solve. Indeed, accommodation is among the problems most often rated as serious in the Erasmus surveys (Maiworm *et al.*, op. cit.). It is a preoccupation which haunts not only the beginning of the student stay, but also the days before departure. In European cities where the number of students, natives as well as foreigners, is increasing without a corresponding increase in terms of quality-affordable accommodation, this issue must be acknowledged as a major concern.

The assistance extended to them in this area varies depending on factors such as host country general accommodation conditions, cities involved,[14] as well as institutions. The number of moves in the middle of the year may be considered as a sign of this predicament, errors occurring more frequently in the case of the first long stay abroad. Students who moved included Matthew during his first experience as an assistant, Franz, Viktor, Bruno, Christian and Thomas in the EAP group settling in Paris, as well as Sophie, Karine, Marco and Hélène in Dublin. They moved because they discovered some disharmony or, to quote Hélène, 'no particular affinities' between them and their surrounding milieu. It must also be stressed that the mode of accommodation selected in the host country frequently differs from the mode students are accustomed to in their home country. As such, this area represents another adventure they embark on without previous knowledge, and naturally induces a degree of error.

The accommodation selected is one of the characteristics which differentiates the three groups from one another. Assistants more often than not have the edge over the others in that institutional help is assumed to be provided by the local school authorities. Erasmus students may benefit from some guidance from the host university, but usually in the form of a list of possible places from which they make their own choice. Two main options arise for Erasmus students: launching into the unknown just like native students, which gives them equal status and encourages mixed cohabitation, or else accepting institutional arrangements with the inevitable consequence of getting into a social network made up of other international students. As for the EAP students, their only option was to find their own accommodation, a delicate task given the property market in Paris, added to some students' lack of knowledge about local practice. Consequently, as Marina and other EAP students pointed out, there were quite a few disagreements. The evidence from our students indicates that by and large both students and institutional authorities were not always aware of the significance of the choice regarding accommodation in the overall integration process, particularly as a core element in social activities and contacts.

Four different types of accommodation were possible.[15] Mixed or international cohabitation implies that foreign students live together, usually in a university residence, sometimes, but not always, with native students. This option was chosen by eleven Erasmus students, one assistant and one EAP student. Cohabitation with natives sets the scene for a different mix where the foreign student is in a minority position while natives represent the majority. It was the choice for most assistants, four Erasmus students and, initially at least, five EAP students. Ethnic or national cohabitation refers to the situation where students from a same linguistic or national group are together. This form of accommodation was selected mostly by two Irish groups of students and by Jürgen. Finally, independent accommodation represents a special case where students live on their own, distinctively adopted by ten EAP students out of twenty.

The data bring to the fore the preferred choice for each group. The majority of Erasmus students opted for international cohabitation, most assistants for cohabitation with natives, and EAP students largely for independent accommodation. These data must be interpreted with caution because they do not necessarily refer to the same reality. However, they reveal the most significant difference between our three case studies and highlight the role of the numerical ratio between natives and students. The first two modalities, international cohabitation and cohabitation with natives, dominate the data, the other two solutions emerging as compromises. The role of institutions as initiators of contacts is also highlighted. The assistance Erasmus students usually receive from international offices and language assistants from their school authorities structures their immediate search for accommodation, while EAP students arriving in Paris probably had to resort to their own devices.

Mixed cohabitation implies that student travellers are not isolated for long. They are assigned as co-residents a group of peers made up exclusively of foreign students or of a stiplulated mixture of foreign and native students. In Trier in Germany, foreign students live in individual flats in a university residence. On each floor, one or two flats are reserved for foreigners, the other eight reserved for native students. On the Louvain-la-Neuve campus, students live in *cots*, a sort of communal apartment shared by about eight students. The composition of students is rather similar to Trier: six natives to two foreigners from different nationalities. A student may not be in the same *cot* as her/his compatriots, but since there are four *cots* in each building, distance is relative, to the extent that Amin interprets this arrangement by saying that the Irish students were 'all together'. He regards this residential facility for Erasmus students as producing a group effect and a 'lack of identity'.

Well, that residential facility in Blackrock, they spend all the time together, they eat together and... you know, even, even, when I, even when I meet them in college, I go for lunch with them, I do all that sort of thing, I arrange to go out at night time, I... just couldn't... I'd rather ring my friends... No, apart from my two friends, but not the others, not the ones who... 'cause they're a big group, I know, it's a big horde to organise. The lack of identity, it's just... they're Belgians, like we were the Irish and it's hard to break. If you live together and spend all the time..., you just cannot break out...

The existence of 'a big group' pushes towards categorisation: 'they're Belgians, like we were the Irish'. The group effect dissuades intimidated natives from trying to meet the newcomers and hinders intercultural encounters between foreign and native students. Moreover, even though Erasmus authorities are generally careful about blending students from different origins, living in a university residence necessarily means that the social milieu revealed through cohabitation is primarily the student milieu. Groups, in this case student groups, whether national or international, protect. But at the same time they fence in on a world closed to the social diversity outside the campus grounds.

Cohabitation with natives is the most demanding mode of accommodation, but potentially the most enriching. Not frequently found among our Erasmus students, it is selected by those who are well aware, before they go, of what is at stake in staying abroad. These students select this residential pattern knowingly, as a strategy to obtain a more intimate entry into the local milieu. Among the few EAP students who tried it out for the same reasons, this approach resulted in a semi-failure for three of them who decided to move out in the middle of the year due to disagreements with the Parisian families they were staying with. The other two who shared apartments with native friends, Thomas and Matthew, are 'experts', the stay in Paris representing their second lengthy stay abroad. The impact of their mobility capital is fully visible in this area. It is also the case for two assistants in Dublin, Nicolas and Karine, who lived with friends they had known for a long time. For these students, it could be assumed that integration started prior to the actual stay abroad.

Cohabitation with natives is the natural choice for many assistants who find themselves appointed in small towns where there may not be other foreign students. In that group, only three students opted for a slightly different version of that pattern: an equal blend of natives and foreigners. Siobhan lived in Bordeaux with a French girl and an English girl. Christine and Jannick lived with Irish people who took in one other foreigner during the year. The qualitative difference is hardly noticeable, foreigners constituting still a minor ratio to the number of natives. Sharing accommodation with local people signals a desire to immerse oneself in their life with the added bonus of constant language practice and of socio-cultural discoveries from the inside. However, relationships which are fashioned in this type of context are immediately set on a more personal footing and as such exposed to the vagaries of subjective affinities.

The significance of this specific type of accommodation was made quite explicit by Hugo: it was the first topic he mentioned in his interview. To succeed in his enterprise, he arrived before the beginning of term because he knew that Irish students chose the place where they would live at that time. He was aware that the very beginning of the academic year determines what is to come: 'the people you meet then, you normally have them for one year'. His knowledge that the first weeks are crucial came from his previous experience with Erasmus students in his own university in Germany.

> I had a certain picture in my mind when I went to Dublin. As I said, because the first two weeks, I think, are the most important, the people you meet then, you normally have them for one year and afterwards it's getting more and more difficult to... change the environment you're in. So... it was very important for me that I just organised the first two weeks.

His strategy was successful: at the end of his year abroad, he had many Irish friends and felt well integrated in Irish life.

Maria is another Erasmus student who availed of this approach, but under duress. She found out when she arrived that the type of accommodation she had booked with the Spanish local university office was the wrong place. So she decided to look for an alternative, but stressed the anxiety this produced ('I was knocked for six when I arrived') and the risk of not finding suitable co-residents.

> I remember feeling very, very anxious quite a lot of the time because I hadn't anywhere to live. It wasn't really that... I was getting anxious about finding where to live, because everywhere I went, the apartment, there was only one room left and you had to share with somebody or, hum, I didn't know what I was going to do. So I finally took an apartment on my own and I looked for the people, so I was in charge of the apartment, then I was terrified that I wasn't going to find three flatmates and I'd have to tell my Dad that my rent was four times higher than it should be. So I was quite anxious until I filled that space and didn't fill that space for another month after that. So that was another month of quite... but it was only worrying about the apartment, space more than anything else. But it was a settling-in factor, finding somebody to live with, I suppose, so it has to be included.

The crucial step of deciding to rent her own apartment, being 'in charge' of her own accommodation and having to find flatmates became a 'settling-in factor'. It is an experience which very few students dare try out. She is anxious at first because she is on her own, but she has the opportunity to choose her group of flatmates among natives: 'I made sure I got Spanish flatmates, this is why, another reason why I rented my apartment: I chose who I was going to live with, I picked them: three Spanish girls [...] I made sure I had the amount of Spanish in my life that I wanted'. In her case too, the risk pays off and her flatmates represent one of the friendship networks she establishes during her stay. Indeed, sharing accommodation with natives is conducive to the extension of social networks of acquaintance or friends outside the professional milieu, and also to facilitating participation in local activities, as we will see.

The last two categories of accommodation, cohabitation with compatriots and independent housing, proceed from the absence of pre-established local contact. This is partly why some students take up residence with fellow students from their own institution whom they already know, as two groups of Irish students did, EAP and assistants. Living on their own is also the first option which presents itself to the EAP students who do not know anybody in Paris and are sometimes isolated from a national point of view. This approach is also natural in a city where one-room apartments[16] or indeed independent bedrooms are a customary form of lodging for students while, in other countries such as England or Ireland, students or young people commonly share a house.

Interestingly, EAP students used different approaches in Paris and in Oxford. From first to second year, the changes go towards more collective quarters (not a single student lived on her/his own in Oxford), towards a greater mix of nationalities, and of gender with both sexes often sharing the same place. The choice of accommodation for the second year was governed by the personal relationships generated at the end of the first year. Iris contrasted the solitude of living alone the first year, when one is looking for new friends, with the support she received from living with other people in Oxford.

> The thing was in Paris I lived alone. I had a room on my own and here it's a lot easier because we have the house and like… if you live together with other people, we support each other a lot, and living alone is sometimes quite difficult because you have to make your own planning and you have to make sure you see people because not everybody is going to phone you… and then you can spend a whole Saturday on your own if you don't phone them up… if you are not going to do it yourself, you have to keep yourself busy, otherwise you get really bored and lonely… but I tried to do that as much as possible and… the thing is of course at EAP last year, when we started, everybody came from their culture to EAP and everybody left their friends at home and basically needed new friends, so the whole group was very open… and now we all have got into small groups of friends and people around you and that is different.

This comment proves that living with compatriots or alone represents a flawed or rudimentary solution to a problem which must be solved urgently rather than a considered choice. On the other hand, EAP students in Oxford did not attempt to take up residence with native students any more than they did in Paris. This might reflect one of the weaknesses of a programme where diversity within distracts from diversity outside, and hardly ever opens up to relationships with the local population.

The question of accommodation could be regarded as the first trial testing student travellers' adaptation potential, particularly their aptitude regarding the material organisation of their life. This issue takes up centre-stage position in the beginning, but its importance declines as new challenges appear more stimulating.[17] It gives students the opportunity to gain experience in an area with which they are not always familiar, finding a place to live in, paying their bills, and so on. When the first choice proves to be wrong, they are in a position to seek an alternative during the year. In any case, the choice they make in terms of residence means that life will take on a different guise for them. Accordingly, between the student community living on an international campus and the broader social community open to those who share their living quarters with natives, the modalities for gaining entry into the social scene through shared activities and social links are quite different and induce rather varied personal experiences.

Conclusion: a new appraisal of space – 'the difficulty with living in one place' (Hélène)

Mobility calls for a new appraisal of space. The essential and complex relationship between individuals and space, spatial fabric sustaining social fabric, is suddenly ruffled, even rocked, in the physical displacement. In the new environment, learning a new spatial organisation means in the first place organising one's own territory so as to move from initial coldness to warmth, from anonymity to gradual recognition, a sign that the visitor has found an entry into social circles. This often proceeds by extension from a central familiar space, usually one's own accommodation, to more and more distant explorations into unknown territory where one progressively acquires landmarks. Organising a personal space one can call home represents the first step towards a feeling of belonging. The choice of accommodation is doubly crucial, as a personal refuge offering security and as the locus of interpersonal relationships, a basis for social relations, as we will see.

In the case of temporary strangers between wandering and fixation, the roots themselves are movable. The experience is an initiation to mobility, which does not mean having no place, but having several potential places, the emancipation from a single spatial affiliation and the extension of the sense of 'home'. Hélène feels the ambivalence of this position when she describes it as an 'enrichment' and a 'suffering' at the same time.

> I remember that once in class [a lecturer] said to us: '*You'll see, when you have travelled abroad, when you have spent time there, you won't be comfortable anywhere, you'll always find it difficult… the difficulty with living in one place, either your… your natural home, or the foreign country where you will no longer be…, or etc.*' […] I miss my home, I miss Hamburg,[18] but I'm sure there'll be things I'll miss from Ireland once I am gone. And certainly, it is a treasure, but it is perhaps also a certain suffering… well, I don't know… (our trans.).

The ambiguous status of strangers in space, the uncertainty and dislocation between several attachments expressed here, conjure up theories about the 'homeless' mind and the 'pluralisation of social worlds' (Berger *et al.*, 1973). The changing nature of space defines the singular position of the mobile person, potentially at home in several places.

Student travellers feel less like strangers as they acquire new social cards to play, a professional role in the local community, a familiar environment where they feel at home, improved ease in communication and a place, even temporary, in the new society. Then, as they say, they feel part of the environment and can go on to more personal tasks. From new spaces, they move on to new places, and then to new faces as their own personal landscape is stretched.[19] This phase of social reorganisation represents a second stage in the chronology of the sojourn. It differs qualitatively from the first stage related to departure, arrival and initial difficulties. It marks a crucial transformation for students from a condition of sometimes overwhelming strangeness to a position of relative strangeness.

8 The new social setting

Introduction: moving in and taking part

The students' multidimensional experience represents a powerful point in time for them, questioning numerous aspects of their life in a dynamism where permanence and change coexist. Special faculties of creativity and enterprise are required so that they can work out strategies allowing them to adapt to the multifold new setting. What options present themselves in their endeavour? Under what conditions may strangers go from outside to inside? In other words, what is the interplay between proximity and distance in the social field for those whose experience combines the contrasting dimensions of another origin with a desire for participation, albeit temporary?

The experience of student strangers from one social space to another may be apprehended at the intersection of two sets of issues, the first related to social contacts, the second to identity, notably transformations as a result of interactions between the individual and environment. In this chapter, we discuss the particular social contacts which pertain to the students' professional and social setting in the new environment. This social setting may be approached in several ways. In the previous chapter, we dealt with the new space as a geographic territory to stake out into a familiar habitat, and most importantly as a personal space with the choice of living quarters. The new social setting is approached here from two different angles: the students' socio-professional roles and their participation in the social scene through various activities. The next dimension which naturally follows has to do with the new setting as the locus for interactions of a different type.[1] All these aspects of social life are interconnected and overlap. Setting them apart, for the purpose of analysis, may obscure their juxtaposition in real life. The degree of socialisation achieved in the end may be assessed by examining those elements which characterise students' responses to the challenge of making the new place their own.

To gain entry[2] into the social space, students must organise not only their physical setting, but also their new social setting. This implies moving from a familiar space of socialisation to another less familiar. First, their new professional setting grants them a specific role. Secondly, the activities they take part in, with others or on their own, represent another way to try and gain access to the local social scene. In carrying out these various tasks, students redefine their territorial, familiar, personal, professional and social positions. Entry represents the moment when the initial worries and uncertainties concomitant with the arrival are progressively alleviated as one problem after another is confronted. Then, the effort towards a new socialisation is fully set in motion. Since institutional arrangements regarding entry may prove inadequate, individual initiative is mandatory.

New socio-professional settings and roles

Following accommodation, the need to establish a familiar territory involves the activities which engage students in their new temporary environment. Several options are available to them. The most obvious revolves around what Siu calls the 'job',[3] or what students refer to as work, in other words the explicit reason why they are spending a year abroad, which grants them a certain socio-professional role. The role of student is subsumed under that heading since higher education may be regarded as the first step towards professional integration. The three groups of students differ in that respect. The main role for Erasmus exchangees is usually that of students, though some of them take up small jobs to help with their financial burden. The main role for language assistants is that of assistant teachers. They are placed in a professional milieu, but quite frequently a few pursue their studies at the same time with their university of origin. EAP students are at the intersection of these two roles: they study for part of the year and go on work experience for the other part.

Each role introduces the students to new ways of doing and being as well as to diverse social contexts. On the one hand, they are familiar in their own society with the role of student, but must get accustomed to new methods and to studying in a foreign language. On the other hand, those who step into a professional role, teaching in a school or working in a company, may not have had previous experience of that sort in their own society and must do so in a society with differing norms.

Each socio-professional situation determines various learning modes. Schild (1962) outlined three principal learning modes accessible to strangers: observation, participation and communication. Used throughout residence abroad, their importance varies over time. Observation, the dominant mode during the initial stages, prompts hypotheses, assumptions, inferences and personal considerations, but strangers remain somewhat on the outside and on their own. Participation implies moving into action and, most importantly, interaction, often on an experimental basis, foreigners trying out various behaviours and appraising their validity from their hosts' reactions. Forms of participation go from minimal forms, such as commercial transactions in shops as a way of surviving, to more complex forms, such as adopting roles usually filled by natives, for example being a teacher. The third mode of learning which pervades the entire stay is communication with natives and others, highlighting once again the vital part language plays in life abroad.

The special position of strangers at the periphery of society means that the social learning situations available to them are limited. In other words, the sample of social situations on which strangers rest their learning is restricted. It could be assumed that the more diverse the social situations they find themselves in and the closer their contacts with natives, the more student travellers will have the opportunity to diversify and refine their learning. Observation is an activity in which any foreigner can engage unilaterally during a period abroad. By contrast, situations which allow participation and communication in the native scene are less easily accessible. Yet, adopting the role of participant may reduce considerably socio-cultural distance between natives and students. What kind of local activities and situations did our students engage in? How did they manage their roles in the new society?

To describe their professional life, students have a tendency to focus on local practice, conventions and behaviours on the basis of their personal observations (of university, school or professional situations). They tend to contrast what they are used to at home with the new system they come upon. These representations, notably the interpretation of differences they observed, must be seen as the inter-action between a foreign reality and a culturally determined person. This is why, to fully appraise their explanations, the two segments or parts of the interaction, outside reality and perceiving subject, must be kept in mind, as already mentioned in relation to culture shock.

University life as an Erasmus student

University life and practice in Europe are analysed by our group of Erasmus students along the same lines as have been documented elsewhere (Flory, 1993; Maiworm *et al.*, op. cit.). The students contrast the different European higher education systems in terms of whether they favour student autonomy or profes-sorial authority, staff–student personal contact or reduced communication, written or oral examinations, different forms of continuous assessment, class attendance or not, memorisation of content or critical analysis. Two areas are frequently referred to: study methods and examinations. For example, Hélène thinks that she did 'more in-depth personal work' in Dublin than in Paris because the department abroad encouraged independent research and reading. This is the reason why an Irish student like Amin found course content in Belgium 'very rigorous': 'I wouldn't say it's any easier, it's just a different system. In Belgium, you have to know everything you are taught in detail because it's all precise questions, there's no choice on papers.' John evaluates the Italian system in a similar fashion: oral examinations based on the lecturer's notes rather than on authors' texts and requiring a high degree of memorisation in the most minute detail rather than personal research in the library: 'on page 328, there are three facts concerning economic development, which are they?', he recalls quoting an exam question. Marco – who is the exchange student in Dublin for John in Rome – explains the system he is familiar with: 'in Rome, the system is based on exams, not on lectures, and you don't attend lectures because it's not possible'. The large number of students, '30,000 students in economics', makes attendance difficult. To obtain a place at a lecture, according to him, you must 'queue for two hours before the beginning of classes'. He enjoyed the new study methods which 'force you to develop your own ideas' and to approach a topic in a critical way. These are but a few summary examples of comments made by Erasmus students.[4]

If they are pleased to discover new study methods, those Erasmus students who are not language specialists stress the difficulty of having to study in a foreign language, particularly at the beginning of the year: lecturers go too fast, they explain complex ideas at great speed, foreign students do not understand some of the key words and dare not interrupt overcrowded lectures. Amin remembers feeling lost.

> Well, ya, because the lecturers move quite quickly and they'd be explaining fairly complex things and you just get, you just get lost, just couldn't catch up... like they would keep repeating words that you didn't know what they meant, key words for some concepts... So you're just lost... And there were big lecture halls, you know, big crowds. I didn't really want to stop the whole thing and say, you know: '*What did that word mean?*' when everyone else seemed to know... Just things that were happening all the time, so you're going to fall behind... Because there's a couple of words that you don't... you don't know what he's referring to, so... you know... keeps referring to a couple of different parameters... and you don't know what they are... So you're lost...

Initial fears, for example of being at a disadvantage compared to native students who are studying in their own language and who are familiar with the academic content and methods, drive some students to work much harder so as to compensate what is perceived as a handicap, as Hélène explains.

> We're not going to be on a par in fact and so to fill the gaps, this discrepancy, well I think that you work much harder and then also because... you're a certain showcase, I mean... we're like representatives, well ambassadors and you don't want to give a wrong impression (our trans.).

Others rely on the clemency of some lecturers towards foreign students who are not always expected to follow as many courses or to do as many examinations as the others. A common strategy which helps European students in their attempts to follow courses consists in asking native students for their lecture notes.[5] However, this kind of request is not necessarily met positively. It assumes that personal contacts between native and foreign students already exist, which is not always the case at the beginning of the year.

Besides academic issues, university settings present differences regarding the quality of the environment and the facilities for community life they offer. University traditions seemingly differ radically in Europe between institutions which feel it their responsibility to take care of their students' social and collective integration and those where such a drive does not exist (Galland, 1995). In the first context, students develop a strong sense of identification with their place of study, which is often also their place of residence as well as the venue for their leisure activities. In the second context, the feeling of affiliation to the university is minimal. Quite obviously, this dimension of university life will have repercussions on the integration of foreign students. For some of them, life on the campus involves more than strict professional aspects and includes experiencing the whole gamut of student social life.

Schools in the life of language assistants

Professional integration in the case of language assistants means that they are introduced to more diverse situations than Erasmus students and are in contact with a greater variety of social actors: their pupils, but also the parents, their fellow teachers in several schools in some cases (Aoife and Emily both taught ten different groups of children in four schools) and the school administrative staff. They do comment on differences between school systems and pick up obvious contrasts like timetabling.[6] But the human dimension and the personal contacts which participation in a professional activity like teaching involves stand out in their comments.

Another characteristic of their situation lies in the strong links which exist between their professional activities and other areas of their life. The school fulfils many social functions. It may be the place where they live, which is often the case in France. It is the locus of their socialisation, colleagues and parents of schoolchildren being a source of social contacts. It may also be the venue for their leisure activities, when the assistants take part in collective activities, school visits for Sophie, school orchestra for Valérie, the basketball team for Aoife. Such contiguity means that professional relationships are extended easily into more personal ones. Sometimes these are even like family relationships, when the language teacher is invested with the role of parental substitute, as happened for Christine in Newbridge, Siobhan in Bordeaux, Edwige in Donegal and Aoife in Arcachon.

Assistants highlight other cultural differences, the local system of administration in France representing a favourite target. The treatment reserved for foreigners by members of the French administrative system is frequently mentioned as surprising, even offensive in its apparent rejection of non-French individuals, including other European citizens. Siobhan is astonished by the heaviness and ridicule of a system where someone is asked to bring back an application for a *carte de séjour* because the identity photographs have been cut in four segments! The cold bureaucratic hostility displayed towards foreigners, to whom such procedures appear beyond belief, produces the feeling that foreigners are 'begging' the right to stay as if they were 'dispossessing French people', she comments. In another national context, Valérie is amazed by what she calls Irish 'obscurantism'. These 'astonishing' cultural differences frequently constitute what is meant by culture shock, as evident from our previous discussion.

Interestingly, school systems provoke fewer comments regarding educational differences among assistants than university systems do among Erasmus students. This may be related to their divergent professional roles. Erasmus students are personally confronted with a different learning system, but they are in a position to observe and reflect critically on it. Teaching assistants are part of a professional corps. They are more directly involved in the local life and may be less prone to observing things from the outside. Overall, the comments regarding cultural differences made within the group of teaching assistants tend to show that they behave as if they were part of the system, inside it as actors rather than as outside observers. Their socio-professional participation in the local society involves them more closely than students who may remain somewhat disconnected from close participation. As a result, when Aoife compared her two experiences as an Erasmus student and as a teaching assistant, she pointed out that students do not always 'feel they are part of society' in the university milieu while she did as a language assistant in a school.

The EAP dual experience

EAP students have a dual experience in terms of socio-professional roles. Their first role is that of student in the international school at the beginning of the year, their second that of *stagiaire*[7] after Christmas. The difference between the two modes of participation highlights the significance of the work experience, which in the opinions expressed by the students outweighs the student experience. All EAP students cite their *stage* as an epiphany in the cultural learning process, notably because it enables them 'to understand the local culture', Iris says. But also, Damien points out, 'the *stage* gets you out of the school, it just starts you thinking about things', in particular about a future professional life.

Initially, their social scene in Paris is very much centred around the school. To many, the institution represents a world apart which functions as a kind of autonomous international microcosm. Damien compares it to a 'bubble isolated from local culture'.

> The school is like a little bubble isolated from local culture in a way… you are all in an international circle, living your experience together of being an international group, studying together etc., all the time and you could be in any country really.

Marina confirms that 'few people have an open vision because really the EAP, they live together, it's always the EAP evenings together, it's always… contacts within the EAP'. She thinks that the second year in Oxford might be different. The risk is great that the predominance of the international 'bubble' eventually renders the local milieu invisible. As a result, at first the only contacts with natives which the students are involved in are limited to functional transactions, such as those required to rent accommodation, and academic interactions. So in the beginning, their main discovery regarding the local culture revolves around French ways of studying, particularly the system of *grandes écoles* which most non-French students find astonishing.

Consequently, the EAP does not appear as a European school for the first year in Paris, but rather, in Damien's opinion, as a French institution.

> I think that is a big contrast on Oxford and Paris. I think in Paris you have 35%–40% French and you are in the French capital. The school is bent towards the French ideas and so on… and it is probably strongest in Paris and I think you find that definitely… and the French definitely think they are in France. They are very open about this. They consider this normal… the EAP is not a European school for the first year, it is a French school, everything is done as it would be and there is very little internationalism.

In other words, in the EAP experience, the first year abroad serves mainly as a phase enabling discovery of the internal diversity within a group of about one hundred young people from various European nationalities. However, some are more curious and eager to seek contacts outside their professional microcosm. Eric, who is an exception in this respect, judges that being open to the culture outside the school very much depends on individuals, their personality and their objectives, 'whether they want to get integrated within the EAP and remain there… or whether they want to look for contacts elsewhere'. But what kind of contacts can students seek elsewhere?

The work placement represents for the vast majority of the group the main situation of direct contact with natives in their environment.[8] It modifies the numerical ratio between natives and non-natives. Damien underlines that 'everybody there is French' and Thomas that 'there are no Germans', as if the native majority group suddenly became visible to foreigners who up until then were mostly involved in an international scene. The *stage* represents a very strong moment in the process of cultural discovery. For Marina, this is close to culture shock when she realises that in spite of a common language, cultural distance sets apart ways of doing things, in this case obtaining information, in France and in her native Luxembourg. Their work experience also introduces them to some kind of social diversity so far inaccessible to the students, as Viktor recalls.

> Like for example, there was a secretary, we had a chat very often, she was very *bavarde* and that's interesting, to see an average normal family… because I never had experience with that before… or at the same time, meeting some… normally I worked in a team of just an assistant and executives, and it's also interesting to see their interests there, like where they go to eat, especially in France it's important… when they have a foreign delegation, when they invite, to see… the social ritual of taking foreigners out to a meal, which for the French is the biggest gesture… .

To Viktor, discovering the way 'an average normal family' functions through conversations with another company employee or finding out about social rituals like taking people out for a meal represents a new way of gaining an insight into French life.

The work placement is regarded as a major factor facilitating integration into the local society, particularly when the first role, that of student, was not welcomed. Josef, who worked before entering the EAP, suffered from his sudden change in social status and reported that he did not feel integrated in the school, but did during his *stage* when he was able to socialise with his colleagues. Regaining the social status which he regards as normal for him makes him feel finally at ease in France. As for Thomas, his work experience enabled him to assess the degree of integration he had achieved: he thought he could live and work in France, even without friends and having to speak French eight hours a day.

> The *stage*... in the sense that there was no, first of all no Germans around because it's like... France... Ya, I felt like I could live or I could work in France, just me, no friends around, just get a job... like '*here's your job*'. Now you would stay there for five years and you would get along with persons and... just talking French just eight hours a day with... the secretary or the chief... But, always it was integration and what they were interested to talk, what they were interested to eat, how they make business, separated from the rest, just among the French... to get along also, you know, to work is a special relation, you cannot walk out, you cannot say '*Ok, I don't work this way*'. You have to make the effort.

He makes the point that the integration process comes about naturally when foreigners observe what interests the locals, their subjects of conversation, their eating habits, their business practices.

It is also during the *stage* that Damien understood fully the benefits of a 'European business education'. He noticed that large amounts of time and resources were lost due to language and cultural barriers between English and French partners in the same company.

> It was a pity because the French side were after spending an awful lot of money on this stuff and they were not going to get value out of it like for years later, because everyone was being slowed down by language barriers and by cultural barriers and because the Anglo-Americans think of infor-mation technology as something they understand and that they dominate and they are not aware that the French have an excellent track record in a lot of this stuff and conceptually they are very suited to it.

This situation made him appreciate the enormous value of a European study programme such as the EAP which enables students to acquire linguistic and intercultural competences which will be of benefit to Europeans working together in an international setting. Their work experience acted as a powerful lever for integration and gave EAP students the feeling that they were getting closer to French culture through entry into a professional structure.

The different socio-professional roles adopted by students depending on their programme provide a certain type of entry into local structures, the door being more or less open to the society outside. As a first step into a process potentially leading to closer interactions, this introduction may not necessarily end up in something else than functional sociability among 'acquaintances'. These relationships usually remain rather superficial, a stage when 'you know their names, but you don't really know who they are as people' (Aoife). Nevertheless, participation in a local structure as a student, as an assistant teacher or as a *stagiaire* represents a valuable entry into a foreign culture which can be either seized to open doors wider or ignored as an opportunity. Whether travellers use it to reduce psychological and symbolical distance or whether they prefer to stay on the doorstep at a distance depends then very much on personal resources and dispositions of the moment.[9] This is where personal efforts towards social seduction will be at work.

Participation in the new social scene: shared activities

Besides their professional context, student travellers have access to other activities which lead to more social contacts and learning situations. Activities shared with others, notably with natives, represent another way of entering society, all the more important that the leisure context calls for direct and informal personal contacts and communication. Answers to the questionnaire reveal two types of activities: those which imply interacting with other people, or shared activities, and those which relate more to individual discoveries, 'cultural' activities in the strict sense of the term.[10]

In the category of shared activities, three main pursuits were cited: casual meetings, regular leisure pastimes, and irregular ventures such as excursions, trips or holidays. Casual events included meeting people for a drink in a café or a pub, attendance at student parties, conversation in the common room of a student residence, visits to nightclubs. The majority of students reported these as weekly, sometimes daily, activities. In this domain, the experience of assistants revealed one major difference: they were the only ones to be regularly invited for dinner by local families in their home. By contrast, Erasmus and EAP students mentioned no invitation of the kind throughout their entire stay, or at most one to two dinner invitations during the year. The only exceptions to the rule concerned the few students who had established friends in the local community before their stay. In the assistant group of fifteen, only three did not mention as regular events meals with families who often became close friends or assumed the role of their family abroad. The scarcity of invitations to native homes, outside the assistant experience, draws attention to the eccentric social position in which most foreign students find themselves.

Sharing a meal, which is regarded in many European cultures as an important socialisation event, is prohibited to student travellers, particularly when their mode of entry precludes sharing a professional context with natives.

Participation in leisure pastimes may equally prove tricky when time, financial means or local resources are lacking. Many students find that their studies are demanding and leave little time for other activities. Others do not know how to go about entering local society through this particular avenue. For a long time Josef believed that there were no clubs in Paris and explained that he did not know how to get in touch with people.[11] A smaller town may indeed prove more promising in this respect. Jürgen notes that it is easier to go canoeing in Oxford where the local sports club is ten minutes cycling away from his house than it is in Paris.

For Erasmus students, opportunities depend very much on the university environment: English-speaking campuses are reputed for the vast array of activities offered to students and the number of student societies. Marco comments on the difference: 'we really go to university to study, here it embraces your whole life, so it's easier to have something to do here'. Where clubs exist, they generally provide an excellent entry into native society. Some students used them to the full: Hugo in the environmental society, Marco in the sailing club through which he went away for weekends. Amin played rugby in Louvain as did John in Rome. Julie, an experienced tennis player, applied for membership in a local club in Trier. Elena swam three times a week with a Parisian girl. Daniel played football with Irish students. The two Spanish students in Dublin attended a weekly aerobics class as well as an Irish dancing course. Hugo summed up the potential social role of student societies, especially sports societies, as providing experiences for members and producing a fraternity based on common experiences.

> Especially societies which do something... like the environmental society is perfect because they actually have ideas and they want to do something. Other political parties, they will know what they want to do, maybe just debate. Especially sports societies, they get you into it. It's because of the experiences you have together. Because... sports or going out into the country, doing something together besides studying is an experience which... you have this experience at home and a similar experience here and the people are the same.

A bridge across social distance is provided. Sharing activities with others, students discover a certain commonness: 'people are the same'. For some however, societies proved a disappointment. Régine and Hélène found some students' behaviour immature and kept away from them.

But Hugo stresses an important aspect of the social scene: 'you have to work at it'. He quotes two German friends who kept talking German to one another and isolated themselves from native students. When they understood their mistake, it was too late to rally local students around.

There is also the problem that you have to work at it, because there were five students in the canoeing society and they didn't really get accepted... First of all, there were two friends, they knew each other and they were talking all the time in German and they did it in the first two weeks, then they realised: '*Well, that's not a… Nobody is talking to us*'. Then, they changed, but it was kind of too late because the first two weeks are very important.

Nevertheless, as already stated, trying to gain admission to a group cemented by a common language and a common cultural system requires strong determination on the part of individual strangers. Hugo had this determination because he was aware of what was at stake before he embarked on the experience. If 'social integration depends on whatever you do yourself', waiting 'until somebody comes to you' is an ineffective strategy.

If you go in the first two weeks and maybe you look stupid and say: '*well, I'm going to these people and try to talk to them*'. Hum… then slowly they just get used to you, they accept you. It's a very awful experience, you have to make this experience at home too if you come to a different environment, you have to be active, and not just wait until somebody comes to you. This doesn't work out very well. Social integration depends on whatever you do yourself.

The individual stranger must initiate contact even though it is 'a very awful experience' because 'you look stupid'. Feeling stupid because of one's accent or because as the newcomer one misses out on jokes and other cultural references, as discussed before, is an unpleasant part of the experience of strangeness. Seeking a social position within an established group implies a temporary disintegration, both personal (self-esteem) and social (outside position), which is hard to accept.

Once again, assistants seem to benefit from more local resources than the other two groups of students. An analysis of the questionnaires filled in by Christine and by Sophie gives a specific image of the assistant experience in its general aspects and in two different spatial contexts, a small town and a capital city. Both shared accommodation with native people of their own age. They had more friends among natives than among other foreigners or their own national group; Sophie talked of other assistants she knew who had 'a level of integration more or less similar to (hers), i.e. they have many contacts and exchanges with the local population'. The two assistants had many opportunities to share a meal with Irish families, teachers in both cases, and for Christine in her 'Irish mother's home', where she felt 'like at home'. Both of them went out for a drink 'very often' and 'exclusively' with Irish people, 'with all my friends from the musical society and my co-residents', Christine adds. They also had regular, if less frequent contacts with other local groups in various contexts: Christine through horse riding, an aerobics class and a local choral society, and Sophie through a ten-week drama studies course, a literature course in a local university, as well as films and outings organised by the school. In the end, they mentioned a feeling of integration in the local community, which Christine measured from 'people saying hello because they recognise you, not as THE French girl or boy, but as someone who goes shopping in the same place, who lives here, etc.'. Christine felt so integrated that she was considering staying on for a couple of years and dreaded thinking about her departure. Sophie judged her integration by other criteria: 'I have a convenient flat, a circle of friends, regular social activities (theatre, cinema, going out to the pub) and a job which is a great factor for integration'. These examples illustrate the cohesion which developed between various elements of their social life, particularly accommodation, activities shared within the local community and the ensuing social contacts.

Indeed, many students stressed that the choice of accommodation had a strong impact on social activities and contacts. Elena drew attention to the danger of 'cultural isolation' which sharing an apartment with three compatriots generated. Lucy explained that in the student residences in Louvain, all regular social activities with natives took place around the *cot*. In some, the students organised a 'common soup' which each student in turn was responsible for, while in others they preferred games, and in others they watched videos together ('we were really excited because it was the only thing we could see', she adds). These activities represented opportunities for native and foreign students to socialise together. On other campuses, the procedure was similar: sharing accommodation enabled lengthy discussions at night.

However, sharing the same living space does not necessarily induce intimate relations, as Régine explained.

> Of course, there were ups and downs, particularly when living with someone you don't know from nowhere… spending a year together, what's going to happen! mostly from a political point of view and all that, we don't agree at all! [she laughs]. But, with small things, it worked well. We had small conventions: '*not this, not that, not that*', general rules of what… it was the first time for me and for her as well, we were somewhere and we weren't under the parents' rule or visiting… we had to find our own rules: no orgy because the carpet is pink! so, no orgy, no drugs, no drunken parties and then, we wash this and that… how many times a week… so we observed these and it worked well, but it's true, we're very different… well at the same time, the national level and in a way it's true because I feel far more French now than when I was in Hawaii, and the political level because I'm more… well not aware, but well I listen to the radio, the news… she doesn't even listen to the radio… and then I am older… it went well. We are slightly distant… maybe we'll keep in touch, I am invited to her wedding and all, but it wasn't a great revelation… (our trans.).

Cohabitating with another person may only lead to a kind of amicable agreement because of different interests. Their relationship ends up halfway between proximity and distance: 'we are slightly distant'.

Relations which obtain from living with a local family, even when not fully successful, are tantamount to a powerful introduction into local society, largely because of the proximity produced by such circumstances. Christophe, Matthew and Viktor mentioned the French home where they were staying as a key resource for 'learning the society', or rather a given strata of society through the representatives of one family. Christophe, who had French as one of his mother tongues, learnt mostly from family conversations while Viktor relied on observation: 'I never asked direct questions, but it was evident, from looking at reality, the way they behaved or their reactions... it was very important'. The kind of relations which the presence of a stranger within an intimate place maps out are ambiguous. Christophe outlines the dilemma: is the stranger admitted into the inner circle or is s/he maintained outside?

> I was addressed as *'Monsieur Christian'*, eh... it was, it was rather amusing, I find, but that, that, I don't know whether it was distance relative to me or distance with me integrated in their small family bubble, relative to the rest of the world... well, I, I didn't mind at all, I found it all rather amusing, rather nice, but... eh... the family themselves were... the *bourgeois* family unfortunately stuck in their... (our trans.).

Sophie also found her family accommodation a privileged place for communication. But in the end, she considered that, if one gained in terms of social proximity, one lost in terms of personal freedom. Indeed, the three students mentioned above moved to other living quarters. On the other hand, the students who were happy in a family home, like Karine and Matthew, listed the many benefits they derived from the experience, notably meeting a diversity of people and finding security in a warm affective spot. Matthew said that 'the best way to get integrated in any culture or the easiest way probably is to go and live with a family if possible', particularly because students are immersed in the language all the time. In such a context, the experience abroad forms a whole and appeals constantly to the three modes of learning: observation, communication, and participation.

'Cultural' activities

The second category of activities refers to information about the socio-cultural environment conveyed through different media, press, books, radio, television, cinema, theatre, musical events, visits or trips. The main result regarding this type of cultural practice is that they vary considerably from one student to another and seem to be dependent on personal needs and tastes, on social customs and on individual resources. For example, under the heading 'books', i.e. reading in the foreign language outside their studies, some answered that their average weekly reading time is about twelve hours[12] whereas others mentioned half-an-hour per week. Two other factors separating students in this regard were their language competence and their major field of study. Régine who studied English in Trinity mentioned twenty hours a week of independent reading. Similar variations may be observed regarding listening to the radio, watching television and going to the cinema, which are dependent on availability. Attending the theatre or a concert hall varies also with personal inclinations as well as age[13] and access. Collette, a language assistant in a small French town, went once to a concert in a nearby town, attended the cinema club once a week, watched television in a friend's home a couple of hours a week and listened to the French radio on her walkman on her way to school. By contrast, Tom commented on the cultural habits of older students in the EAP by saying that for those lucky enough to afford it, Parisian culture meant 'good wines, good restaurants, theatre, opera, cinema and symphonic orchestras'. These activities would be out of bounds for younger students who have to work every summer to finance their studies. So reasons for not taking part in these types of activity are most of the time strictly material: no television at their disposal, not enough time since their 'two priorities are to study and to make friends' as Marco specifies, and lack of finance to attend the theatre or the concert in expensive capital cities.

As a result, activities in that area were restricted. Lucy summed it up by saying: 'we did little, we'd stay together and we did very little…'. Yet, 'cultural' pursuits are usually considered as an essential source of information on a foreign culture. Students who tried to justify this lack of practice in their daily life highlighted an important specificity of the stay abroad. Julie explained that she read the papers and watched television because 'it is a fantastic way to learn the language', but she did not read books 'on the political system and all that, no…', implying that such pursuits are not as relevant in the context of the stay. Marco went on holidays in Ireland with a group of foreign students at Easter because he was curious to discover the country. He took this opportunity to read two guide books and a few history books, which helped him to 'understand better all the problems…'. He also obtained some information through discussions with his 'exchange student' in Rome, John. The conflicting reports he heard regarding problems in Northern Ireland created doubts in his mind: 'I don't know what to think… it's very difficult'. Hugo who worked hard on his social integration used another strategy. He followed his native friends' interests. At home in Germany, he reads the paper, but if they do not read the paper, he will not do it in Ireland: 'If it doesn't interest them, then it doesn't interest me'. His knowledge on the local culture came largely from what he learnt from his friends. To these students, 'cultural' knowledge about a country, for example of a historical nature, may be learnt on one's own and outside the country, not necessarily during one's actual stay. It can be done either as groundwork before departure or as a concluding step after the event. Hugo compares the learning process to the way children who are first immersed in their native culture learn about it later at school. In other words, for the students, live knowledge takes precedence over book knowledge because it is the specificity of the learning experience.

Moreover, what students seemed to reject under the heading of 'cultural' pursuits was first and foremost a role. Generally speaking, they assumed that when pursuing this kind of activity, they took on the role of tourists who consume information, but remain on the outside as distant observers. By opting for life abroad, they chose a different role. Direct face-to-face contacts are opposed to indirect contacts which insulate visitors. The former are particularly sought during the stay abroad because they cannot be reproduced at home, while the latter may be dealt with away from live interactions. Tourists differ from sojourners precisely in the nature and quality of contacts they establish with the local cultures.

Learning a foreign culture abroad

The cultural discovery process has many facets. In this respect, the role of the cultural informants or intermediaries is crucial, but also confined by its lack of representativeness. We saw in the previous chapter that the existence of such intermediaries greatly assists the students at the very beginning when they arrive in the new context. Here, we see their role as cultural guides who alert outsiders to the complexity of local realities. In the next chapter, they appear as key-people, who play an important part in the students' personal relationships. Students like Hugo, Thomas, Aoife and Matthew, who lived with natives, mentioned that their flatmates or lodgers acted as cultural intermediaries, 'explaining society' to them on a daily basis, particularly when conflicts arose: they are 'always there to help if there is a problem, a misunderstanding or something', says Matthew.[14] Then strangers begin to feel that they are 'inside' the foreign culture.

The cultural intermediary is the person who presents her/his culture and explains it formally, as a translator or teacher would, which is often the profession of these individuals, helping travellers through potential hazards and cultural enigmas. Aoife met a teacher, described as 'a link between myself and French society', who explained 'different mannerisms' to her: 'if there was something I didn't understand during the week, different expressions, she would explain them to me'. They started off with French grammar and expanded into a variety of other areas. These choice language or culture informants give the rare student travellers who benefited from such guidance the opportunity to rationalise their live experience which otherwise might have remained puzzling. The advice from a seasoned mentor enabled these students to develop their knowledge and go beyond the level of spontaneous occurrence into reflection. Experience becomes knowledge.

Thomas contrasted three cultural informants who made him see different aspects of their culture. One introduced him to French culture, politics and history and enabled him to advance deeper in his cultural understanding: 'he... brought me more into French culture, took me more into French culture, like *politique de la 5ème République*, in the language class and he was very into politics like... de Gaulle and Giscard d'Estaing'. They talked a lot about French society and 'as he was a professor, he could tell me a lot of what was going on in France, you know... it was just a view of the whole nation'. His other informant during his stay in Aix was the teacher whose house he was sharing. She urged him to 'understand' the culture by reading Sartre and Vian.

> She knew the French literature, she said: '*Now, you are in France, what you have to do is read French books, watch French TV, go to friends around, you have to understand...*'. She said: '*your aim is to be like this*' and that impressed me, to understand... Because she saw also the whole culture and the whole nation as a whole, and she said '*to understand, you have to read Sartre and Boris Vian and this and this and this...*'. So, '*I give you a TV and you have to see TV*'. I took this as good advice. So, I took out French books and it was really hard to read French books when you don't speak the language, but I just said '*OK, you have to learn, and if everybody talks about Sartre, you have to know who is Sartre*'.

This supposedly 'very French' concern for understanding through the medium of a certain kind of culture, even when it enables students to comprehend contemporary realities in a larger historical context ('the whole culture and the whole nation as a whole'), is nevertheless based on selective judgement. Thomas's other informant was his flatmate during his Parisian sojourn.

> We talked for hours..., well not about culture or about history, more about daily parties, she was my age, or about cooking... you know, saying '*oh, what are you doing? it's disgusting! I would never eat cheese in the morning, I would never...*'... and so, I got to know the French taste, what do they eat, how do they work, the French things of what you should not do and what you should do, like what people think: '*this is not really ... or this is not good what you do*'. You have to take all this... and she had a sister who was studying at the Sorbonne and that was the cultural part, like she studied history and she explained to me '*you know, the French and the English, they did this and they did that*'... and... she took me in Paris showing me around: '*this is that and this is that...*'. So I had more history with the two girls.

The contrast between various intermediaries illustrates the complexity of choosing one's informants or rather, since they are few and far between, of assessing the place of their particular voice in a larger social context. What kind of information needs to be given and according to what ranking? The choice made by the majority of our students is clear: information of a 'cultural' type is often deemed secondary and discounted as a valued source of learning compared with face-to-face interactions.

In fact, comments made by students often challenge definitions of culture and the way it is learnt. When asked about their discovery of 'culture', they practically always answer in terms of people.[15] In this context, how does one approach a foreign culture? Some students highlight the 'natural' way foreigners learn *in situ*. According to Philip, one learns without really being aware of it in the course of daily interactions, as a participant observer. In any case, what is meant by 'understanding' a foreign people and culture? Elena rightly draws attention to the natural limits of such understanding: 'I don't think anyone completely understands everything'.

I did not really say to myself before I went: '*I want to understand French society and culture*' because I assumed it would happen. It didn't really happen because I don't completely understand the French... I don't think anyone completely understands everything, so it wasn't one of the things I said to myself before I left... I did assume that it would happen naturally living in the country... which to some extent it has, but as I say...

She considered that she had achieved some degree of 'understanding' because she felt 'much more relaxed' in a French context. In other words, fear of the unknown which makes foreigners anxious about ordinary dealings had receded and been replaced by a degree of familiarity with a social scene.

Philip quoted two key experiences which marked the cultural discovery process for him: a summer camp with a group of French people and preparing for the EAP *concours* in France.[16] The summer camp was his 'first real cultural immersion': 'it was all French people... a very French group of about 20–25... a real immersion... because I was speaking French all the time, living French culture, French language... I learnt a great deal in those short three weeks'. But the moment he begins to 'feel really integrated' coincides with preparing for the *concours*.

That's when I really started to get an insider's view of French society because as I said, I was there as a foreign student, so you still have a certain way of looking at French culture. When I started to study for the *concours*, real French culture, that's when I really felt that I was integrating into French culture... [...] I mean that you understand how people think from that perspective. Sometimes I can take a step back and take a look at them as an English person, but still understand exactly what they are saying. And that is what I understand by integration.

The kind of integration he alludes to touches upon ways of thinking. It consists in considering the natives from a foreigner's point of view while at the same time understanding their point of view. It means going from being simply a foreigner looking at another culture to getting an insider's view through adopting a native role, here the preparation for a local exam. Experiencing this kind of process requires time and can only be done slowly, 'bit by bit' as Hugo said. After a while, a degree of strangeness has been conquered.

Conclusion: from space to society

Student strangers organising their familiar territory through participation in professional and socio-cultural activities feel that they are progressively more and more part of the environment, or at least that they are no longer set apart from natives. They start feeling at home. Sharing activities, whether professional or social, means that you become 'impregnated with people', as Mathilde says, 'otherwise you'd probably need to stay longer... because there are aspects of things one doesn't see'. So, duration and quality of contacts are related to the mode of entry: when sojourners share activities with natives, the process is faster and more complete. Mathilde underlined that as an assistant, 'it's all the time, you jump into the water practically twenty four hours out of twenty four, you are in a context... you touch all areas at the same time'. She stipulates the conditions to be met for successful integration: close social context, frequent contacts with natives, participation in local life, and language competence. These coincide with the three elements which most students consider as the basis of their social life: work, friends, and language as the foundation.

To sum up, the nature and quality of social integration depends largely on the various modalities students choose as a way of moving inside society. The impulse to become involved in society varies with each traveller's personal motivations at the time, but also with the type of sojourn selected. It seems to be the case that a professional role engaging students in a work experience provides a more complete cultural immersion than the role of student. It also seems to be the case that students who share many activities with local people will integrate faster than those who stay on their own. As such, 'cultural' interests which can be pursued on one's own, like reading, do not appear as productive as activities where a common interest brings about direct interactions. One of the characteristics of the stay abroad is precisely that one learns from people. The benefits to be derived from actively taking part in local society should be stressed before departure so that students can organise themselves mentally and concretely in this area. The type of sojourn, more importantly the social context it defines, may also imply that foreigners feel more or less free to brush aside the local society and to take refuge in a world of their own. Someone working as an au pair, as an assistant or as a *stagiaire* may not find it easy to 'ignore' the surrounding society, as Lucy puts it. By contrast, a student might well decide not to become involved for one reason or another. This is a danger against which students should be warned.

9 The creation of a new social fabric

Introduction: social seduction

Social contacts, as Simmel or Park and Burgess define them, imply reciprocal relations between individuals or groups. Reciprocity matters, for at first the social relationship between newly arrived strangers and their social environment is given as asymmetrical and unequal.[1] As Josef underlines, if the stranger tries to gain entry, the others do not necessarily want her/him to. Indeed, most are indifferent to strangers in their midst.[2] This initial disparity, linguistic, social, cultural and symbolic, explains the vulnerability of newcomers, which sometimes generates a feeling of social devaluation. At that particular moment of their stay, distance separating from others appears maximal. How can strangers restore some equilibrium and social parity? More specifically, how did the students go about achieving this?

Simmel defines the mobile person as someone who comes into contact with a great many people with whom s/he has no prior relationship. In this chapter, we review the main types of contacts or networks students resort to as support for the length of their stay. These are the ethnic group where they have recourse to their compatriots and home culture, the international group as their most common social resource where they find the core of their new friends, and finally the native network which represents a more uncommon course meant for the most enterprising. Each student has access to the three networks,[3] but will mix members from each in an idiosyncratic blend to create her/his own social fabric abroad. In other words, students may opt for a predominant network, for personal or circumstantial reasons, but nevertheless avail of the other two for different functions within the overall relational framework. The distribution of primary and secondary relationships within this composite whole shows an inner circle made up of a few close friends, another circle of less intimate friends with whom one goes out and an outer circle of acquaintances. The ratio of natives and foreigners in each circle is different. For example, some students may rely heavily on the native network in their daily interactions, but have a mixed circle of close friends.

In this enterprise, not everyone possesses the same hand. As already stated, the context of entry into society, accommodation conditions, previously established contacts and contextual circumstances draw the lines of a certain social scene, which determines the kind of situations and contacts to which students will have access. Another variable which figures high on the list of student mobility research (Klineberg and Hull, 1979) highlights the quality of welcome extended by natives, particularly native students. Here the hosts have the winning hand: they may well refuse to enter the game and turn to their natural ethnocentrism favouring their own ingroup. In this case, do strangers possess cards outside obligatory contacts with members of the local community? Another significant variable concerns the travellers themselves and sets the spotlight on the personal part played by each student, notably the qualities called upon to bring to fruition their aspiration towards social integration. The term 'seduction' attracts attention to the personal zeal required from strangers to charm their entry into the circles of established society. Evidently strangeness is mutual, but native members do not have to try and reduce the distance separating them from foreigners. This is why students sometimes find it easier to turn to other groups to populate their social environment.

The challenge for student travellers consists first in trying to establish contacts and secondly in transforming these fugitive contacts into more lasting personal relationships. The relational dimension of the stay is paramount in the eyes of students as a major incentive and expectation.[4] Most research also shows that satisfaction in the new country is tied to host country interactions in general and to the development of close friendships with host nationals in particular (Gareis, 2000). Intimate, rather than casual, friendships with host nationals are assumed to facilitate adjustment and to help modify international images. Yet mere co-presence is in no way a guarantee of positive contacts. Believing it does rests upon the delusion that intergroup contacts have positive effects on cross-cultural relations (Amir, 1969). On the contrary, spatial proximity may well generate mental distanciation, sometimes even animosity, tension or rejection, and sway the whole relational scene in an undesirable direction from the very start. The very transient character of the students' sojourn implies special conditions. What kind of social contacts will they seek and obtain abroad?

Social contacts and degrees of strangeness

The social fabric refers to the whole system of relationships an individual builds up on the basis of available contacts. It is made up of different networks, i.e. smaller sets of people linked together through communication, exchanges and interactions. Contacts are the elementary form of social interactions, and come about from exposure to varying contexts. Contacts set in mutual presence a stranger, alone or in company, and others either foreign or native, in face-to-face interactions. When *in situ*, direct contacts are all the more crucial in that they form the basis from which representations or attitudes regarding the foreign culture are derived and then often generalised as judgements and opinions. The fact that they are grounded in 'factual' observation grant these cognitive outcomes a kind of cogency which is seldom questioned, let alone contextualised, by inexperienced travellers.

Contacts do not come easily, we know, and strangers have to impress their interlocutors 'in that conversation', Amin remarks. He found 'it quite hard to convince them of who [he] was' because 'you're exposed actually, you're just exposed, they really take you for what you are in that conversation and there's no... they don't look around to see how you're dressed'. By exposure, Amin means that 'your true personality is exposed' because the social cloak has disappeared. The fleeting time given in a conversation is all strangers possess to make an impression. As a result, he discovers the importance of time in intercultural interactions.

> Well I just know now that it takes, that with someone from a different culture, you just have to take longer with them, you have to give them more time, they have to give you more time... and they were natural, they were natural... you can't, I think also... when you meet someone from a different culture, you can't tell as much about them as quickly as somebody from your own culture... [yes] there are kind of subconscious signals that when you meet someone from your own country, you, you categorise in so many different ways so quickly, but from a foreign culture, you can't and in some ways that's good because, you know, your preconceptions...

The relative social nudity results from familiar social signs being unreadable, which defeats speedy categorisation.

Foreign students leave a familiar social scene to discover a new world with which they are more or less familiar. From a position of no previous knowledge at all in the local language and culture, rare in their case since most are at least proficient or experienced, sometimes expert,[5] to an advanced level of familiarity for those who benefit from local friends among the native group, various positions are likely. In most cases, however, student strangers go from an existing social environment at home to a relational void abroad. Transforming a superficial level of communication into a more personal one implies crossing several degrees of strangeness. It means transforming contacts presented as secondary into primary ones. The students' choice of words discloses two main levels of relationships: 'acquaintances' and 'friends'. In the beginning, relationships usually belong to the first category, since they stem from the wider social spectrum where one meets people randomly. At this stage, the primary network has not been formed or is restricted. From this starting point, how do students create their social fabric? What choices will they make so as to stretch their relationships beyond the mere functional sociability alluded to in the previous chapter?

In terms of access or the range of contacts available, different social settings contribute to the students' social encounters, as has been shown, notably their living conditions, professional life and activities in the local environment. Of these, the professional setting is particularly prominent. Language assistants tend to socialise with members around the school environment, Erasmus students with other students around the university, and EAP students with other students in their school or with co-workers during their company placement. Access to social actors from the wider stage may prove more elusive.

The amount and quality of personal contacts eventually forged is assumed to have a profound influence on any evaluation of the experience. The problems students meet are usually solved at the end of the stay, but their elucidation depends on the contacts which they set up. Thus the quantity and quality of social relationships which students manage to generate determine both the learning which ensues and the degree of satisfaction at the end of the stay. It has also been assumed that significant relationships with host members play a vital role at all stages of the adaptation process.[6] However, Furnham and Bochner revised this hypothesis, showing that 'it is the amount of support that is seen as crucial rather than who provides it' (1986: 129). To what extent is this the case in our three groups?

The ethnic group

The first social network which comes about as if naturally is that of the ethnic group, disclosing the ingroup tendency which Siu analysed in the case of the sojourner. Sojourners, on the basis of their common interests and culture, tend to associate mainly with people of their own ethnic group, usually around a specific area, symbol of their social segregation. Similarly, students sharing a common language or culture will have a tendency to gather in a group, unless they have willingly chosen not to do so. Two attitudes seem possible: either student travellers try to avoid their compatriots or on the contrary they lean on them for affective and moral support, particularly at the beginning of the stay. Hugo, Marco, Julie, Maria[7] and Thomas, for example, made the strategic choice of not mixing with their compatriots. Most of the others did not.

Relying on the ethnic group is first and foremost a method for the recreation of a primary relation around the native culture, a kind of 'home away from home'. Relations within the ethnic group hinge upon the contrast between cold and warm contacts.[8] Private relations are then centred around the monocultural group. However, friendships outside that group are not precluded. The Irish group in Louvain illustrates this type of arrangement, analysed here by Amin. The distance he established initially between himself and native students made it difficult for him to get closer later. So, when his compatriots arrived, a group of Irish friends spontaneously came into being.

> I found I really... I didn't have much in common with the Belgians. I mean I spoke to them, we went out sometimes together for a few drinks... But what they enjoyed, I didn't enjoy and vice-versa [...] I ended up... well, I, I, I ended up really going out with my Irish..., with Irish friends who came over in the second term because it... in some ways, it was because we all had wanted to do the same thing, we wanted to travel, we wanted to go... we wanted to visit different places and it suited us to...

The eight students concerned knew each other beforehand, but were not necessarily friends. They formed an Irish group even though each of them lived with a majority of native students in a *cot*. When visiting friends on Erasmus exchanges in Strasbourg, Tom noted a similar tendency to recreate a community outside the home country, particularly with Irish students. Similarly, Amin remarked that the Belgian group who came over to Ireland the following year also leaned towards the formation of an ethnic group. What exactly is the function of this arrangement in the student experience?

Eric stresses that seeking the familiar seems to be a reflex action which helps to dispel fear of the unknown: 'when you arrive in a foreign country, you look for... what you know... probably because you are afraid of what's coming from the outside'. In Paris, at first he sought the familiar, students from Luxembourg or Belgium living in the same university residence, or indeed for familiar food, invested with the power to recall home. Then he became more outward-looking. In Oxford, where he feels at odds with the environment, he looks for familiar elements through indirect means, reading things he has already read or listening to music he enjoyed at home. This search is impelled by a need for security. Jose and Iris, who both belong to linguistic minorities within the larger EAP group, do the same. They need the refuge of their language and cultural home as an interlude from the pressures of life in several foreign languages.[9] Recourse to one's culture and language is a course of action which expresses continuity with ties resisting disconnection.[10] Elena, discussing the role of this social structure, uses the image of the 'cushion' protecting against immersion.

> I think we were cushioned to some extent because we went over as a group, say, of Irish students studying at a French, you know at the college. So, we were cushioned, to some extent, from total culture shock. I think a lot of people in Paris that I met, the strange thing is that a lot of foreigners in Paris I met had often retreated to their own cultural groups. Like I met some Irish girls who didn't see anyone else except Irish girls and they had met maybe one or two French people and that was it.

The issue then is to balance out the comforting shelter[11] of the native group with other more adventurous associations. Otherwise, the foreign experience is limited to meeting members from your own original network.

If the ethnic group is comforting, its negative side is that it separates from the natives thus in some part defeating the object of the stay. Hugo exposes the outcome for students maintaining the use of their own language and culture.

> As soon as you talk with someone in German, and an Irish person is there, some friend of yours, it's first of all very rude and they're not interested in talking to you because they think '*ok, you're in your language and your culture, you're not here*'. So I just tried to prevent this.

This behaviour is interpreted as social absence, in spite of physical presence: 'you're not here'. John throws light on the comparative merits of the ethnic group and other possible arrangements by saying that, though he would have loved to find a group of familiar friends on his arrival in Rome, this would have resulted in his making fewer native friends. The ethnic group operates like a screen, reassuring, but alienating natives.

> I would have made a lot less friends, I wouldn't have been as approachable because I think... people would have seen me as '*Oh, he's got a friend...*'. I think people are less inclined to talk to you when you're with others than when you're on your own, especially in the Erasmus case. I think my whole experience in Rome would have been a lot more limited, or sorry not in Rome, but in a different country, I wouldn't have been exposed to as much, I wouldn't definitely have learnt as much.

Students are less 'exposed' when surrounded by their familiar group, which means that they are less vulnerable, but they also become less accessible. Amin too understands that it is not a good strategy to obtain entry into the local community, but finds it hard to make a break.

> When I was there, the whole time I was aware that this group thing wasn't really good, it wasn't a good idea, but I, I mean, I lived with these people and... it was just, always just that little bit... it was hard to make a break. I think the best way to have made that break would've been not to live there in the first place.

The group effect encloses into an arrangement which produces segregation from others and categorisation into a group to the detriment of personal identification.[12] For similar reasons, going away with one's best friend may be a mistake because travellers mutually hinder each other's take off, as Lucy explains.

> It depends on what you want out of the year. Definitely, if you want to get involved in..., to go with your best friend is not a good idea. You end up just growing on top of each other and you never branch out 'cause it's too difficult. You can't say: '*Now I'm going to meet Parisians... thank you,... because you're just Irish*'.

Attractive in the beginning, this particular social option often loses its cogency over time.

Indeed, after a while, students recognise the limits of staying with compatriots and try out new friendships among the native community. However, Amin, who met two Belgian students 'who took an interest' in him, is quick to comment on the limits set by most local people: coffee, but not much more.

> They were in my class and I got to know them... They, they, they took an interest... they took an interest in me and I took an interest in them... I found also that people were prepared to spend, maybe go for coffee with you after class, but generally speaking,... after that, their willingness to... you know, put time into you... It was just... they were doing their own things and, you know, you don't know much about the country... you're generally receiving...

There is the crux. For a relationship to be personal, mutual interest is necessary. However, in their vast majority, local students do not have time to devote to foreign students who are in the uncomfortable position of being on the 'receiving' end. The lack of symmetry is clear here. Josef strongly feels the inequality of the situation: 'you want to have experiences, but the others, the Parisians for example, they are not interested at all'. Communication is one way. Members of the majority group, established in sedentary comfort, are heedless.

How can the ethnic group be avoided? Amin again comments that accommodation determines social relations to a large extent. He adds that, if he had to do it again, he would choose to live with a local family, the choice his two Belgian friends in Dublin made, so as not to stay with their compatriots.[13] Lucy, who defined her situation in the ethnic group as 'at the periphery', opted for a different strategy to 'escape' from the group: she went away to her sister in Germany every weekend.

> [My friend] got more involved in the sort of Anglo... in the group, there was an awful lot of English people and other Irish people, whereas I wasn't involved in it because I was going away nearly every weekend. ... I think there was a lot of people who were very dependent on the group and I think that's quite unsuccessful for when you've gone away. [...] I think the fact that I used to go away for the weekend was almost good, otherwise... you couldn't really escape it.

The existence of this large group impels her to stay away, but others depend on it. The word 'escape' illustrates the ghetto effect created by the double fencing of being on a university campus with an exclusively student population and staying with one's ethnic group.

The unsuccessful outcome of this option is that the initiation into the new culture is restricted. Students find themselves in 'a rut', according to Lucy, bogged down on a well-known route rather than setting off along new avenues. She adds that the ability to 'close off' the local culture and to do 'exactly as you would have been doing' at home depends a lot on the context of entry. While the local culture is imposed on the au pair student who cannot ignore it in the capital city, as an Erasmus student on a university campus, it is easier to 'close it off'.

> You can't ignore Paris, you can't ignore a lot of the atmosphere, the social life. But, also... in Belgium, it was different, we were with Irish people and you can ignore it. You can get yourself into a different, you know, a rut of Irish people. You're doing your own thing, you're doing exactly what you would have been doing in Dublin, you know, and that makes an awful lot of difference. I don't know if it was Belgium or Belgian culture, I don't think it's as strong as French culture... Maybe that's because we were in a university town and there was an awful lot of foreigners there as well. We, I, made friends, we all made friends with the people we lived with... but apart from that we just did what we could have done in Dublin. [So what you're saying is that the immersion situation is crucial?] Yes, you can close it off very easily, depending on how strong the culture is. You can close it off, you can isolate yourself and you can do exactly what you would have done in Ireland quite easily... We did that in Belgium. I don't know, I think my sister did that in Paris. I think she stayed with... sort of Irish people. I came back from Paris listening to French music while my sister didn't at all, you know...

The learning which goes on is deemed to be on a par with the degree of exposure and the involvement students are ready to engage in.

Preference for this social arrangement is made possible where there is a sufficient number of students from the same national or language group together in a foreign location. It is frequently the case with large national or language groups, particularly on university campuses. The risk being greater for these groups, it may be worthwhile warning future candidates and highlighting the potential benefits to be derived from more diverse interpersonal relations.

The international group

This kind of network, very likely the most common in the student experience, denotes that contacts among foreigners predominate as the essential social resource abroad, the ethnic and the native groups playing a minor role. The social scene in this case combines diversity of origin and unity of purpose. Its weakness may lie in this potent blend which might discourage students from being more adventurous. Thomas, discussing his language school, conjures up the dilemma: 'the language class had a lot of English people, Dutch people, German people which... they stay easily together and you go on parties... so it's hard to get to know the French culture'. The tension between the appeal of the international group and that of the native people creates what he calls 'a social problem', students finding it hard to sever the link with peers in order to experience the natives' company.

> But I was always in between, I was never completely with the French, there were always Germans around which is a social problem. You cannot deny, when you go to language classes, you say '*ok, we're friends, but I don't talk with*

you any more because you are German or Dutch, and I want to learn French!'. It's
impossible! So you cannot.… If you go somewhere in a village in France,
then you are completely inside, but in Aix it was not possible to go
completely in France.

He confirms here what others mentioned about the spatial context: it forces a
certain type of relations. In a village, it might be easier to be 'completely inside'.
This proved to be the case for the assistants staying in rural communities. To be
in a town or a city exposes strangers to more international contacts.[14]

John's and Marco's examples illustrate this specific social network. John
explains that his first friends were mostly from the Erasmus group in Rome, in
particular some Scandinavians with whom he shared an apartment, and they
would have parties together. His opposite number in Dublin, Marco also
mentions parties at the start of the year as a key moment in international gatherings. He explains that if his main source of friends derives from other Erasmus
students, it is largely due to his late arrival in Dublin.[15]

> People were already in their groups at that stage. I met them in a class, so I
> could know them, but they weren't really looking to know somebody else.
> The foreign students were more open, at least at the beginning of the year,
> they didn't have their own groups.

A late arrival deprives foreigners of the opportunity to get into a group otherwise
difficult to penetrate. By contrast, international students appear easily accessible.
They are in a similar situation: available, seeking friends and often living close by.
Parity is regained. This is how the well-known phenomenon of 'international
ghettos' on campuses evolves.

As a consequence, contacts with natives are usually limited in this particular
structure. For example, John in Rome 'made some Italian friends from playing
football, rugby', but found that Italian girls were 'very aware of men in general:
they believe if you talk to them, you're trying to chat them up and, you know,
become very intimate with them… so it was quite difficult to make Italian girls
friends, and that was the case for the vast majority of Erasmus students'. Marco
as well became friendly with Irish students through the windsurfing club and
spent two days racing with them. John was invited about four times to private
homes in Italy,[16] but found that on these occasions he remained very much 'the
Irish'. His status as a foreigner was unchanged and these relationships remained
'categorical' rather than personal.

Why are students in the Erasmus context more inclined to opt for the international network? The two main reasons quoted relate to the numerical ratio of
the foreign contingent in relation to the native contingent and to the size of host
universities. In the first instance, two opposite situations lead to a similar result,
separation from native students. Sometimes, foreigners are submerged in a mass,
nobody knowing them because they are indistinguishable. For example, Marco
explains that in Rome there are about two foreign students for a thousand

natives. In other cases, student travellers form a sizeable group which remains separate. In Trinity, the group of international students represents about 15–20 per cent of the total, he says, a minority, but large enough to be independent.

> Oh, there is not, I think, in Ireland a big problem in a… in Trinity, because there are many, many other foreigners. So every professor more or less knows your problems and while in Italy professors don't know these Erasmus. So I think there is the average of 2 per 1,000 students who is Erasmus and here it's at least, I think, 15 per cent or 20 per cent or even more. So there is… exchange. Actually most of the friends that I have here are foreigners, so we more or less stay between foreigners.

Consequently, Erasmus students do not feel isolated because they can always rely on the international group. But their personal friends are rarely from among natives. Generally speaking, European students find native groups 'very closed' because 'there are too many Erasmus… foreign students lose their appeal because there are too many people from different nationalities' (Hélène).

Another reason has to do with the size of some European universities. Large universities constrain their students to a life of anonymity. As a result, local students tend to stay together in small groups where familiar relations already exist: 'there was always some link that linked them to the past', John observed. As a result, 'friendships' or 'acquaintances' are very different in the two universities he knows, La Sapienza and Trinity College.

> One big difference would be… friendships, very big difference, acquaintances. They… because of the size of the university, the friends they have in college or university, 90 per cent of the time they are school-friends, that was very noticeable, or family… one or the other.

Marco confirms that many Roman students rely on their old friendships as social network: 'many of my friends were friends from school'. Networks from the past are continued mainly because the size of the university prevents students from coming together easily. Every class involves new partners, new faces.

Native students who find themselves distanced from established networks are in a similar situation of strangeness. John's description conjures up the 'impersonal' feeling of the newly arrived 'wanderer' against the warmth of small groups.

> If you're in a class of, which is quite normal, 250, 300 people, you're sitting next to a different person every day, very impersonal. So the feeling on campus, in general, would be very impersonal. There'd be very warm groups that you'd see having a good chat, you know, and they kiss on each cheek, very much warm. That'd be in their own little group. So you really saw a little… a group here, a group there, all over the place, and then wanderers, people from Calabria, down the South, Sicily, they came from

little small towns on their own. They'd be on their own a lot of the time. Maybe they got their friends from their apartments, but not as close bonds as you got with the Romans themselves or people from Calabria who knew each other. So very much family-linked or school-linked.

Continuity with the past being broken for strangers, it is easier for foreign students to become friends with native travellers. Régine's friends came from Northern Ireland, 'because Dubliners are already established', and John had an Italian friend who came from southern Italy.

Other reasons contributing to distance being maintained may relate to personal factors, such as maturity or mobility experience, or more importantly to contextual factors such as the length of the stay. Régine stays away from Trinity students, whom she finds 'immature', but becomes friendly with an Irish family, accustomed to travelling and 'less afraid' of foreigners, according to her.

> Well, it's always the same, they are people who have travelled a lot, I mean they have been to France three times since the beginning of the year, they lived in Saudi Arabia, so they are probably less afraid because… the Irish I'd met, it's fine meeting people in a pub, but getting them into the intimacy of your home, that's more difficult. Eventually, I made very few close friends apart from the other French girls, and it's the first time this has happened to me in a foreign country, eh… *to shift back to French people*[17] (our trans.).

As an expert traveller, she is surprised when she has to 'shift back' to her own group for friendships. Native indifference is a major force driving student travellers to connect socially within their own ethnic group or the international group.

Julie highlights another important factor, duration of the stay and the time needed to establish personal relationships. According to her, the combination of cultural differences, age differences, maturity and motivation ('people are there to study') account for the slow progress of sociability with natives. The development of friendships spans over several stages and can only proceed 'gradually'.

> And people are there to study and they realise that sort of… like I usually met people for lunch and coffee as opposed to meeting them in discos. And then sort of afterwards you sort of progress to the stage of… you'd go out. But it was first of all, meet for coffee and then lunch and then… so it would gradually progress, but… I think maybe the culture in which you are determines how you integrate.

Each culture determines a certain way and pace at which these interactions are to take place. But the precariousness of relationships between strangers and natives is a major difficulty which students have to meet frontally, devising strategies to counteract its negative effect or to try other takes.

A special international group: the EAP social scene

The international group *par excellence* is the EAP group, which Damien compares to a zoo, that is a place where strange behaviours are observed. As previously mentioned, the school forms a world apart where students are somewhat isolated from local culture until they go on their company placement. As a result, their social fabric in the first year was quite distinctive and different from what it is the following two years of the course. Students generally agreed that two main groups remained distinct within the overall student population: the native group, here the French, and the foreign group.

The first group, French students, was perceived by many other European students as young, inexperienced, notably in terms of mobility capital, and rather insular. Damien described them as quite innocent, unaware of the image they presented to others because they were 'in their own habitat' and 'had no image of themselves as anything other than French'. The fact that they were a minority within the school did not matter to them since they were socially at home.

> A lot of them hadn't travelled outside France much, so they were very unselfconscious about how they were behaving. They had no image of themselves as anything other than French and no image of how things might look to outsiders... So it was like being in the perfect zoo: they were behaving like they would in their own habitat... the fact that they were being observed, they are outnumbered in the EAP, the staff are all French and the environment is really French, but they are outnumbered in terms of students... and peer pressure is less important to them in some ways than it would be in an Irish university or an English university where your image is sort of very important... the fact that the criteria changed and the game was... they thought they were still in France, they were still in France geographically speaking, but you are being observed by people who are looking... Sometimes they were very childish, but they were very natural because I know we were quite guarded.

The opposition between being 'natural' and being 'guarded' encapsulates the contrast between the ease which goes with being on one's own ground and the self-consciousness attending the experience of being in new surroundings.

The slightly 'artificial' character of an international institution set on a particular national territory comes out strongly. It is, as Philip says, a 'different world', 'not English, not French, and not German either', signified by the variety of languages spoken in the corridors.

> We certainly do live in a different world. Listening to languages that people talk in the hallway here, French, native French and English with a heavy accent, the same goes for English, Spanish and German. So this is the environment which is artificial, not English, not French, and not German either.

International society within a national society, issues of identity, notably national identity, are constantly challenged in such an environment.

The other EAP group, the foreigners, is perceived by students from a national minority, as dominated by German students, in larger number than the other nationalities. German students also differed from the majority in age and experience. Jose contrasts three general profiles of EAP students, 'the French, the Germans and the others...'.

> There are two or three things that distinguish them and those are: they probably worked before, they are older, they are more mature, and very important, they have chosen EAP. The French student when he gets to EAP is 19 years old and did nothing else but to study *prépa*,[18] he has had enough of studies, and most important, he's in EAP because he didn't make it to HEC,[19] whatever... And that obviously has to cause a conflict! The other students... it depends a lot... because basically we are one Portuguese, two Spaniards, one Italian and three or four Danes, so you don't feel a community. You usually talk in terms of the French, the Germans and the others... and the others sometimes have more the German profile having worked, older, more mature, chosen EAP, some have more the French profile, younger, less experience, end up in EAP because... whatever...

The unbalanced distribution of members from various European member states drove students isolated linguistically and culturally to different strategies. Some decided to 'let go', others to prove that 'the work you do is better than theirs' (Jose). They also found friends among a few French students who were not from Paris. They met 'to discuss their region and to drink and to eat their regional specialities' and were generally more interested in non-French students, as was the case with John and Italians who were not from Rome. Here again, a common situation of strangeness led to greater openness towards other minority groups.

Do contacts with the native milieu really matter in the EAP experience? It does not seem to be the case, at least in the first of their three years abroad. Besides their professional work placement, students have few contacts outside the school.[20] They usually do not meet other local students because, according to Josef, the school is distanced from other universities, which precludes from participation in student associations or activities. Their major local contacts come about through French students within the EAP.[21] Marina considers the EAP tendency for inner-oriented rather than outside-oriented discovery as fairly natural given the wealth of diversity in their own milieu.

> As a matter of fact, there weren't that many [contacts outside], but it wasn't probably that important granted that there were all the people we were getting acquainted with in the EAP... and so... who became really good friends now, so... we didn't look for as much, I'd say, hum, contacts outside the EAP. Now (in Oxford) well we all have our friends more or less and... in fact one might be looking for something new, or different.

Interestingly, Marina draws the line between the Paris and Oxford experiences. While the first year is absorbed by the formation of a primary network of friends within their own international group, the second year could bring about different prospects in the area of social relationships, as if strangers needed to establish a close social network before embarking on further discoveries.

Social groupings change and evolve. The contrast between the first two years of the EAP experience highlights the dynamics at play. Progressively, original groups expand or explode. At first student travellers on their own linguistically and culturally may stay aside, as Bruno did out of a linguistic inferiority complex. But as they gradually regain confidence, Eric points out, students become more intrepid and venture outside either their own national group or the group they initially identified with. Marina mentions that group work is a method which frequently allows students to break free from their initial apprehension and to get out into different groups. She takes Eric, her compatriot, as an example because his desire 'to get into Parisian life' prompted him to break free from existing groups faster than others. Finally, the last stage of development comes about when students cross the divide between socialising within an international group on the basis of fortuitous and 'superficial' encounters, as she says, and socialising with a mixed group on the basis of personal affinities and friendships.

This step is critical because it coincides with students going beyond national identification. As a result, in Oxford, 'the houses are really mixed… there are lots of nationalities in them', comments Marina. In the process, the disintegration of initial connections proceeds in the direction of more personalised relationships and greater individuation. As Elena points out, 'it's so easy to talk about cultural differences, but at a very superficial level'. In other words, interpersonal relations are progressively less subjected to cultural interpretations. Eric suggests that when travellers have gone beyond the level of cultural 'surprise', they are prone to discover more personal aspects both in themselves and in others: 'you go away and you discover yourself… and you live the way you want to live eventually… that's probably the attraction of life abroad'. Even if the ultimate goal proves to be a personal discovery, discovering diversity within a multicultural group remains the fundamental attraction of a course of study such as the EAP: 'what makes it valuable is really being with such a varied group of people' (Tom).

The 'seduction' of the natives

Some sojourners choose to seek primarily contacts with natives. Overall, this strategy means that the majority of their contacts are with native people, other contacts, less numerous, being with foreign people, from either the same or a different nationality. This particular social network is mixed like the other two, but the dosage between the various sources of contacts which coexist is different. Here, the main social component is on the native side and requires special ingredients. The context of entry, frequently mentioned, appears to make this option more accessible for assistants who are often one foreigner to many natives, less so for EAP students in their own multicultural milieu, while Erasmus students are halfway between.

To illustrate the range of personal characteristics at play in this specific choice, let's take the Erasmus group. Three students opted for this strategy: Maria, Hugo and Julie. Their choice was made before they left. In particular, they had made up their mind to try and live with natives rather than with other foreign students. Being quite aware of the language stakes inherent to the experience, they had also decided to have as few contacts as possible with their own language or cultural group.[22] With a good mobility capital, being experienced or expert travellers, they embark on the stay abroad a length ahead of others and master the social game surprisingly well. We remember that Maria weighed her contacts when she talked about making sure she had 'the amount of Spanish' she wanted in her life.[23] She is expert at combining various groups of social contacts, as she does in her hometown. Hugo and Julie appear similarly quite mature in their social relations. In other words, personality and maturity certainly matter, but circumstances, the moment and place, equally play a part.

As an example, Maria has four different sets of friends and acquaintances, two of these entirely Spanish. Her accommodation setting provides a first network of contacts resting on spatial proximity. She shares an apartment with three Spanish girls, newly arrived in the local university, but does not regard them as 'friends'.[24] They provide her with the linguistic practice and social introduction she is looking for: 'I wanted to learn Spanish and I knew that it was a way of meeting Spanish people... If you meet Spanish people, they must know somebody... [...] I knew I wanted to live with Spaniards, so I went for it'. The second group consists of people she goes out with. This is where Maria is different from the majority. She goes out with three Spanish students she met at the university and becomes 'the fourth' in that group. Through them, she penetrates the local society while her flatmates, Spanish but from outside the town, remain isolated. She plays the card of the novelty she represents, which adds to the social value of a native group, all the while being careful not to shock them so as not to be rejected. A true social chameleon, when she goes out, she dresses and behaves like her new friends, Spanish style at night, going back to her usual style in daytime.

> They used to bring me out and they loved this 'cause they had a new curiosity among them... People wanted to be with them again, 'cause you see: '*Oh, yes, you've a new friend?*'. And I am quite traditional anyway, so I'd be the same as them in sort of dress sense, drinking patterns, behaviour with boys, I wasn't making a show of them. So they felt quite happy to bring me around. OK, I dressed differently during the day.[25]

Apart from these two groups, Maria possesses two other sources of contacts, the international Erasmus group on the campus and a couple of friends from the English-speaking community, though she is keen to dismiss this English parenthesis ('it was for a few hours' on a Saturday night). She adds that the native friends fulfil the same integrative function as a sport team does for boys' integration: 'and the team would think that they were part of the group, they were in…'. The dividing line is between 'being in' and staying outside.

What is at stake in this social game is integration into the local society, as Julie's strategy shows. She employs similar methods in her endeavour to meet German people rather than international students. Before her departure, she had 'definitely made a conscious decision to hang around Germans as opposed to… being friendly with the international students', and to go about it by joining a tennis club: 'you know, sport is a great way to get to know people'. The social construction proceeds in a chain network: one meets people, meets them again, they become friends, 'as well as friends of theirs'. The deepening of relationships progresses slowly over a period of time, with repeated encounters focused on a community location and a common activity. She ends up getting a job at the club, spending all her weekends there, and being on one of their teams. Her previous knowledge of the language and people serve as a springboard to ease her effort 'to get in'. Nevertheless, she feels vulnerable at first ('there is nobody there for you') and even though she is prepared through her familiarity with German 'characteristics' ('I knew the situation'), she stresses that arriving strangers 'have to make a big effort to get to know them [the local people] initially'.

> I'd been there to Germany for many summers and then once I met Germans, I really felt like I was integrating properly in the culture. Because, maybe I was very lucky with the people I met, they were all very friendly and they all sort of brought me in and sort of inviting me with them every-where. It wasn't sort of me tagging along or anything. I really sort of integrated well with them.

The tennis club served as a 'good opener', enabling her to find real friends among native members, with whom she now stays on her trips back to Trier.[26] In spite of these choice contacts with native members, at the end of the year, Julie's closest friends are among the international group.

The major deterrent for relationships with natives is their precariousness.[27] Hugo tries to juggle this stumbling block by announcing from the start his concern for continuity. According to him, when local members learn that travellers intend coming back, they invest more willingly in a primary rela-tionship. Such a strategy, he suggests, offsets the discontinuities inherent to the relation. Usually, when foreign students leave at the end of their stay and others take their place, relationships patiently established over the year are jeopardised.

> …it worked out very fine. I have a lot of Irish friends, like I'm really into the Irish life. I have this feeling because… there are a lot of people coming over this summer to visit me, Irish students, and… and this is also because I have

this long-term plan to come back after one year here to Ireland, maybe to work there or to stay for a longer time... So, the people, if they hear that, they are more interested. That's one major problem, they say *'Well, eh, you come here as an Erasmus student and then next year, there's another generation'*, and it's really hard if you just get friends like, it's over after one year. So it's not a real friendship normally. So if you signal to them, *'well, I'm interested in more. I'm coming back and you can come to my house if you come over to Germany'*... Yes, it works a lot better.

The success of his strategy may be gauged from two signs: he expects Irish visitors to his German home over the summer and he made a lot of good friends among Irish students.

The option of constructing a social fabric composed mainly of native contacts is not very common in the student experience, as our discussion on contextual constraints imposed on EAP students and to a lesser extent on Erasmus students illustrates. However, this particular option predominates in the experience of language assistants or indeed of au pair students.

Lucy, whose first experience of adaptation abroad derived from her year as an au-pair in Paris, highlights the role three native families played in her integration. The three families, that of her French penpal who had become a close friend, her boyfriend's, and the family with whom she was staying and working, provided three different entries into Parisian society. The privileged contacts she enjoyed with natives are the reason why she did not seek the company of her compatriots or other foreign girls from her language school. Local families provide an invaluable patronage, a real passport guaranteeing strangers access to a new social territory.

The situation is similar for language assistants. The majority of their contacts are almost inevitably with native members, particularly in the spatial context of a small local community. As discussed earlier, the correlation between physical proximity and social proximity greatly assists and promotes the process of integration. Like Christine,[28] Cecilia described the formation of her social fabric as a process which evolved through progressive growth and extension. The ingredients are familiar ones: professional context and local activities. The first local family to welcome her was the school principal and her husband who offered her temporary accommodation on arrival. They introduced their niece to the Irish girls and from there, a whole set of new people arrived in her social life. A second social entry was offered through a teacher who drove her to school and invited her several times for a meal. Since their interest was mutual, the relationship was on an equal footing.

She had me for meals and they liked Ireland. Every summer, her family used to do a house-exchange with Ireland or England. So she was interested in me as I was interested in her. We *'profiter'* ... there's no English word for it, 'make use of'.

Outside the professional milieu, they met other French people, friends of friends. To open up the social scene, they organised a weekly evening which enabled them to meet 'lots of friends', Irish and French.

> I met those people through the school. And then we met other French people along the way: friends of friends, and then my uncle's friend, Philippe, went fishing in Mayo. So, he was another link. He was very good to us and very helpful. He used to bring us out for drinks and to meet his wife. And then we met a group of Irish people in Bordeaux who began to set up an Irish pub. They knew nobody, because it was new. They wanted to meet French people. So we said: '*We'll arrange one evening a week*'. We'd go out to a restaurant, fifteen or sixteen people, half French half Irish. We met lots of friends through those evenings: a different restaurant every Friday night. It was fantastic! Old Bordeaux, two tables together, conversation flowing …

The distinction in this case is that their relationships are linguistically and culturally mixed, but limited to two national groups, close to a bicultural network (Furnham and Bochner, 1986).

For these students, the process of social formation developed gradually. Starting with their initial fear of speaking English most of the time if they remained within their 'own little circle', they consciously decided 'to go out in French life'. Once the first step was made, they mixed easily with others. In their case, social construction proceeded in a concentric fashion in a snowball effect, a small group opening up to more and more new partners, and they ended up having a rather large set of personal relationships from different settings. All of them were not close friends, but the creation of a circle of social contacts including natives in large proportions, sprinkled with international people, co-nationals or other foreigners, together with a few key people one can rely on for guidance, produces a rich social fabric for a year abroad. The students who enjoyed a social scene of this sort ended up very happy with their stay.

'The key to getting on with people' (Marina): key people

Within the inner circle of close relationships, there are fewer people, but relationships are deeper. This circle is made up, more or less equally among our students, of either natives or non-natives. Overall, it seemed that students who had the majority of their contacts with natives looked for a close friend among other strangers from the national or international compound, while students who had a majority of contacts with foreigners looked for a close friend among the native group.

Many students usually found close friends among the international community with whom they have much in common and feel on an equal footing. For example, Maria's friends were English-speaking like her. Her American friend introduced the same kind of difference in her world ('I don't know anyone like that in Dublin') as her Spanish friends might do. Interestingly, she felt that their relationship was mutually beneficial in terms of adaptation, though her friend was married to a Spaniard, a mother and six years in Spain.

> Rather than actually helping my adaptation, I helped hers more because my Spanish was good, her Spanish was bad. So I used to teach her Spanish and then I'd bring her out with me and I'd introduce her to Spanish people that I'd met in the university and she'd start chatting to them. So she'd give me emotional support and I'd help her adapt, I think.

John too was relieved to meet a compatriot in Rome, and they became 'really good friends'.

> ...and we became really good friends. Great girl! She ended up only living a few miles from our house and we knew people, the same people, and she made things a lot easier and we leaned on each other all year. When I was down, she'd be there for me, when she was down, I'd be there for her. We really helped each other. We had similar..., you know, friends, backgrounds, everything, and it really helped. There was somebody else there for advice. I helped her out a lot of problems. It was great to have someone else of your similar... culture there, I think.

The friend who shares the same language and culture institutes a link with the past, common references and language rest, relaxing from the effort necessary for social seduction. Students in a situation of linguistic and national minority, like Jose and Iris,[29] yearn for the same, in vain. The main functions of these relationships are to provide linguistic relief[30] as well as 'emotional support', in short to afford breathing space, as mentioned in chapter 5. Students can say what they would not dare say to natives. Hugo also mentions being with compatriots as an opportunity for not 'being on your guard', loosening the tension inherent to unfamiliar interactions. But above all, he sees this type of relationship as an opportunity to talk about the experience with peers involved in the same venture and to reflect upon it, which enhances the process students are living through.

Only a handful of students reported that they established choice relationships with one or two native individuals. These key people can become personal friends, when they are the same age, or have the role of cultural intermediary or family support, when there is an age difference. What are the characteristics of these relationships?

First, the native person must be open. Thomas's French friend is interested in German culture and 'ready' to invest in a foreign friendship. Interestingly, the native becomes a bit foreign in his talk as a gesture of goodwill towards his new friend.

> There are two things. He was interested in German culture. It was the first time he had met a German. He was prepared, he spoke easy French, that you could understand, like friends of his were saying: '*you talk like a foreigner finally*' because he liked to... make it easier for me.

He goes halfway and their intercultural learning becomes a two-way process. Similarly, Elena and Suzanne met a French student, outside the EAP circle, who had spent one year in England: 'he was really open and he invited everyone to his house for dinner'. They had lengthy discussions about cultural differences and understanding French culture from a foreign perspective. Again we note that natives who are ready 'to invest time' with foreigners are those who possess a curiosity for foreignness or previous personal experience of life abroad.[31] On European campuses, these natives are often ex-Erasmus students. They are links between travellers and sedentary members on their home ground. Together with the new student travellers, they form a pool of mobile individuals which should be invested with greater awareness and status, as well as a sense of belonging to a growing social group, the new stranger experienced in border crossing.

Secondly, as we know, friendships require a mutual investment, particularly if the contact is to be other than transient. Then, according to Jürgen, you 'get to learn the culture, but it's not a conscious process'.

> If it happens, it just comes along the way... you just meet somebody, you get to know them, get to like them, go out together, you have dinner together. Certainly while you go out together, there are certain elements in the behaviour, in their behaviour which are not necessarily familiar to you, but it is this social aspect which is a lot more important than... in fact, it's what is exciting!

Communication leads to spotting 'certain elements' which are not familiar and to 'exciting' social discoveries. The personal and cultural elements are intimately linked in such intercultural encounters. But, Marina points out, just as Elena did earlier, that 'you're no longer that interested in other people's differences. You tend to take people not as Germans or less as Germans, French, Irish, I don't know, rather as individuals'. Clearly, as Wood highlighted, categorisation becomes less potent as culture learners uncover the personality behind the national mask.

The difficulty of striking the right balance between several types of contacts is brought forth by Lucy who considers that at least one local friend outside routine activities is vital as a resource to go and talk to about whatever is happening in your life.

> The more native people that you can meet, without being completely obvious about it you know... But, if you can have friends from there that aren't going to stifle you, but that are going to help you out, you know,

when you need it. I mean, it's quite a difficult balance to strike, but if you can have a friend that you can go to, say on Sunday lunch, and talk about what you've been doing the rest of the time, not necessarily that you've got to be doing it together or whatever... But somebody that you can go and visit, being from the country, and they can help and show you where to go...

This friendly contact, who benefits from a native grasp of the local scene, acts as an affective, sometimes material, source of assistance which may be called upon only occasionally, but nevertheless helps strangers to find their way around more efficiently in the new society, so that the 'field of adventure' may become 'a shelter'. This is the role fulfilled by key-persons, family or personal friends, who soften 'the landing' in foreign territory, in Matthew's words, because the stranger does not feel alone. In this instance, the quality of contact makes up for its numerical deficiency.

The new personal contacts which students manage to establish during their stay form an essential part of a social learning which resembles a new sociali-sation and grants them a specific social knowledge, relational ease, which Marina describes as 'the keys to be able to get on with people... really, we are given the tools and the key, how to behave with others so that it works... with other nationalities'. The special and privileged intercultural situation which social contacts abroad entail places students in a maximal learning position, 'as if I had jumped four steps all at once', Marina adds. Her words echo those used by Simmel: the key to open the door ('*tür*') and the bridge ('*brücke*') to cross from one side to the other. These two metaphors, emblems of interconnection and communication, also encompass images of separation and dissociation, both from the past and for the future. The duality of strangers' social position, when assessed positively as a life experience, teaches travellers the art of combining proximity and distance in their social relations. This is why, after a while, the social attributes they master allow them to contain the feeling of strangeness or, at the very least, to acknowledge that proximity and distance are variable.

In a context more ephemeral than others, travellers have to forego the idea of a welding sociability, the ideal of a transparency in social links. Instead, they are in a position to appraise the symbolic interval which separates from others and the importance of the interaction context. The quality of the performance is visible in the travellers' capacity to appreciate social links in their lightness, in the fluidity of co-presence and conversation. As Lucy put it earlier, one needs to acknowledge that foreign relations may only be 'flippant'. Travellers must not be too demanding, but rather understand that 'friends come and go'. Learning precariousness, they have the freedom to engage lightly in social relationships where everything is played in the instant of conversation rather than in a substantive fusion. In order to think of social relationships in this way, an approach which pays heed to the most minute detail in a life, a situation, an interactional space, a moment, a particular figure, is required.

Conclusion: from new spaces to new faces – social relationships as home

The social links students establish differ depending on the institutional context of their stay and consequently sway what Maria calls, in a metaphor reminiscent of the jungle, their 'social hunting'. Each network plays a different role and their respective importance varies at different times of the stay, promoting or delaying the adaptation process. Natives may not form the exclusive take, particularly when access is limited. Some students prefer to play the hand of international diversity with its fill of surprise as their major. The compatriot network has a punctual function to be circumscribed. For most students, the emerging social fabric is motley and comprehends an assortment in variable quantity of secondary and primary contacts with other strangers or with natives. The social-support hypothesis should be slightly altered in their case. First, if the diversity and quality of their social contacts influence considerably their appreciation of the stay abroad as a whole, these social contacts extend beyond the native group which plays a minor role in most students' stories. Indeed, the international group, which promotes relationships among 'equal' strangers, usually represents the main interactional resource in the student experience, the other two playing lesser roles. Secondly, the learning outcomes in the end go beyond mere social learning. The enrichment which students derive from the experience comes from a deeper sense of who they are and what resources they can avail of in unusual social circumstances. This double edge may be summed up as twin gains: discovering otherness and discovering oneself.

The creation of a social fabric is similar to a conquest, a triumph over distance between self and others, which is more or less successful depending on individuals, their starting point, their motivations, their previous experiences, their personal ambitions and talent, the context of entry into the local society, their knowledge of the language and country, and the links they maintain with their original context. This complex process stages a variety of individuals, natives or others, who create a given social landscape from which travellers will, if they choose, construct their personal social milieu. The undertaking is far from easy. It implies in the first place the identification and search for those contacts one wishes to create, sometimes having recourse to specific and reasoned strategies, and then the transformation of those distant external relations into close ones within the time constraints imposed by the stay. A few months to build up a set of social relations seem insignificant. The necessarily limited duration of their stay gives prominence to the challenge represented by the venture. Some students try to overcome this particular constraint differently, by playing the international game, by announcing continuity of friendships in the future, by creating a family type of exchange with a few chosen individuals, all strategies aimed at penetrating an existing social milieu frequently closed to passing visitors.

After a while, the ambiguity of being in between leads to the question of who you are, a stranger at home and abroad or at home in both places. This is summed up by the question Hugo asks: 'Where are you?' Park describes this oscillation, a consequence of being uprooted, as the hesitation characteristic of any transition period. It corresponds to the time when old habits are discarded, but have not been replaced by new ones. If the migrant lives through this stage in a state of internal turmoil, Hugo suggests that temporary travellers may solve the dilemma differently, by redefining home. Travellers begin to realise that 'home is strongly related to your social relationships'.

> Then that's another problem: where are you? And then... I feel here as a foreigner sometimes very strongly when I am walking, like in traffic, where you're just moving and you're not with your friends. As soon as you're with friends, you are not feeling a foreigner. The same in Germany. So you suddenly realise that home is strongly related to your social relationships. And as soon as you have social relationships, you can call that home. Hum... at airports, everybody feels a foreigner.

The feeling of strangeness may dominate in specific circumstances, but it recedes when students are with their friends. So, home is where you have relationships. Affiliation to places becomes relative and ends up transmuted from places to faces. For Jose, the fact that he has other homes in a sense means that he 'basically has none', but that he feels 'comfortable everywhere'.

> During 21 or 22 years, there was a place that I have always called 'home', always, there was no doubt: that was home. And all of a sudden, it's not any more because... you have other homes and euh... as you have other homes, what it means is that instead of having different homes, you basically have none... and you feel comfortable everywhere [...] I basically think that now, if I want to refer back to home, I would have to, to... each home has special moments and that's why you refer to that place and not because it's home. What I tend to, to... every time that I refer to Lisbon now, it's not because it's Lisbon or Portugal or I was born there, but it's because of what I lived there... and when I refer to Paris, it's the same, and in Oxford and in Berlin, it will be the same for sure, and Estonia and Africa... So... it's not a place where I live that I belong to, but it's somewhere where I have lived an experience.

Experiences lived together with other people create a sense of home wherever you are. 'Homes' multiply and grow: they are the places where one has lived and experienced a part of one's life. As such, 'home' is no longer a place of belonging. It becomes portable and moves with travellers. Hugo adds that 'you transport and... build your environment and take it with you... a process of getting older or mature'.

This process of social creation of one's personal environment wherever one lives is felt as a maturing process. To relativise one's childhood environment, as Jose and Hugo did, implies a step towards greater independence or the emancipation Park heralds. Then space no longer conveys an intimidating strangeness, but promises of exciting experiences to come. Liberation from one's origins is no longer considered as a loss, but more as a step towards 'a new space of freedom' (Sophie). Identity may then rest 'on becoming rather than being, biographical (or historical) experience rather than the fatality of origin, derived from something more like a curriculum vitae than a birth certificate' (Wollen, 1994: 189). Space redefined, 'where we live no longer matters', writes Harry Clifton (1993) about the Irish diaspora. Where we live no longer matters once being a traveller or a migrant is not summed up in a postal address, but implies a realisation that one's life space may become mobile and changing.

10 Adaptation: chameleon or clam

Introduction: adaptation, state and process

Adaptation implies the notion of change. Adaptation also refers to the state resulting from that change. The term is both dynamic and static depending on whether it indicates the process or the result of that process. It is generally understood that the change is positive, that it increases chances of survival for individuals in the milieu where they are located, and that it represents a gain, an added value. Consequently, it is suggested that individuals exposed to a milieu other than theirs by origin will come out greatly enriched and enhanced. Their life and their personality are supposed to become fuller than those of non-travelling fellow beings. This enhancement would manifest itself as a capacity to function in another destination or more precisely in more than one given environment. But how can this competence be defined and what are the signs which would allow its assessment?

In this chapter, we deal mostly with the process, looking at the way the students define the term, the personal qualities they identify as facilitating adaptation, and the signs which reveal the extent to which they have succeeded in becoming members of the new society. We gather the various threads running through the narrative. More specifically, students' definitions of adaptation bring to the fore the need to change one's behaviour under the pressure of the new environment in order 'to fit' in. This change involves imitating or borrowing other cultural practices, in order to extend one's range of cultural tools, rather than changing one's identity. The image of the chameleon adopting a different colour according to the environment expresses this quality. That of the clam closed on itself expresses the opposite. We suggest that the range of factors which students list as influencing their integration, i.e. personal attitude, social participation, personal relationships and capacity to adapt, may be considered as signs by which to measure their progress at the end of the stay. As regards personal qualities, students underline that openness and self-confidence are the two crucial dispositions which make adaptation possible. Finally, the students' own assessment of their final position in the host society enables them to see the road travelled since their arrival. In the end, adaptation appears as a multifaceted process which tests individuals in many different ways, the final result being on a par with the investment made by each traveller.

The concept of adaptation is understood chronologically. It usually refers to a passage from one condition to another. The passage may not be linear. It generally involves different stages. In the student experience, the overall course of the sojourn tends to draw a cyclical line, revealing strong fluctuations with movement forwards and backwards as on a choppy sea.[1] The idea of final growth (Kim, 1988) implies the notion of progress, but progress at a price which has to be paid through some degree of hardship. To what extent is there necessarily progress at the end of the journey? The overall level of satisfaction at the end of the stay is generally very high (Maiworm *et al.*, op. cit.) and the amount of students with lasting difficulties usually very low (Church, 1982). Nevertheless, some individuals might 'move' very little or even end up damaged by an experience for which they were not ready or fit. The metaphor of the initiation journey during which individuals, when they come out triumphant, acquire a certain immunity against difficulties illustrates this point. Adaptation implies adjustment, becoming used to, but the effort and labour required may be forced upon by outside circumstances and unwillingly conceded to. In any case, even if the end result is positive, the process of transformation may not have been continually enjoyable. The individual case studies presented in this chapter illustrate the range of factors influencing the overall process as well as the contrast between individual trajectories.

It is also worth noting that adaptation to a new context is such a general human process that it may be likened to many other experiences of transition. Indeed, students tend to liken their adaptation abroad to other efforts they had to endure such as changing schools or moving, mentioned in the discussion of their previous experiences. To what extent does the process of adapting to a foreign culture reveal signs which are specific to that experience and not applicable to others? The answers presented here gather together various threads of evidence dispersed throughout our discussion.

Defining adaptation

To the first question, 'How would you define the term "adaptation"?', the students provided different answers. Generally speaking, they defined adaptation as the capacity to change one's behaviour under the pressure of circumstances, as the ability to transform strangeness in a new environment into familiarity, and as a gradual process leading to various degrees of discovery.

There would be a general agreement with Philip's definition, that 'adaptation as a verb [sic] or as a noun is somebody who modifies his behaviour in a certain way so as to fit in more with the local customs'. The word we often heard, 'to fit', accounts for the necessary tailoring and matching which must take place between a given environment and a newly arrived person, who initially feels out of place because of different manners. However, two different desires, to move closer to the local community or to maintain one's original identity, notably through one's use of language, alternate with each other. Philip explains how the balance between the two evolves over time.

> When I first started studying there, I was really eager to become as good at French as possible. That was always my target. I wanted sort of to speak French like a French person so that nobody would even recognise that I wasn't French. But as the time drew on, as I became more accustomed to the French way of life, I realised that although I would still like to speak very good French, I wanted to maintain an English identity.

At first the ambition to speak like a native so as not to be identified as a foreigner dominates. But as familiarity with the foreign culture progresses, the aspiration towards maintaining one's native identity asserts itself strongly. The foreign accent to which so many long-term non-native residents cling is a way of signalling a dual identity.

Since strangers are noticeable, adapting would consist first in modifying the very characteristics which differentiate strangers from others, so that their visibility becomes less glaring. John hints at how one may become less of a stranger. He also differentiates several degrees of strangeness, varying according to the duration of their sojourn. At the end of his stay, he could not be mistaken for 'a foreigner who'd arrived yesterday' because he had adopted native ways, dress code, way of communicating through gestures, 'sayings,… movements and actions'. If he remains a foreigner in the natives' eyes, these signs nevertheless disclose that he has lived 'there for a while'.

> Well, for example, by the end of my time in Italy, I was wearing their blue sunglasses, I was wearing my jeans like they wear them, I'd bought all the shirts, had the shoes, had my soccer jersey, I'd wear their clothes, I had… I came back I was all this (*gestures*), everything I was talking was very much hand signals like they use. Very much all this sort of stuff, just from being immersed in the whole culture. I was still a foreigner, but to a native one could see that I wasn't a foreigner who'd arrived yesterday, that I was living there for a while, that I'd picked up their… their sayings, their… movements and actions.

Adjustment is contained here in the verb 'to pick up', which infers that foreigners not only acknowledge the value of a different practice, but also borrow from it and try to copy it. In this sense, the capacity to imitate cultural signs, habits and customs (non-verbal language, movements, actions, clothes) constitutes a first level of adaptation. Tailoring your manners so as to conform to new external surroundings implies a functional adjustment. It may be regarded as the most external level, taking place almost by osmosis. It is similar to the 'ecological' level of the adaptation process, mentioned by Abou (1990), which refers to accommodation to the physical milieu, climate, habitat, places.

Sometimes, even local traits rejected at first as exasperating or shocking may be borrowed after a while when they prove operative, as Christine remarked about timekeeping.

> The Irish are laid back… at first, it got on my nerves, but now I'm like that… before I couldn't stand being late, now if I'm late, I, people are not waiting, I don't mind at all, hum… I know that, that has changed my character in some way (our trans.).

She ended up adopting part of the local philosophy and found herself more relaxed while 'before [she] would easily lose [her] temper'. Philip did the same. As an expatriate in Paris for a year before joining the EAP, he found that 'on a very general level, people in Paris are very rushed, pushed, pushy, quite often arrogant, aggressive'. After a while, he realised he had become 'more aggressive because that was necessary to survive in Paris'. Eventually, he considered that this change might be 'an advantage later in life'. For him, this process of cultural borrowing means increasing the gamut of cultural solutions available: 'when something pleases me about a culture, then I will try and use it, maybe replace that, for example… sometimes I might behave more in a French manner, even when I am in England because I think the French way of doing something is nicer'. He gives the French way of greeting people as an example of a practice he borrowed willingly. Being able to function sometimes as a French person, sometimes as an English person, as one likes, inevitably expands the set of tools at one's disposal for self-expression or social communication, as Thomas also noted.

To epitomise the notion of adaptation as imitation, Maria conjures up the image of the costume which one wears as in the theatre, the social cloak belonging to a given stage. Adapting to life abroad involves staging one's life and playing unexpected and untried roles. Maria adapts easily because she enjoys being an actress adopting the 'local costume'. Indeed, to her, dress norms represent a mandatory passage and a marked sign of adjustment.[2] We know that others, Valérie and Sophie in particular, also called attention to the mask one wears when interacting in a foreign society. Valérie indicated by a gesture that the mask is two-sided: one side displays one identity, the other side displays another. The two sides are not visible simultaneously to the onlooker, but the person concerned is aware of their coexistence. Cloak or mask, these familiar references to the stage highlight the inner tension and duality inherent to the situation of foreignness. Could it be the case that life abroad affords actors an opportunity, as in Greek drama, for a catharsis enabling beneficiaries to emerge renewed?

Similarly, the image of the chameleon encapsulates the process. It is used by Maria and by Viktor, who speaks about 'absorbing influences from other cultures'. Like a chameleon, a foreigner may temporarily change to suit a particular community or environment without changing one's own inherited traits.

Hum, I think 'adaptation' is the ability to change like a chameleon, to suit other people's needs, without changing your own inherited traits, just changing your pattern of going about doing things differently. You don't actually have to change, but your method of doing the thing might need a little bit of alteration.

(Maria)

It is important to underline that adapting does not imply changing the core of your personality, but just the manner of doing things which is more superficial. Some newcomers may want a personality change, a new life, as a result of the changing environment,[3] but this is too rarely the case to be taken into account. Changing one's personality would be unrealistic, Hugo points out. It is more a question of adjusting the person you are, your character, 'which has something to do with your culture as well', to the society. Individuals who try to fit into the new society in this fashion are working towards another level of adaptation, not just physical or ecological, but social and personal.

Feeling 'comfortable' or 'at home': acquiring 'a history' over time

Adapting is not synonymous either with adopting the native culture or exchanging national affiliations, changes which would be too radical for student travellers. It is more a question of feeling 'comfortable' to the extent that the student would consider the possibility of living there for a while, if they so wished. Two expressions are repeated in most narratives to signify this crucial element: feeling 'comfortable' or 'at home'. They usually refer to the stage when problems are solved, social contacts have been established and students are entering a constructive phase. Cultural differences start to fade, contacts become more intimate and common experiences accumulate.

What does feeling 'comfortable' mean? Evidently, each student would have her/his own definition depending on personal history and circumstances. But, Matthew's captures the general intention: 'when you are adapted, you feel completely comfortable, you can function 100 per cent in that culture, you're relaxed, you're not stressed... being able to interact confidently with the people from that culture'. This description emphasises the restored predominance of positive feelings over the initial negative elements. He adds that the outcome is that 'you feel part of that culture, you no longer feel a stranger or a foreigner'.[4] In other words, the relationship between foreigner and surrounding culture is qualitatively modified. This change may result in different degrees of adaptation. Hugo quotes two examples, an American friend's and his own.

He's perfectly into the society, he's behaving very well, and they like him, he has a lot of friends, but he will... if he comes back, he will be back as a tourist, he won't visit people [...] these contacts he has are not so strong that… […] what I mean is he likes the stay here and he really appreciates it a lot, he made great experiences, but it's not adaptation in a sense… you can call that adaptation, it's a perfect adaptation in one sense, but not in the sense that he thinks he could live here.

By contrast, he says: 'my adaptation is not that I would become Irish, but I feel very comfortable here'. He defines his degree of adaptation as the knowledge that he could live and feel comfortable in the new society.

However, no longer feeling a foreigner does not imply that your core personality changes, nor the culture which sustains it. Rather it is like having a 'blank piece of paper' which you fill up with new experiences, alongside your own culture.

> …because when you go into a new culture you have to be very open and ready to try out new things and new experiences, so basically when you go in there you still have this core in yourself, your personality and your own culture behind that because you are going to make a comparison but you have this blank piece of paper and then you go in there and then with your experiences this paper fills up and it works alongside your culture. Your personality is still there.

The two sides of students' life, the original and the new, advance simultaneously. The enhancement manifests itself in the form of an expanding personality rather than an altered personality. In this case, the transformation does not really correspond to a total change because beliefs and values retain their integrity. It resembles more a mutation, in the sense of a change of orientation or circumstances. Jürgen says that you cannot forget twenty years of your life, but that you end up being as comfortable in the new destination as in the original one: 'you feel you could stay there'.[5] If other data revealed that this feeling was shared by a large amount of students at the end of their stay, then the European ideal of fostering the right to study, live and work in another member state would be fulfilled.

The adaptation process is gradual and slow. It requires time since it involves changing an initial situation of linguistic and social isolation into a situation of personal comfort through communication and interactions. The process contains two facets, often referred to by students as the environment and the people. For Julie and Hugo, the experience proceeds from the outside to people. Students start with building up their environment[6] and then 'get accepted by the people as part of their environment'.

> …it changes very slowly on a day to day basis, very small amounts. As soon as you build up your environment and you feel '*ok, I'm slowly getting control of my life*' and you get accepted by the people as part of their environment, and they don't ask you questions, like when you talk to them, the themes you're choosing are not any more about Germany and Ireland, the differences

or…, so you just talk about day by day, what the Irish are talking about. So this is changed.

(Hugo)

Interestingly, the steps forward may be ascertained from conversations. First, the fact that natives do not change their conversation topic, but carry on as if foreign students were a normal occurrence, is a sign of integration. A second and most important sign is presented when interpersonal discussions no longer focus on the issue of cultural differences. Indeed, many students refer to the initial stage as a period when cultural differences or national identity 'stick out all the time', (Matthew). It appears as a kind of mandatory passage at the beginning of the stay because national contrasts acquire greater visibility abroad. But as we saw earlier, Marina, Elena and others noticed that over time, interest in other people's differences wanes. Categorical judgements lose their power and are replaced by a more personal approach to others.

Then, the construction of a common history may take place. For Sophie, it means 'sharing certain joys, certain moments, certain… with someone considered as a foreigner, but the difference is not overpowering… it really is when you're on the same wavelength…'. The specific moments when this sense of community becomes a live reality may be an evening watching television together at home, as for Sophie, or else group work in intercultural teams within the EAP, for Marina and others, or a weekend spent canoeing, a situation which Hugo describes as 'a very dense situation' which enabled him to 'learn a lot about people'.

> And you also realise what we were talking about, that you get a past, that you get a history. And eh… it's very slow… how you behave and in fact… it comes from experiences together… Only the time… one year can be a very long time. There are a lot of these dense situations, if you live somewhere or, I'm doing canoeing here, and if you go… like one weekend somewhere, to Scotland, we went canoeing and we camped there, this is a very dense situation and you learn a lot about people. This was like the… steps which brought me further.

Sharing experiences contributes to the emergence of a common history between foreign students and natives. In the process, the foreigner gets 'a past' or 'a history'. S/he is no longer a person without history. Besides a common past, integration into a group may be seen when new friends talk about the future and make plans together for common projects. In this way, student travellers become part of their friends' life and the relationships are set in a continuous span.

Critical factors relevant to the process include the social strategies used by each individual, as detailed previously, but equally, personal factors. This is why it is impossible to predict who will adapt or not, according to Hugo, Philip and Thomas. It depends essentially on the person and on the circumstances, almost fortuitous, of the encounter between this person and a given culture. The outcome may be positive, but it may equally be negative. However, the individual 'controls' the process, s/he has the cards in hand and decides whether or not s/he wants to play the game. When a traveller is 'not interested', i.e. indifferent or not happy with life generally or has no desire to adapt, like Lucy in Louvain, it is likely that adaptation will not take place. As a success story, Hugo quotes his own strategy of avoiding other Erasmus students and trying to get integrated into a native group. Sophie confirms the decisive role played by personal motivation in the overall process. She also thinks that simple curiosity or indeed a negative impulse, such as the need to leave one's country, are not enough as an impulse to leave. 'You need something like a pain or soreness to start with… so that you can really accept even the shortcomings… in others… to reach this point… because if you feel comfortable at home, why?, why leave?'. She may be pointing in. the right direction to explain why so many students are sedentary: they feel too comfortable at home.

What is needed for settled individuals to go and leave for a different scene goes beyond mere interest: inquisitiveness is required. A spirit of inquiry implies a special kind of attitude combining specific mental gestures, such as a willingness to ask questions, to investigate beyond appearances, to engage in communication, to question familiar customs. For some, the stay abroad may be a non-event because they refuse to get involved in this demanding process, particularly when self-questioning is part of the adventure. So what are the factors which can facilitate adaptation?

The adaptation process: four facilitating factors

Each person adapts differently and some adapt faster than others, John thinks. The choreography changes accordingly. Different students hint at different variables. Individual variations put in play 'your mindframe and also […] your situation', says Lucy who emphasised as a situational factor the opportunity to have friends 'from there… that are going to help you out when you need it'. They equally put into play gender, according to Amin, who noticed that the girls in his group were more willing 'to make an effort with people' than the boys. They are also a function of age or the moment in one's life according to Hugo, who considers that a young person could be more open but may have less self-confidence than an older student. They certainly put into play contextual factors, "the country, the people" as well as personal qualities of sociability, which Maria depicts as the ability to hunt 'down the kind of people you're going to get on with'.

> The country plus the people, depending on how good you are at hunting down the kind of people you're going to get on with. Because if you don't meet anyone you like, you're not going to have a good time, 'cause I think

every country has both good and bad people in it, it's just… you know, I'm sure if I went to Germany, I'd meet nice people, but in general I think the Germans are boring, so it might take me longer to hunt down somebody who's kind of like me, you know what I mean? So it depends on how quick you are at that process.

They also put into play initial perceptions of other cultures, particularly those related to national stereotypes, prone to present obstacles or at least to hinder social discoveries. All in all, depending on these contextual and individual factors, the adaptation process will be more or less speedy, lengthy, or even avoided.

When asked about factors which in their eyes influence integration into a foreign community, the students mention four main components which somehow sum up their view of the overall process.[8] These four semantic sets convene aspects which were disclosed in other parts of the discussion orally. They highlight the general competences around which the adaptation process is structured. The four components quoted as the main pillars supporting life abroad, illustrated in Table 5, include personal attitude, social participation, interpersonal relationships, and an aptitude for communication and adaptation.

The first component, personal attitude, refers to aspects listed previously, in the area of motivations in particular, but also in the area of personal qualities needed for success. Christine for example mentions 'a forceful will to get integrated', which means that 'the foreigner must go towards other people'. Sylvie quotes the necessity of a 'real psychological openness to the new cultural environment' which means that the approaching person 'has to be extremely tolerant towards the local population'. Collette says that one has to be highly motivated language-wise so as 'to learn the language and try and speak it as

Table 5   The adaptation process: four facilitating factors

Personal attitude	Aspiration to otherness and openness (mental disposition) Psychological competence
Social participation	Activities (integration in the social milieu) Socio-cultural competence
Interpersonal relations	Relationships established locally (contacts and friends) Interpersonal competence
Adaptation and communication aptitude	Ease (autonomy and control of circumstances) Strategic competence

much as possible', a necessity which Jürgen confirms. Birgitta calls attention to 'the degree of personal determination and necessity to adapt to the foreign culture' and Ania to the need 'to be interested in different cultures'. Daniel refers to 'the desire for integration in a foreign community' through an interest in the local social life. All these written answers point to the mental and psychological attitudes required to engage in the experience. They overlap somewhat with what we analyse further as 'openness', an attitude which means, Matthew says, that 'you are always ready to try out something new' or, Kurt says, that 'you try and maximise time spent abroad'. Christine emphasises that 'openness of mind leads to openness of mind', the students attitude inducing a similar response from their hosts. To sum up, what students describe here is a mental disposition, part of a psychological competence, which acts as an internal engine fuelling the experience from inception to finish.

The second factor revolves around socio-cultural participation and spells out a practical requirement, the benefit derived from foreign students taking part in various activities within the local community. Access to this 'community' may be more or less straightforward depending on the host environment, as we saw. Marco, for instance, considers that 'Ireland is much easier than England'. Christine found that the benefit derived from sharing activities is that natives and stranger are united around a 'common interest' on a more equal footing: 'sharing all sorts of activities, clubs, societies, etc. enables one to receive and to give at the same time around a common interest'. Some students, particularly those who lived in a capital city like Sophie or Régine, enjoyed the 'cultural immersion' provided by musical events, cinema or theatre, but recognised that 'it all depends on the level of personal development, tastes, interests, motivations'. Valérie stresses that knowledge acquired previously, e.g. 'politics, a bit of history', facilitates 'cultural absorption'. Others mentioned regular activities around the pub as an important source of their socio-cultural life. But, in order 'to find personal ways of discovering a culture', Mathilde adds that students must have free time:[9] one of the great advantages of being an assistant is that they can welcome the unexpected because their timetable is not full. This set of factors outlining ways of 'getting in' through a variety of activities refer to a socio-cultural competence. It may be at this level that individual stories differ most widely.

The third set of factors focuses on 'contacts and friends' and highlights the relational dimension of the experience. Students generally agree on the centrality of this aspect, which engages the sociability of travellers, their 'personal character' as Louis writes, in particular whether they are 'extrovert and friendly' (Collette) as opposed to 'timid', an obstacle to contacts mentioned by Daniel. Christine stresses that 'in order to meet a maximum amount of people, to speak, to learn, to read, to share, you must not have a passive, but an active behaviour'. An introvert with a tendency to close in on her/his world has less chance of achieving integration. 'Contacts with natives' are essential in this respect because 'you learn so much from others' (Ania) in this particular setting.

Learning abroad takes place through the people students meet. These people are invested with the fortuitous role of unwitting carriers and symbols of their culture.

What students mean by contacts here ranges from the widest, e.g. 'human relations' (Marina) to the most specific, e.g. 'parties' as a great opportunity for personal encounters (Kurt). Birgitta draws attention to the role of 'living conditions, accommodation, etc.' in setting variable conditions for relations with natives or other. Marco quotes 'friendships with natives' as an influential factor, endorsed by Sylvie who recommends 'attempting total immersion and trying to avoid compatriots'. Several students stress what Sophie calls 'the essential notion of exchange at all levels', which means that integration depends largely on attitudes, the natives' attitude, whether they are 'receptive, encouraging or indifferent, hardly cooperative, etc.', and the travellers' attitude. She adds that student travellers should not expect too much from others and that 'one only reaps what one sows at the start', highlighting once again the reciprocity of social relations. This set of factors regarding the interpersonal or relational competence represents a test for them, but also a great source of satisfaction. Besides, the capital acquired through learning to manage contacts with a great variety of individuals is transferable to other situations and continues to grow.

The fourth set of factors relates to what the students call 'ease' or 'self-confidence'. This element is proteiform. Régine explains that 'ease is a generic term: it may be geographic or territorial, it may be the language and the accent which come more naturally...'. Ease implies that the traveller has lost 'the rigidity you feel at first when you are newly-arrived', and is akin to flexibility. In the first place, most notably among assistants, ease is defined as a linguistic attribute: 'the degree of autonomy and mastery in the foreign language' (Sylvie). The language dimension, which is so crucial, is combined with another dimension, the capacity to adapt to a foreign context. This means first being able to solve 'all the common problems' which accompany arrival and which Josef lists as: 'finding accommodation, work, having problems with your car, looking for a tennis club, cooking French style, etc.'. This aspect of adaptation generates material autonomy and personal independence, an outcome frequently mentioned, but which varies with each student's previous experience, as Jose specifies. Caroline and Amin highlight that adapting to a strange context implies a road which is onerous and where travellers are on their own: learning to accept possible feelings of social isolation, alienation or marginality without too much stress is a prerequisite (Nash, 1963). Maria says that travellers feel 'at ease' when they no longer 'suffer from insecure attacks', when they feel confident about 'going and doing daily things that fit in with their culture'. Damien too relates ease and 'a sense of security', which induces the self-confidence required to communicate and go about meeting people. It also signals the 'maturity' of the individual concerned. Overall this strategic competence through its many facets of linguistic, material, personal, social autonomy is the one most closely associated with living abroad. It puts side by side the aptitude for adaptation to a strange culture and the aptitude for communication in a foreign language. These are two elements which are specific to living abroad and make it so special. If the experience produces more self-confidence, Matthew explains, it is because 'if you can solve complex problems in a language and in a country which are not your own, you can certainly do most of what life requires'. Adaptation to a foreign language and culture produces learning outcomes significant enough to be transferable to other life situations.

All these elements are interdependent and mutually supportive. For instance, Julie and others explained their itinerary, starting with their taste for languages which drew them to open up to foreignness and generated the desire 'to go into the culture'. Then, they chose to meet mostly natives, not their own group, as a learning strategy and ended up integrating easily, which in turn increased their self-confidence and overall satisfaction. The kind of advice students offer to prospective candidates illustrates this circularity: 'perseverance, confidence, open-mindedness' (Matthew), 'to keep their eyes and ears open: be ready to discover Ireland or any other country in all its various aspects, never judge too quickly, take time to understand' (Mathilde).

To prepare themselves mentally, travellers could remember the following: 'prepare yourself to live alone', 'do not have expectations', 'organise your practical life', 'plunge into the environment', 'overcome your fears and launch into adventure', 'stick it out'. In terms of social participation, they are advised to 'go to the cinema, go out, share as many activities as possible with people', 'try all the experiences related with the local culture, e.g. travelling around the country, trying to know a lot of local people', 'take time to see and to understand'. In order to facilitate their interpersonal relationships, they are advised to 'integrate with as many natives as possible', 'be interested in others', 'avoid judgements', 'be ready to make the first steps without losing heart', 'distance yourself from your culture, and be open'. Finally, they are advised to 'talk to people', 'be flexible', 'learn through life experiences, immediately'. The whole process engages travellers in a complex interaction during which awareness of self and others undergoes a metamorphosis.

Personal qualities of good adaptors: openness, tolerance and flexibility

The personal qualities required of good adaptors appear at several stages in the course of the interview in answers to questions related to personal dispositions and taste for travel, to the kind of advice they would give newcomers, to factors facilitating adaptation, and finally to the personal changes they perceive in themselves. All in all, they form a kind of personal kit. First, they exist as a promise drawing a potential itinerary; in this respect, they predispose individuals and motivate them to travel. Then, they are energised and reinforced during the stay abroad. Since success is predicated on these qualities, they are presented as advice given by seasoned travellers to aspiring candidates. Consequently, they emerge in the data as either prerequisites or as outcomes of the process. What are these personal qualities of good adaptors?

Two sets of answers dominate the data.[10] The first semantic set hinges upon the qualities just mentioned, which students identify as 'self-confidence' or 'ease'. This embraces the capacity to be autonomous and to live alone, the talent for communication and sociability, as well as the degree of awareness of self and others in interactions. Some of these were discussed when we outlined the personality features of the potential wanderer, in particular sociability or the aptitude to communicate and connect easily with individuals one does not know. We will not dwell any further on this aspect.

The second set of answers brings to the fore the central quality of 'openness' and its two facets, tolerance and flexibility. These personal characteristics are found repeatedly in students' comments, indicating a consensus. They are present in most descriptions of life abroad and, more specifically, in assessments of cross-cultural or intercultural adaptability (Byram, 1997b; Kelley and Meyers, 1992). But can we circumscribe these malleable concepts in greater detail from the evidence presented by the students?

Openness is an attitude which characterises student travellers before their departure[11] under the guise of curiosity and readiness to change. Philip emphasises that a person who will adapt easily is 'somebody who wants to discover new cultures, new ideas, somebody who is really prepared to change', outlining the very predispositions mentioned earlier as motivating factors. The often precocious invitation to travel, yearning for elsewhere, attraction to otherness, international vision, represent so many required preparatory stages which constitute a budding competence for freedom or emancipation. In this respect, the voluntary aspect of the project crucially impacts the outcome. 'If somebody is forced to go to a different culture, they will change very reluctantly', adds Philip who quotes two English ladies in his French neighbourhood[12] as examples. One of them came 'quite reluctantly against her wishes to France', she refused to interact with locals and 'has maintained very much of her Englishness'. The other lady was 'much more willing to move to France', is outgoing, teaches pottery in the village, is involved in the local community and is 'very integrated'. In other words, predispositions and motivations play an important part in swaying the direction of the sojourn in certain ways.

Openness may also be defined as the attitude by which one accepts 'that people are the way they are', says Christine, who gives the example of her male flatmates who expect girls to do the housework and are careless about cleaning. She decided to accept that attitude rather than fight it. For Lucy, openness is indeed synonymous with adaptation. So, 'you have to be open before you can adapt; if you're closed, you're negative, there's no way you can adapt'. Openness of the mind translates into one's personality. It means being 'the kind of person who goes to people and starts talking to them instead of staying in your corner waiting for something to happen', Siobhan explains. She adds that failure stories are stories of foreigners who 'hate the experience and look for every opportunity to go back home'. According to Damien, travelling experiences contribute to the development of this competence: the more one travels, the easier it is to open up and end up 'accepting new ways of doing things'. The opposite of being open, John says is insularity, which he defines as 'thinking that your own place is the best place in the world', a definition singularly close to that of ethnocentrism. Insular people will find it hard to adapt. Closure into one's world is contrary to the desire for expansion which living abroad symbolises.

Again, the movement of opening up is dual, from self to others and from others to self. Lucy underlines that this is why you have to make an effort: 'you have to ask for acceptance'.

> It's, it's, you have to want to basically. I mean you have to want to and you have to be able to make an effort because it's actually not... you know, you have to ask for acceptance. Also other people... You have to be in the environment before you can actually adapt to that environment. So you have to be open to the environment, you have to go out trying to meet people. I mean it's quite a difficult thing to do; it depends on your mind-frame, how confident you are and stuff. I mean it's definitely worthwhile, but it's...

Opening up to the environment and to people is far from easy, but 'it's definitely worthwhile'. Lucy refers to an English student in Louvain who was 'unsuccessful' because she was closed to the experience, did not want to learn the language ('she did maths and didn't need much French'), she did not try to communicate with her Belgian flatmates. She 'had a very successful academic year', but she 'didn't get on with anybody' in the native community and reverted back to the English-speaking group for her social life. Having an open mind in this light is an attitude which students can cultivate before the experience and which will translate in the field as willingness 'to accept what people have to offer', says Jose, from the most unfamiliar food[13] to more intimate aspects. To be open means to be willing to allow some flow of communication between self and the outside so that bridges are established, making social interaction possible.

Openness of mind is almost synonymous with tolerance here. It leads to understanding others, to recognising the differences which generate distance, to realising the role culture plays in life. Tolerance is mainly a mental attribute, the opposite of narrow-mindedness. In Régine's opinion, it is a function of knowledge because narrow-mindedness and ignorance are synonymous, she thinks: 'each time you say someone is *narrow-minded*,[14] you say that they are ignorant... and the term "ignorant" means both that you're an idiot and that you're *narrow-minded* while it really means that you don't know something'. For others, tolerance comes from the social experience which encourages individuals to extend their relational circle and to move out of their social cocoon: 'I became friendly with people I would never have got on with at home', Birgitta acknowledges. The experience expands socio-cultural knowledge, in the dual sense of cultural information and social relations, and broadens horizons. Maria analyses the process from the initial position at home where one may have 'a secure kind of social position', which means that 'you don't have to tolerate other walks of people', to the road travelled. 'When I went abroad, I realised that people that I would never have got on with in Dublin, I was now making friends with and I think I became more tolerant.' She talks about receiving 'a comeuppance', a lesson for being so sure of herself.

Indeed, the opposite of tolerance is arrogance, somewhat disturbed by the move. For Christine, tolerance consists in becoming 'a little bit less French', in softening some traits in her character which end up being altered by the experience. She finds herself becoming more patient, less rushed, and says that she learnt 'to have a sense of humour, wit to answer back… to be less arrogant than the ordinary French person generally is…'. The paradox is of course that at the same time her sense of national identity is heightened because 'you see what your country represents outside'. For Hugo, arrogance proceeds from being on the defensive. It occurs when foreigners feel troubled in their new situation. Tolerance comes when you dominate your fear of others and when you are ready to launch into the challenge. In any case, whether it refers to intellectual, social, personal or relational openness, tolerance contains the notion of difference. What students indicate is a broadening of their mental horizon in the way they perceive others, which allows them to break free from their own frame of reference to try and penetrate that of others. Tolerance is oriented towards otherness, even if it implies working on self. In this sense, it is a true adventure.

Flexibility is more oriented towards self. It refers to a specific behaviour, a response of the individual under the impact of changing circumstances. Sojourning abroad represents a radical social change, as we argued previously, which profoundly affects the world of taken-for-granted habits and customs. When Damien says that 'you bend, but you don't break', he conjures up the flexibility required to adapt to newness in a foreign context. This capacity has two sides. Faced with difficulties inherent to the new situation, foreigners must bend. But, they do not break, that is they do not let difficulties take them down. On the contrary, they learn how to become flexible which means taking up or learning some new characteristics while remaining true to themselves. Damien gives the example of a friend who left because 'he was certainly less flexible than us', maybe because he was older. The image of nature bowing with the tempest without cracking exemplifies the individual experience of travellers confronted with hardship in their surroundings and is here a metaphor for the labour requested in adapting.

By contrast, those who do not adapt are people who are rigid, who are 'in a system' and refuse change, Daniel concludes. 'Bad adaptors, they're just too set in their ways, they're in a system, they're systematic people who cannot change and I think they don't adapt.' Maria quotes two counter-examples. First, she met Spanish girls in Trinity who could not adapt because they were 'just not willing to let go, the way Irish people let go, they keep everything neat and tidy'. Their inability to be in unison with fellow students different in their ways maintains a distance between them and natives. In a similar fashion, the English students

Maria saw in Spain never became accustomed to the environment: 'they weren't willing to change their way of portraying themselves even though it was going to work to their advantage'.

> The boy they were living with used to say: '*look, why don't you come out? we'll do this, we'll do that*' and they would go: '*Nay, nay, will be full of Spanish people gabbling in my ear*'. They didn't want that, they just didn't and anyone who was English was very welcome in their group. They had a massive gang.

Refusal to go out with local people and closure on the ethnic group immunise against the risk of local infection. But, as Stonequist stated, strangers are only strangers if they do not remain in their original group and have contacts with natives. The break-off point is crucial. Otherwise there is no experience and nothing happens. Rigidity is the refusal to allow any change to touch you. Life abroad inevitably implies multiple changes. Failures are predictable for travellers who will not be moved.

Refusing to bend under changing circumstances may be due to individuals clinging to their own values, according to Jürgen. For those, 'home values are such absolute values that they would not be willing to accept that there could be different values'. He illustrates his point with the 'French breakfast culture', which appears non-existent. This maddens some students: 'those French never have a decent breakfast!'. People who react negatively like this tend to 'criticise every day, every time you see them', from the slightest cultural area like food[15] to more important differences. Lacking the plasticity to integrate external differences into their personal life-world, they remain in their original position. In this case, the change in location is purely geographic and the mental journey is null and void.

Flexibility is a disposition related to change and novelty, but above all it may be an antidote to the prejudices and expectations which often mar the game prior to direct contacts. Abroad, Elena stresses, travellers should be less inclined to produce distance-maintaining judgements because they are not familiar with local rules and symbols related to social identification.

> I think being flexible, ready to change yourself as well and not come over with these preconditions, you know, '*someone wearing that sort of clothes, I am not going to talk to him*'. It is so easy to do here[16] because when you are [at home], you can identify groups of people from say, what clothes they wear, what pubs they go to, but when you are in a new place, you don't know the pubs and you don't know the custom in the clothes, so you are flexible and you will talk to someone, you know, anyone... then you are at an advantage, I think.

Such unfamiliarity promotes mental flexibility, whereas in one's home environment social signs constitute so many screens which filter interpersonal contacts. The immediacy of familiar social identification compels a biased interpretation of others. But student travellers, who are not acquainted with foreign signs and

conventions, are in a more advantageous position. This characteristic, the positive side of social nudity, affords foreigners a certain social elasticity. Indeed, in
the two types of personalities which make good adaptors (Nash and Schaw,
1962–3), the 'autonomous' person, 'devoided of prejudices', possesses the
attribute of flexibility, which facilitates a more rapid adoption of host culture
norms.

Assessing adaptation: three contrasting narratives

An examination of some individual itineraries and the specific adaptation
process they reveal throws light on the variety of factors to be taken into account
in order to assess the relative degree of success of a stay abroad. The main
factors reviewed as characteristic include age, language competence, mobility
capital, motivations for departure, initial representations of the foreign country
and people, perceived cultural proximity – distance, expectations prior to the
stay, choice of accommodation, professional integration, social activities,
personal relationships, links with the home culture. They can be taken into
account altogether and reflected upon separately, either by candidates aspiring to
prepare for a period of residence abroad or by returnees assessing their progress.

The three cases illustrated in Table 6 represent contrasting narratives, taken
from the three different groups analysed. In the first instance, we chose Josef as
representing a special case among EAP students. He is somewhat different from
the average student. He is older and chose to go back studying after working for
two years with a German firm. He thinks that his sojourn in Paris had a limited
impact on him.

The second narrative is quite different. Mathilde is a language assistant who
lives and works in Dublin. She exemplifies a most advanced level of competence,
combining language ease with a deep knowledge of the local culture through her
literary studies. She was placed in the category of experienced students because
she did not have previous experience of a long-term stay. But her position in the
end and the quality of her learning places her ahead of many others. Her experience taught her about language, one's own and that of others, about otherness
and what it means to be a stranger, and her self-knowledge was greatly
enhanced. She sums it up with the image of the clam: abroad, one withdraws
within oneself in order to open up to otherness at a later stage. She thinks that
her year abroad 'will stay with her for a long time'.

The third narrative illustrates a route which is marked by lack of movement.
Louis is happy with his stay and said that he 'had a good time', but he could
have been anywhere. He actually did not find many differences between his
home environment and the new. His stay was a non-event: not much happened,
he did not change, he did not discover anything and he did not regret his relative
isolation from the local people. His answers during a very short interview were
monosyllabic and he had very little to say about the experience. It seemed to
have had no impact on him. Interestingly, he is the only student who identified
himself as a 'tourist' at the end of the year.

Table 6   Different tales of adaptation

Josef:

Age	He is older than most other students in the EAP (about 27 years old).
Language competence	His mastery of French or English appears limited, at least orally. It is not easy to understand what he says in English.
Mobility capital	His mobility capital places him in the category of experienced students, but his previous travelling experiences are mostly of a touristic nature.
Motivations for departure	He decides to follow the EAP programme of European studies for explicit professional reasons. He is focused on his task.
Initial representations of the country and people	He has an idyllic touristic vision of France before coming over and his expectations regarding French reality are extremely distant from what he discovers. He is disappointed.
Perceived cultural proximity –distance	He is shocked by what he perceives as the French sense of superiority, particularly the way French people can glorify their history when this is not possible in Germany.
Expectations prior to the stay	He did not expect to find many cultural differences among Europeans and is unsettled by those he perceives.
Choice of accommodation	He lives in an apartment, on his own at first, then with a compatriot.
Professional integration	He suffers from his status as a student in France, rejects the EAP and feels infantilised.
Social activities and personal relationships	Most of his social contacts are with his own national group, rarely with natives. He does not know how to go about engaging in activities other than his studies.
Links with the home culture	He frequently travels back to Germany where his girlfriend lives. When he does not go home for the weekend, she joins him in Paris.

Mathilde:

Age	She is very slightly older than most, 23 years old, has two degrees already and is doing an MA thesis on an Irish author. The level of reflection on otherness she manifests reveals her maturity.
Language competence	Her level of competence is extremely high and she says that very quickly she did not have to go through French to express herself.
Mobility capital	She started travelling young and went back regularly to stay with people with whom she got on very well. These were not commercial contacts. Personally, she adapts easily. She derives great pleasure from contacts with other languages and people.
Motivations for departure	She wanted 'to get lost in the language' and to study the culture.
Initial representations of the country and people	She did not have preconceptions about Ireland, but an advanced knowledge through studying the literature.

Perceived cultural proximity –distance	She did not share the usual stereotypes about Ireland, she says. She is aware of the intercultural proximity – distance phenomenon and takes her two roles of foreigner and ambassador of her country seriously. She explains that the stay allows her to be in a state of 'constant cultural absorption' and that she enjoys the live dimension of the experience because it facilitates a kind of 'anthropological observation'.
Expectations prior to the stay	She had no special expectations.
Choice of accommodation	She shares a house where foreigners and natives are mixed.
Professional integration	She found the teaching experience rich and interesting.
Social activities and personal relationships	Living in Dublin, she engaged in many 'cultural' activities, notably the theatre and cinema. She mixed with many different people, avoiding her co-nationals because 'among French, they speak about France'.
Links with the home culture	Her boyfriend is also in Dublin on a work experience. She had already acquired her own autonomy from home.

Louis:

Age	He is 22, the average age of many Erasmus students.
Language competence	His level of English is intermediary. He is capable of functioning and studying in the language, but was disappointed with his lack of progress.
Mobility capital	His mobility capital is low, made up of holiday trips.
Motivations for departure	He followed 'the others' because 'everybody said that it was a good experience'. The idea of leaving was also 'a bit like a holiday'.
Initial representations of the country and people	He did not have much knowledge of Ireland, except that it was supposed to be a stress-free place. He chose it over England because it meant being in the capital city. He is not disappointed.
Perceived cultural proximity –distance	He does not find 'a great change' between Ireland and Belgium. The two countries seem quite close to him.
Expectations prior to the stay	He had no particular expectations and did not experience any culture shock.
Choice of accommodation	He lives in a university residence with his Belgian friends and says that 'it is like being at home'.
Professional integration	He had no problems and felt integrated in Irish student life.
Social activities and relationships	He did not use television, newspapers or radio. He acknowledged that he did not learn much about the local culture and lived in a kind of 'bubble' outside Irish culture.
Links with the home culture	Nothing to mention.

These three travellers' tales highlight the wide range of potential individual responses which may be actuated in the course of a broadly similar experience. Besides the natural diversity of human experience, diverse contextual or organisational factors direct each traveller's itinerary in a certain way. The contrasts surfacing between the various tales as well as between the three case studies provides evidence of those factors which tend to facilitate or retard the adaptation process. Similar narratives, analysed along those lines, may prove useful to prepare aspiring students before their departure so that they maximise the conditions of their stay.

The students' rating of their final position

Another sign revealing the students' perceived degree of adaptation is the rating they assign to their 'final position' in the host culture. This rating indicates the membership orientation obtained at the end of the year. Five degrees were suggested[17] to the students: 'tourist', 'survivor', 'resident', 'near citizen', 'citizen'. Though rudimentary and arguable, this question proved valuable because of the results it produced. The data reveal a high degree of consistency within each of the three groups studied, which vindicates our choice of contrasting several student experiences. Most Erasmus students positioned themselves in the category of 'residents', assistants overwhelmingly in the category of 'near citizens', and EAP students alternated between these two categories.

Being a 'resident', according to the students' explanations, refers to someone who lives in a country, has a professional role there, such as studying, and has contacts and friends in this milieu or, in Hélène's words, 'a small social fabric'. Such a person would be familiar with a certain territory. Régine specifies that she would know the shortcuts and where to buy bread, would have familiar landmarks and would feel adapted within a relatively limited world. But, she would not master the complexities of local history. As a result, the 'resident' is someone who created a personal environment in which to live in, implying a certain length of time in the same place – a major difference with tourists whose visit is brief. 'Residents' may be 'survivors' at the beginning of the year when organisational, linguistic and social difficulties are prominent. 'Residents' may pass for natives after a while when they adopt the specific local signs related to physical identification which John outlined. But they can be 'heard' through their distinctive speech. The 'resident' denotes above all a person whose stay will be temporary. The return home is always part of their future.

The 'near citizen' is the person who got involved in society to the extent that s/he may stay on for a while. The same comments are reiterated from the assistants' group: Christine would like to live there for a couple of years, Karine could see herself living there (but would not like the weather), Nicolas plans to go back to Ireland and open up a restaurant, Edwige is going to stay for a while, Sylvie would like to stay another three years. Siobhan would like to declare herself a 'near citizen' but thinks that she lacks the necessary knowledge about French history. Valérie is settling in Ireland since she is engaged to an Irishman. Their experience is marked by a higher level of membership. This category of travellers is distinct from that of 'citizen' because of the absence of shared memories and history and also because of their language. However, even when they share a common language, they may remain 'near citizens'. This is the case for Christophe who feels perfectly integrated in France, but remains Belgian. It is also the case for the Irish students in England who describe themselves ironically as 'tourists who speak the language'. This membership category is close to the first generation migrants, if they stay on. If they remain attached to their home culture in a constant search for the past, they are closer to Siu's sojourners.

All in all, these findings reveal that student travellers at the end of their period of residence abroad situate themselves between levels 3 and 4 on a scale of 5. The threshold or 'acculturation' level is supposed to be between 2 and 3 (Acton and Walker de Felix, 1986), a crucial step forward being made when a certain level of language competence is achieved. Our results vary with the context of entry determined for the three groups considered. But a more advanced level of integration is noticeable among the professional linguists in spite of their lower mobility capital at the start. This observation substantiates the centrality of language in life abroad, though the assistants' experience is also distinct from the other two groups in other ways, as we have shown. The experience of the professional linguists calls for further studies, particularly in relation to other cases of student mobility.

Besides language, duration is a crucial variable. It could be correlated to the degree of language competence assuming that linguistic knowledge acquired previously guarantees students a position ahead on the starting line, language capital complementing mobility capital. The academic year abroad is perceived by the majority of students as necessary to achieve the level of adaptation they expect in order to feel 'at ease' in their host society. But this length of time is not always deemed sufficient. Two different representative cases emerge from the data. Some students may not be entirely satisfied with their stay, which they consider was constrained by the duration of their stay ('a year is not enough'). By contrast, other students feel so much 'at home' in the host culture that they are apprehensive at the idea of breaking away from their new belongings and returning home to their original ties. Re-entry shock is another dimension of the experience which is worth including in research to come. Our students' plans for the future reveal two principal orientations, at least among the assistants and the Erasmus group:[18] they wish to come back or to stay. What happened? Did student travellers pursue the new links they had established while abroad? Have they extended their experience of foreignness to other places, as is necessarily the case for the EAP group? Or else have they reintegrated their places of origin and stored away this part of their life once and for all as a fading photograph? Their chosen route remains an enigma worth unveiling in another study.

Conclusion: 'a life lesson' (Hélène)

Adaptation, as it is defined by the students, is a dynamic process at the same time territorial, mental, linguistic, relational, socio-cultural and personal which strongly puts individuals to the test. Life abroad places students in a situation where transformations are called for if they are to maximise their life conditions. It represents an extensive natural learning situation which Hélène calls 'a life lesson' and John 'a learning experience of life'. The final word from the students was in all cases positive, when not superlative: 'great!', 'exceptional', 'happiness', 'transformative', 'educational', 'would do it again', 'a personal discovery, a discovery of where you are'. Even the student who was not happy with her stay acknowledged in the end that it was 'enriching'. As for the very few students whose experience seemed to have been innocuous, they were nevertheless happy with it.

The difficulties which accompany the initial period of the stay disappear when students acquire the social attributes which open up a world of new affiliations. The self-ascribed final position is the sign of an opening of their social space, a suggestion of what has become possible. The students are ready to start again, to leave again. One of the main benefits derived from an experience which perturbs them is that the learning gained contributes to their overall capacity to adapt to other difficult passages in life. Individuals who have gone through this emerge stronger, asserting their individuality. During this new socialisation which students manage on their own, they become emancipated.[19] Most students mention this kind of elation, of enlargement of their world and of personal opening, as 'growing up'. Then the stay is truly vested with the value of a rite of passage and a 'life lesson'.

The experience means that individuals, urged to move under pressure from the environment, adopt certain strategies so as to modify their behavioural responses. This places students in an intensely formative situation. However, adapting does not mean changing one's identity, but rather adopting and accepting the local 'colour', like the chameleon, so as to fit harmoniously with the environment. Student travellers may also choose not to move and to remain in their initial position, refusing the language, contacts with natives, participation in local life, withdrawing within themselves like a clam, but without opening up in a second movement. The outcomes depend both on external circumstances, over which individuals have little power, and on personal options which put into play their own initiative and resources. Results are on a par with the efforts made. They are also determined by the four facilitating factors discussed above: mental attitude before the experience, social participation and interpersonal relationships established locally, sustained throughout the stay by the crucial aptitude for communication and adaptation. It must be noted that adaptation implies the notion of variation within a specific context, but it does not refer to a norm. There is no model to follow. Each person will adapt differently to a foreign culture while retaining her/his original character and identity. Student travellers adopt solutions to the problems which confront them and, in doing this, soften their personality, 'discard some baggage' as Damien says, extend their range of possible memberships and sometimes acquire the freedom of the potential wanderer. This process multiplies space and affiliations for them in the sense that 'each culture tends to give a lesson, and you tend to be more complete', as Jose says. Their world is an expanding, open, wider world.

Conclusion

This study has been concerned primarily with the interior world of European student travellers. An attempt was made to see the students' experience as they see it themselves, to compare their different narratives, and to explore their specific story alongside other accounts of strangeness. The aim to describe and understand experiences of strangeness today led to general questions about their meaning. It also led to more specific questions related to the European student experience abroad, how it proceeds and what its main characteristics are. These questions were open to the diversity of interpretations offered by the respondents. The interpretations were modified as data were collected and examined in a 'continuous process through which observations and interpretations shape and reshape each other' (Mishler, 1990: 416). The process involved a constant dialectic interplay of theory, methods and findings.

Much previous research consisted in sanitised attempts to evaluate a composite experience. The nature of yes/no or multiple-choice questions cannot convey the enormously complex character inherent in a year in a life. While producing a sample which some would deem statistically unrepresentative because of its size and selection method, the richness of the responses and the ways it links in with existing theory enable one to advance our approach as a more meaningful alternative to strangeness in the context of European mobility. The presiding logic is that of understanding a phenomenon rather than testing its 'truth'. The 'truth' in an inquiry-guided study comes from the observation of a concrete research territory and emerges from the data. Validation is thus redefined as 'trustworthiness' (ibid.: 419[1]). The proof is not built into the research protocol, since the data are not collected to test specific hypotheses, but it materialises in other ways. First, the approach has validity if observation and hypotheses fit. Secondly, internal consistency may be obtained after a small number of individual cases have been examined. The third line of coherence comes from the force of the empirical results themselves, which produce a new theory based on this specific research.

The fit between observation and hypotheses became progressively visible. First, Simmel's essay provided a plan for the observation of strangers' situation and how it can be identified as a specific experience in time, in space, in the social, cultural and symbolical world. These, together with the added dimension of identity changes which appeared in later texts, delineate the major anthropological dimensions of the phenomenon. Secondly, a close analysis of the texts selected presented an in-depth template of the formal characteristics of various strangers in different social conditions, which provided the missing conceptual architecture for our study. From one analysis to the other, the same concepts and their resonance in different contexts are explored. They served as working hypotheses contrasted and confronted with ongoing observation through interviews.

Thirdly, one important pattern was noted from the various discussions of strangers' itineraries. Although different, the strangers discussed have in common the strangeness of their situation, a special blend of distance and proximity which puts to the test boundaries between self and other. The lived experience of strangers arriving in a new culture, whether as a migrant hurled by political or economic forces or as an expatriate stimulated by a vision of personal and professional development, is a relatively stable and permanent phenomenon, particularly in its initial period. It follows a chronological development which sets in motion the same components: external circumstances, personal circumstances, motives, agency and choice, duration and purpose of the stay, type of social involvement sought, languages and cultures in contact, language competence, representations and attitudes, socio-professional setting and status, personal relationships, home links, personality. These preside over the experience and can be applied across a variety of situations. Consequently, the main hypothesis emerging from the first set of data was that the experience of European student travellers could be understood in the conceptual and empirical framework of the sociology of the stranger.

Our specific findings in relation to student mobility show that some concepts and issues are more relevant than others. For example, the concept of the marginal, in between two looking glasses, was found to be inappropriate as an interpretation in the narratives of most students. But it appeared as an adequate description in two or three individual cases, where students' words echoed some of Stonequist's own terms. By contrast, Schütz's analysis of the cognitive shock incurred by the stranger fits remarkably well with most students' testimonies.[2] The same is true of most of the other characteristics relating to dislocations in space, to discontinuities in time, to the need for a new socialisation involving the construction of a new social world. In this book, the dimensions of symbolic position and identity issues were not explored in as much depth as they deserve and would benefit from further investigation of the data from this particular perspective.

The narrative of European student travellers follows a similar structure to that of other migrants and covers a similar range of issues, but from a specific vantage point. It takes as a starting point the anticipations and expectations of the experience, in other words the mobility capital and the motives for the decision to spend a year abroad. It progresses to the difficult period of the arrival, when strangers are thrown into direct contact with otherness, particularly linguistic otherness, in an unmediated holistic contact. This difficult phase is then followed by a phase of active social construction, where students are starting to accommodate to a given space, entering the new society via their professional role and social activities, and are establishing personal relationships. The next phase comes about when the process and the outcomes of the year abroad may be assessed and lessons drawn. It represents a time of reflection when the experience as a whole is weighed up. These issues represent the substance or structure of the student experience.

Each of them could be probed in greater detail than was the case in a comprehensive account such as this.[3] Our ambition was first and foremost to present a coherent picture of the overall experience in a framework general enough to be relevant to other descriptions. Besides, the narrative is limited in time to the year abroad and stops at the end of the academic stay. It leaves in the dark the future, what happens to those who stay on, as two of the students intended doing, in the form of a more advanced acculturation, or what happens a few years on to those who have gone home or on to more experiences abroad. Further studies of a longitudinal nature are required, following the itinerary of a young traveller in adult professional life, to fully gauge the impact of the experience in the long run.

The main research outcome is that practically everything in the European student experience may be assessed as a benefit. In other words, even the negative or difficult aspects of the stay are eventually perceived as enriching, adding significantly to their life experience in the present and potentially beneficial in the future. By comparison, other migrants in differing migratory conditions may find that the costs outweigh the benefits, at least for a long time. Sometimes the entire life span of the migrant is that of a sojourner or perennial exile, forever turned to and yearning for her/his original home from a permanently foreign base. The undeniable qualitative difference between the migrant's progress and the mobile person's route highlights the diversity of interpretations and situations. It poses two crucial questions, which need to be further explored. First, what is the lasting impact on the experience of the duration and purpose of the stay? For example, what are the crucial differences between short- to medium-term sojourns and long-term sojourns, particularly in relation to social integration? Secondly, to what extent does the geo-political context influence each individual trajectory, particularly in terms of choice or agency, the golden expatriation being opposed to the forced displacement? The relevance of the analytical model from the sociology of the stranger could be probed further if other categories of strangers were selected for study, using contrasting criteria, such as duration of stay, age, gender or motives. The kaleidoscope of the stranger would be enhanced with more empirical observations of various demographic groups.

The fit between data and hypotheses is most visible when echoes are discovered between the spontaneous interpretations offered by the students and the historical data from a different era. For example, Schütz writes that the stranger is a person without history and Hugo echoes this comment when he explains that, as you get accepted by people as part of their environment, you realise that 'you get a past, you get a history' from having experiences together. Siu mentions the social nudity which strangers experience and Amin speaks of being 'exposed' socially. Park writes about the emancipation and opening of space and Jose speaks of the freedom which follows from redefining home as 'not a place where I live and belong, but... somewhere where I have lived an experience'. The duality and the image of the two-faced mask is found in Stonequist, but equally in Valérie's and Sophie's words. The two Simmelian metaphors of the bridge and the door are echoed in Marina's testimony. In other words, personal interpretations of the experience of strangers are embedded in enduring metaphors which express the event through a specific, yet generic vocabulary. This claim enters an even more general arena when it is validated by observations outside the particular topic of investigation.

For the fit is also perceptible when other personal narratives, relating to longer expatriations this time, are included. For example, Huston (1999) in her recent account of life abroad for a foreign-born citizen mentions the disorientation strangers feel, which induces 'a sometimes painful awareness of a number of realities which preside unwittingly over the human condition' (ibid.: 19). Disorientation comes first as a geographical exile, a break between before and now, there and here, compelling strangers to keep their other life silent. The ensuing duality results in a kind of schizophrenic mental state, where the self is perceived as divided. She explains that the mask is the necessary guise for the 'theatre of exile', where strangers try in vain to imitate, but remain forever alien. One wonders then where the real self is. The issues reported in this and in other personal narratives (Beirao, 1999; Buijs, 1993; Hoffman, op. cit.; Makine, 1995; Mukherjee, 1999; Said, 1999a) point to a strong correlation between descriptions of the experience produced in totally different historical, geographical, personal and social contexts.

Another line of coherence comes from the force of the empirical results themselves, which produce a new theory, based on this specific research. In other words, the results match a life with a theory (Plummer, 1983), by providing a set of observations relevant to a specific social phenomenon – student mobility in Europe. They bring to light a number of significant constituents of the experience, summarised in Table 7.

These constituent elements of the experience may be regarded as units facilitating the analysis of other student mobility case studies. They represent temporary conclusions which need to be compared with other empirical data.

The empirical validity or internal consistency manifests itself after a number of individual cases have been studied. The overarching observation is that similar elements are mentioned again and again from one interview to another, imprinting the narratives with a certain *déjà vu*. But, if the substance evokes the same stage setting, the lighting within each narrative varies. The number of interviews and the selection of three case studies allowed for regularities and divergences to be detected from interview to interview and from group to group. In particular, dominant group reactions or practices were revealed. For example, the study of motivations highlights the different weighting assigned by each group to the main ingredients in this domain: language, work, friends and other personal attractions. The claim for the internal consistency of the emerging model is enhanced by previous empirical studies, such as Martineau (1995) where, as mentioned before, the same chronological presentation and analysis as well as similar themes are to be found. These cross-sample similarities endorse the validity of the social model. The inclusion of several European study programmes as well as greater cross-national diversity opened up the empirical framework, allowing for finer distinctions to be made.

A comparison between the three case studies essentially shows the relative significance of some properties in the development of the stay and their varying repercussions for the experience. The main difference is to be found in social immersion and how it proceeds differently depending on the context of entry. Each group of students has access to different social situations because of the environment in which their life takes place. As a result, the amount and diversity, and to a certain extent the quality, of their contacts with native members differ. Other differences between the three groups include their language competence, the family history of foreignness, their mobility capital, as well as the dominant motives presiding over their decision to leave. But, these differences are assumed to have a lesser impact on the overall experience in the end.

These findings represent a new conception of the student experience in Europe. However, the subjectivity of the lone researcher who carried out the successive research tasks of data collection, transcription, analysis, interpretation and reporting for such a large sample, must be acknowledged. Different researchers, a different observation protocol taking in a longitudinal approach with a series of interviews or else based on a variety of research instruments, like diaries or ethnographic tasks, different analytical methods and rules for the selection and treatment of meaningful segments of texts, might have thrown a different light on the experience. Much remains to be done. Student mobility is barely emerging as a research area. More studies are called for, multiplying case studies of programmes and groups of students, focusing on specific dimensions of the experience, e.g. the personal transformations ensuing a student period of residence abroad or the development of attitudes and representations, and above all addressing the serious issue of the large majority of sedentary European students. In terms of pedagogy of the stay abroad, it would be necessary to assess the institutional and pedagogical repercussions of the experience so as to appraise its role in viewing 'intercultural experience as education'. It is believed that this hermeneutic study complements and deepens existing research, providing students and teachers with a rich cartography of the experience of the student stranger. This cartography, along with its conceptual toolkit, may then be used as the basis for the comparison and contrast of the individual experiences of present and future student strangers in the evolving context of European integration.

The student traveller is a new stranger, identical to, yet different from, other strangers. European mobile students are more aware of the language stakes intrinsic to intercultural communication than their predecessors. Their somewhat privileged circumstances and attribute of youth mean that they can travel more lightly than those whose departure is a constraint rather than a choice. Their experience is less dramatic since their in between position is only temporary. Their attachment to or detachment from the home culture is merely

Table 7 The student experience in Europe: a taxonomy

1 Spatial dimension
Previous experiences and learning abroad
Choice of destination
Spatial setting and its impact on social relations
Strategies for the appropriation of space
Choice of accommodation

2 Time dimension
Family history of foreignness
Personal taste for travel in a life story
Mobility capital
Motivations and choice of residence abroad project
Expectations prior to the stay
Preparation for the experience
Links with home culture
A future-oriented migratory elite

3 Social dimension
Socialisation deficit of the stranger
Language as stigma, linguistic fatigue
Arrival as a rite of passage: perceived intrusion in the established group
Culture shock as a step towards discovery
Return home
Professional integration
Social activities and relationships

4 Personal and intercultural dimension
Evolving social representations and cognitive boundaries
Personal qualities of potential wanderers
Strategies of social seduction
Adapting as a chameleon
Personal qualities for successful adaptation
Learning outcomes

loosened rather than seriously tested. The difficulties which they encounter are usually transient rather than lingering. If they experience an identity crisis, it may remain superficial rather than profound. Travelling and living abroad for a period of time in this context implies crossing into a new time–space, discovering new horizons where old and new blend, going through tempest and calm, avoiding rocks and perils, unearthing strange customs through secretive languages, pioneering new methods and strategies to negotiate the unexpected, exploring one's resources, meditating over sameness and difference, trying out potential identities, and all the time learning. From migration to mobility, the new strangers question the notion of borders and the meaning of home. Their travels have no final destination and, whether physical or virtual, space opens up for them with the 'proposal of perpetual displacement' (Chambers, 1994: 246). Places are just locations, where one can work, live and love, and distance on both sides may lend enchantment (Iyer, 1998). Home becomes one's languages and friends, a house one carries around as a portable commodity. From places to faces, home is where interactions and conversations with different others are within reach.

Annexes

Annexe 1. The experience of strangers crossing borders: general properties

1 Before the experience: objectives and motives
- Circumstances and motives for departure
- Family history, life story and personal choice
- Mobility capital: previous experience of strangeness
- Duration of the stay abroad: brief, temporary, permanent
- Membership orientation: visit, residence, permanent membership
- Professional task in the new culture and objectives
- Language competence

2 Adjusting to the new environment: the process of adaptation
- Degree of culture shock or personal crisis
- Process of adjustment into the new culture: language and other strategies
- Professional role and status
- Social contacts and activities in the new environment
- Communication and links with the native culture
- Representations of self and others: perceived proximity–distance

3 After the experience: outcomes and transformations
- Cognitive and linguistic development
- Social integration
- Intercultural learning
- Personal changes
- Degree of socialisation achieved

Annexe 2. Study abroad questionnaire

I Motivation

1   Could you summarise under three headings your original objectives in

joining the Study Abroad Programme?
2   To what extent have these expectations been fulfilled?
3   As a result of your year, what further expectations, if any, do you have?

II Previous experience
4   How many months in total had you spent living abroad before:
         1 to 3 months;
         4 to 8 months;
         9 to 12 months;
         1 to 2 years;
         more (indicate number of years)?

5   How many cultures did you rate as familiar, i.e. feel at home in, before
         your year abroad:
         one;
         two;
         three;
         more than three?

III Initial contact
6   What is the biggest cultural shock you experienced?
         (a) in a social context;
         (b) in an academic context;
         (c) in any other context.

7   Could you list three essential elements which should form part of pre-
         departure preparation for future students?

IV Length of stay
8   What do you think is the optimal and the minimum length of stay in a
         foreign culture for the experience to be more than tourism?
         (a) 3 months;
         (b) 6 months;
         (c) 9 months;
         (d) 1 year;
         (e) 2 years;
         (f) more than 2 years.

9   When, if ever, did you no longer feel a foreigner? Why?

V Immersion in the host culture
10   Could you describe your living conditions, e.g. single room; shared
         accommodation; living with a host family; other? If you shared a flat,
         with whom did you share it?
11   How many native friends did you make? Within your study environment?
         Outside?

12   How many non-native friends did you make? Within your study -
        environment? Outside?
13   What type of contacts did you have with native people and how regu-
        larly, e.g. dinner in someone's home; going out with native friends;
        having a drink with friends; other?

VI   Exposure to the local environment
14   What facilities in the local environment did you use to familiarise your-
        self with the culture? Can you rate your weekly exposure to the
        following in number of hours: newspapers and magazines; books; radio;
        television; cinema; theatre, concerts, etc.?
15   In which local activities did you partake, e.g. clubs, etc.?

VII Personal development
16   To what extent do you now feel at home in the local community?
17   Please list some factors which you consider as influencing one's integra-
        tion into a foreign community?
18   In what areas do you feel you have developed personally?

VIII Intercultural learning
19   How do you rate your progress since you arrived in terms of the
        following?
        (a) knowledge of the new culture;
        (b) ability to interact with the natives;
        (c) ability to interact with foreigners;
        (d) other competences.
20   What, in your opinion, accounts for the progress/absence of progress
        you made?
21   What kind of advice would you give future students in order to
        maximise their intercultural gains during their stay abroad?

Annexe 3. The interview schedule

I Previous experience of foreign living and personal background
1   What kind of experience of living abroad did you have before?
        Used to travelling? On your own? With your family? What kind of
        travel?
        To what extent did these first experiences influence you?
        What does travelling represent to you?
2   Influences: family or friends?
        Are members of your family used to foreign contacts, in what form?
        Are your parents favourable to your travelling?
        What about your brothers and sisters: did they have the same experi-
        ences as you had?

Other influences?

3   Personal dispositions and motivations?

Why did you decide to go abroad?

What did you expect?

In terms of your personality, what makes you interested in travels and other cultures?

What were your attitude and expectations before you went away?

How did you prepare yourself for the experience?

4   Host environment: perceptions and images.

What images did you have of the foreign country or of the experience before you left?

To what extent have they changed?

How important is the foreign environment in facilitating adaptation?

How would you define a foreigner?

II *The actual experience*

5   Immersion in the foreign environment.

How did you immerse yourself in the local environment:

(a) living conditions: what kind of accommodation?

(b) local activities: societies, clubs?

(c) media or culture? cinema, theatre, etc?

(d) contacts with the native community? in what form?

Did anyone serve as a cultural intermediary, a person helping you to understand the culture better?

6   Social networks and friendships.

What kind of relationships did you have during your stay abroad? With natives? With other foreigners?

Who were your friends? Locals, i.e. natives or non-natives? How many friends did you make during your stay abroad?

Who helped you in the process of social integration?

7   Contacts home.

How frequent were your contacts with your family or others at home?

Trips back? When? How often?

How did you feel on those trips back home?

8   Key experiences, moments and phases.

Were there key people who helped you?

Were there key moments/situations?

Did you encounter any difficulties?

Were there different periods or phases during your stay?

Did you experience anything like the U-curve?

When were the lows? When were the highs?

Did you experience something like culture shock?

9   Degree of integration in the host culture.

How did you feel in the foreign society?

When did you feel that you had 'adapted'?

As a result, how did you feel in the end in the local environment, on a scale of 5:

1 tourist;

2 survivor;

3 resident;

4 near citizen;

5 citizen?

What advice would you give to newcomers?

What is needed to be successful in adapting to a new culture/environment?

III Assessment of the experience: outcomes

10   The process of adaptation.

How would you define the term 'adaptation'? Can you describe it?

Examples of people who adapted well and people who did not adapt well?

What makes people capable of adapting or not? What are the qualities needed?

What are the signs which show that you have adapted to life abroad?

How does the experience compare with other experiences one may go through in life?

11   Personal development.

How do you assess what you learnt from the experience?

Do you feel that you have changed during this year abroad? More than if you had stayed at home, for example?

What changes do you perceive in yourself?

How would you describe yourself now in terms of your identity, i.e. national or otherwise?

12   Intercultural learning.

What have you learnt in terms of other cultures?

(How) has your perception of your own country been altered? Your perceptions of people?

Did the experience 'teach' you something you would not have discovered otherwise?

13   The future: outlook?

How will that experience affect your future choices?

How important do you think this foreign experience will prove to be in your life as a whole?

What word would you use to sum up the whole experience?

Annexe 4. Interviewee profiles

Erasmus students

Most interviews were carried out in Dublin in 1994, 1995 and 1996.

1 **Daniel** was from Belgium and studied economics at Trinity College, Dublin. He comes from a mixed family and spent most of his childhood holidays in Italy. He lived in a university residence and did not make many local friends. He was satisfied with his experience, except in terms of language achievement.

2 **Louis** was from Belgium and studied economics at Trinity College, Dublin. His mobility capital was low. He was part of a group of French-speaking students and did not become involved in many activities outside university. He was shy and thought that he had become more outgoing as a result of his stay.

3 **Caroline** was from a bicultural Belgian family. She studied economics at Trinity College, Dublin. She had a high mobility capital and an open personality. She was involved in many activities. She made one 'very good friend' among native students and met many other foreign students.

4 **Birgitta** was from Germany and studied history at Trinity College, Dublin. She was an expert traveller, had spent a year with an English family and spoke good English. She made many friends in Dublin, both natives and foreigners. She did not experience any culture shock.

5 **Ava** was from Spain and studied education at Saint Patrick's College, Dublin. She had a very open personality and spoke good English. Her mobility capital was low, but she found that the interview raised her awareness of many issues. She said she was very happy about her stay and that she had changed a lot.

6 **Ania**, from Spain, studied education at Saint Patrick's College, Dublin. She had a low mobility capital, but always wanted to go for a year. She 'needs' to travel, she said. Socialising within a multicultural student group, she did not experience difficulties in adapting, was happy during her stay, but was happy to go home.

7 **Hugo** from Germany studied economics at Trinity College, Dublin. He started with a high level of mobility capital.. The interview revealed great maturity in the analysis of his stay. His choice of strategies was quite different from most other students.

8 **Marco**, from Rome, studied economics at Trinity College, Dublin. Studying was his main motivation and interest. His mobility capital was high and strongly influenced by his family. He socialised mainly with a group of international students, but also with Irish students. He enjoyed his stay.

9 **Hélène** was a student from Paris who studied English at Trinity College, Dublin. She had travelled, but had no long-term experience of adaptation. She spent her year abroad trying to isolate herself in order to reflect on her life. She did not enjoy the year, particularly since her fiancé was in Germany.

10 **Régine** from Paris is bilingual, having spent her childhood in Hawaii. She studied English at Trinity College, Dublin. Outgoing and reflective at the same time, she had an interesting experience which she enjoyed analysing. She made good friends in Dublin.

11 **John** is a Trinity College economics student who went to Rome. His mobility capital was good. His level of Italian was intermediary when he arrived. He had a mixed experience, with highs and lows, but came out delighted in the end, having benefited considerably from his stay.

12 **Lucy** was an Irish student who went to Louvain-la-Neuve to study economics. She had a high mobility capital and very good French. The Erasmus stay was her second year abroad (she worked in Paris as an au pair after school). Her Erasmus experience was mixed because she did not try to integrate into the life in the host country.

13 **Amin** came from a mixed background and went to a bilingual school as a child. He had not had a long stay abroad until his sojourn in Louvain, where he studied economics. His stay produced mixed results according to him.

14 **Julie** was an expert traveller. She studied business and German at Trinity College, Dublin and her stay in Trier was part of her degree. She managed well and integrated quite effortlessly in the host culture, with which she was already familiar. She stayed on over the summer to work.

15 **Maria** was an Irish student of business studies who went to Spain for a year. She is an outgoing and talkative person who obviously enjoyed speaking about her experience. She had a good mobility capital, mostly through her family, but had not spent a year abroad before. Her stay was most interesting and her choice of strategies quite different from many others.

Language assistants

Most interviews were carried out in September 1993 for the Irish students who had returned from France and in the summer of 1994 and 1995 for the French students before their return to France.

1 **Aoife** had not travelled much. But she was very open, curious and really wanted to go. She spent a year teaching in Arcachon and said that her stay was a 'dream'. Her French improved a lot and she met a lot of people locally, mostly natives.

2 **Cecilia** came from a background similar to Aoife's as well as the next two Irish students. They all came from Saint Patrick's College, Dublin, where they studied education and French. She said that her year abroad had 'changed [her] life' and she wanted to return.

3 **Fiona** had travelled very little and was anxious before going to Bordeaux, where she shared an apartment with Cecilia and Emily. Although they lived together, the three girls socialised with a large circle of friends, mostly French. They were very involved in local life and Fiona said that 'it was the best year that could ever be'.

4 **Emily** had travelled more than her friends, particularly to France. She

mixed well in the local milieu, took part in many activities together with her compatriots and made many friends. She said the year was the most important in her life so far.

5 **Nicolas** was French, but had travelling genes through his parents. He had planned his stay from his first year at university and did everything possible to be accepted as an assistant. He loved Ireland, knew many people and had worked there in the summer. His year was a resounding success and he wanted to stay on.

6 **Christine** had an average mobility capital, but knew Ireland and wanted to come back. She was appointed to a small town near Dublin and integrated perfectly into the local environment, with her school colleagues, with her co-residents, with the larger community. She became involved in many local activities. Her narrative is representative of a painless adaptation and integration.

7 **Sophie** was appointed to Dublin and took part in many cultural activities there. Apparently, her experience was mixed. She underwent difficulties, which may have been personal, but emerged strengthened. Her analysis of the situation revealed a great maturity.

8 **Valérie** was an experienced traveller, multilingual and European, with an experience of life in several border areas. She found herself living in Dublin in a residence with seminarists from Northern Ireland and went through severe culture shock. She became engaged to one of the seminarists and intends settling in Ireland.

9 **Karine** was appointed to a school in Dublin. She had a privileged experience because she is friendly with an Irish family and lived with them during the year. She did not have much to learn, but wanted the professional experience. Her stay seems to have been easy and effortless.

10 **Jannick** had travelled quite a lot and was mature. She was a keen linguist and student of Irish literature. She was closely involved in many activities and with different groups during the year and said that she 'absorbed' a great deal.

11 **Mathilde** was appointed to a small rural town. She had travelled extensively and, having lived away from her family, was autonomous. She loved languages and travel. She experienced no difficulties and tried to 'take in' as much as she could from the environment around her. She ended up tightly integrated into the local community.

12 **Siobhan** had travelled more than her friends from Ireland. She was a student of education and French who was appointed assistant in Bordeaux. She met quite a few French people, became friendly with some of her pupils' families and learnt a great deal from dining at their homes. She did not take part in many activities. She said that she had changed and had a very positive learning experience.

13 **Sylvie** had a high mobility capital and had already spent one year in Dublin as an Erasmus student. She was an assistant in a rural town and found it hard at first. She was torn between a desire to be

independent and free and a strong attachment to her roots. She had many literary interests and put on a play with her pupils. She said that the experience had an 'enormous' impact on her.

14 **Edwige** loved languages. She was appointed assistant to a distant rural community in Donegal. She was welcomed there and her tale is a success story: no culture shock and easy integration into several local groups. Yet, she said that openness was not easy for her. She wants to stay in Ireland.

15 **Collette** was an Irish student who was appointed to a medium-sized town in France. She had never been abroad until university. But she quickly took up the opportunities offered to her. She adapted easily in France and enjoyed her year.

EAP students
Interviews took place in Dublin, Paris and Oxford in September and October 1993.

1 **Elena** was younger than the others and was 19 when she went to Paris after two years at Trinity College, Dublin. She was a very dynamic and open girl who took full advantage of her stay, though she shared an apartment with three friends from Trinity. She felt that she had become more international at the end of her first year.

2 **Tom** was a traveller (three passports) who grew up in New Zealand, came back to Belfast with his parents and studied economics in Dublin for two years before joining the EAP. He was looking for 'a place where [he] would like to stay'. His French improved in Paris. He had many international friends and they were what he valued in the EAP. He thought that his year in France 'was not particularly interesting' because 'it was not a big enough change'. Damien said that Tom was 'the one operating the furthest from home'.

3 **Damien** had a good mobility capital (three passports). He had a good knowledge of French and of France before joining the EAP after two years at Trinity. He valued the European education he was receiving in the multicultural environment of the school, but said that he learnt most from his work experience in Paris. He had a good understanding of intercultural interactions.

4 **Viktor** was from Moscow and had spent eight months in Italy before joining the EAP. This was his first stay in France. He had some French, but was not fluent. He stayed with a French family at first and learnt considerably from that situation. His company placement was also an important time for him. He felt comfortable in France, less so in Italy and in Oxford. He hesitated to say that his year in Paris was the most important in his life.

5 **Christophe** was a trilingual student from Belgium who thought a great deal about life in several languages and nationalities. He was

accustomed to crossing borders. He chose to study at the EAP so as 'to enter a world which resembles his personal experience'. France and England were not 'foreign' to him, but provided 'an experience of another culture'.

6 **Thomas** from Germany had extended international experience before joining the EAP, and his family are travellers. He said 'the world is small'. For him, 'the key factor is the language'. He was a dedicated language and culture learner.

7 **Josef**, a German student, left his job to join the EAP in Paris. As a mature student, he felt outside both the student group and French culture. He socialised mainly with German students: 'it's a question of experience' (the others were younger). He did not integrate into French society and remained, he said, 'an outsider' and 'a foreigner'.

8 **Jürgen** had already lived one year abroad in the United States and had moved a lot in Germany. Aware of stereotypes, he tended to reject cultural explanations. He had quite a few French friends in Paris, outside the school. He had mixed feelings about his integration in Paris, but felt 'very much at ease with his personal background' there.

9 **Philip** was Anglo-Italian, but not bilingual. He had already spent one year studying in Paris before joining the EAP. His mobility capital was high and he felt European. His year in Paris was easy. He had obviously spent some time analysing his experiences.

10 **Kurt** was a German business student. His mobility capital was high. He had worked in a French factory at the age of 15 and had two lengthy language and study sojourns in Paris before the EAP. His first one-year stay learning French was trying, but he had a strong will to succeed. He did not experience any difficulty adapting to the EAP.

11 **Marina** was from a multicultural family and, coming from Luxembourg, knew 'the three EAP languages'. She felt European 'as a solution to pluri/multiculturalism', she said. The choice of the EAP seemed natural to her. She felt integrated in Paris from the moment she had her own place. She said that the experience gave her a 'more global view'. She enjoyed analysing the whole experience and talking about it.

12 **Eric** was also from Luxembourg and from a mixed family. He described himself as a 'hybrid'. He quickly felt at home in Paris and rated his final position as that of a 'citizen'. He liked reflecting on intercultural phenomena.

13 **Jose** was a student from Lisbon. Given his high mobility capital before joining the EAP, he already had an international profile. Open and dynamic, he adapted well in a city like Paris, but missed his country's climate. His analyses reveal his experience.

14 **Suzanne** was an Irish student from Trinity College who had worked and travelled abroad, but not spent a year in another language culture.

She always wanted to go away, she says, but was apprehensive before her departure. She adapted well in the EAP and had French friends even though she lived with Irish students.

15 **Christian** was Danish and slightly older than the others. A keen linguist, he had studied French and German at university and travelled quite extensively, staying for long sojourns in these two countries. He had a strong sense of relativism which led him to question his national origin. He adapted easily to the French lifestyle.

16 **Matthew**, from Scotland, had already spent one year in France as a language assistant. He had then a trying, but interesting experience. He always wanted to work abroad. He had many friends in France and lived with a native. He felt adapted from the very beginning of his year in Paris and 'loved it'. He felt 'foreign' in Oxford.

17 **Iris** from the Netherlands had travelled quite a lot. She was competitive and had opted knowingly for an international career. Her Parisian sojourn was her first long stay abroad. She found the language situation trying and tiring at first. She lived on her own. She said that she knew 'the culture quite well' in the end, but not French people. After her work experience, she felt completely at ease.

18 **Franz** was from Germany. He knew France well before entering the EAP and had a 'positive image' from his first visit. He was fascinated by foreignness. The year did not start well because he was not happy with his landlady. By spring, he 'felt at ease' and said 'the experience definitely changed my life'.

19 **Bruno** was from Northern Italy and was accustomed to changing locations. He always yearned for a long stay abroad and wanted to move out of Italy for personal reasons. He kept his distance from the EAP group, partly for language reasons (he felt his French was not up to their level). From May, he felt 'calmer' and happy. His year in Paris was not easy, but the international dimension of the EAP produced 'changes in the head', he said.

20 **Juan** was an expert student from Spain who was sent abroad by his father early in life. He was used to being independent. He felt at home in the United States where he had spent some time. He had his mind set to enter the EAP and worked on improving his French for this purpose. He adapted 'really fast without even noticing' to the EAP and to the new culture. He thought that he 'could go everywhere and not be afraid' after the experience.

Annexe 5. Nationality of interviewees

	EAP	*Assistants*	*Erasmus*	*Total*
EU-12				
Germany	5		2	7
Belgium	1		3	4
Denmark	1			1
Spain	1		2	3
France		9	2	11
Greece				
Ireland	3	6	5	14
Italy	1		1	2
Luxembourg	2			2
Netherlands	1			1
Portugal	1			1
United Kingdom	2			2
+				
New Zealand	1			1
Russia	1			1
Total	20	15	15	50

Annexe 6. Students with mixed families[1]

Daniel (B)	Italian parents, resident in Belgium.
Caroline (B)	Flemish mother, father from Wallonie, resident in Brussels.
Ava (E)	Spanish, but grandfather from Belgium.
Hugo (D)	Polish mother, German father, resident in Germany.
Marco (I)	German grandmother, Hungarian grandmother, both married to Italians.
John (IRL)	Polish sister-in-law.
Amin (IRL)	Moroccan father, Irish mother.
Maria (IRL)	Sister married to a Spaniard, Spanish stepmother.
Nicolas (F)	Russian mother, Franco-Swiss father, early childhood in England.
Valérie (F)	Franco-Swiss mother, Belgian grandmother, French residents.
Sylvie (F)	Sister married to an Irish man.
Tom (NZ)	Parents from Northern Ireland emigrated to New Zealand.
Damien (IRL)	Born in the United States, father from Northern Ireland, mother from the Republic of Ireland.
Christophe (B)	Born in England, British mother, Francophone father from Flanders.
Philip (UK)	Italian father, English mother, resident in the UK, then in France.
Marina (L)	Serbo-Croatian mother, father from Luxembourg, German

grandmother.

Eric (L) Italian father, Belgian mother, grandparents emigrated to Luxembourg from Belgium.

Annexe 7. Previous experiences abroad[2]

Erasmus students

Daniel* (B) regular one-month holidays with his paternal family in Italy as a child; end-of-school trip to Crete; holidays in Spain.

Louis (B) several one- to two-week holidays.

Caroline* (B) six consecutive language summer courses in a Flemish boarding school from the age of 10[#3]; two two-week language-study periods in England; one work-placement, one with a family.

Birgitta (D) several European holidays, with her parents first and then with friends (in Spain, Portugal, Italy, France, Greece); eight months with a family in London aged 17.

Ava* (E) two one-month language-study periods in England.

Ania (E) three language-study periods in England.

Hugo* (D) visits to his maternal Polish family; European trips with friends (USSR, Poland, Yugoslavia, Italy, France, Spain); stays in the US, once for four months[#]; one summer working in the USSR, Ukraine and Poland.

Marco* (I) many family trips; family expatriation for five months in the United States aged 10; three language-study periods in England aged 8, 11 and 13; one summer studying in the United States aged 16.

Hélène (F) language-study periods in England and Germany; three months in the United States aged 16; followed by the return visit of her American correspondent staying with her own family for a year; two Irish trips as a student.

Régine (F) seven-year family expatriation to Hawaii between 6 and 13 years of age[#]; international family trips; one month as an au pair in Switzerland at the age of 14; two months visiting friends in Canada at 16; student trips, inter-railing in Europe or overseas (India at the age of 18).

John* (IRL) family trips to England; family holidays in France; from 12 years onwards, regular language-study periods in France, two of them in schools; inter-rail in Europe; trips to Poland to his sister-in-law's family.

Lucy (IRL) three language-study periods in France, with a correspondent, the first one at 14; visits by foreign students to her home; one year as an au pair in Paris aged 18.

Amin* (IRL) bilingual Anglo-German primary school; visits to French friends as a child and as an adolescent for a few months; one year in an all-Irish boarding-school at 11[#]; inter-rail in Europe

	aged 19; one summer working in the United States aged 20.
Julie (IRL)	language exchanges, the first one at 12[#], then every year alternating France and Germany; three summer jobs in Germany as a student.
*Maria** (IRL)	two-month stay in Spain aged 13[#], one month aged 14; at the age of 15, one semester in a Spanish school, followed by one month language-study period in France[#]; at 16 and 17, more stays in these countries; one summer working in the United States aged 19.

Language assistants

Aoife (IRL)	home contacts with Irish diaspora; ten-day school trip to France; six-week university exchange in Paris.
Cecilia (IRL)	two family trips and two school exchanges in France; one ten-day school trip to Russia.
Fiona (IRL)	two-week school exchange in France; one student exchange in France.
Emily (IRL)	three summers in France as an au pair aged 16, 17 and 18; visits to her sister who lives in Paris; one six-week university exchange in Paris.
*Nicolas** (F)	lived in England as a child; family travels; aged 14, one-month stay in the United States; aged 15, six-week language-study course in England; aged 16, one month in Ireland; aged 17, three-month summer job in an Irish hotel; followed by three consecutive summer jobs in Ireland (restoring monuments, tourist office).
Christine (F)	three visits to Germany with a choir; two language exchanges in England; a two-week tourist visit to Ireland as a student.
Sophie (F)	family and school trips to England and Spain; one-month stay in Florida as a student; five short (one week) European trips; three-week language-study course in England.
*Valérie** (F)	German exchanges twice a year from the age of 12; a two-day school visit to Brighton; European travels with family or friends; one sojourn with Italian friends.
Karine (F)	family trips to nearby countries; one school-stay in Germany; three stays with an Irish family.
Jannick (F)	several school visits (a few days); aged 15, language-study courses in England, then one every second year; trip to Spain; sports weekends in Germany.
Mathilde (F)	personal contacts with foreigners through twinning and sports activities; two three-week language-study periods since the age of 14 (UK, Ireland); one two-month Tempus programme in Poland.
Siobhan (IRL)	European school trip at the age of 15 (UK, F, D, NL); student programmes: one-week exchange in Belgium, six-week university exchange in Paris.
*Sylvie** (F)	aged 13, language-exchange trip; aged 16, stays in Ireland in

	her married sister's home; short trips to London; one summer working in Scotland; one Erasmus sojourn in Ireland (during the third year of her studies).
Edwige (F)	family trips as a child, two to England, four camping in Austria, one in Spain; one five-day school trip to Spain; one three-week language-study stay in England as a second-year student.
Collette (IRL)	two university exchange programmes: three weeks in Quimper and six weeks in Paris.
EAP students	
Elena (IRL)	family part of the Irish diaspora; four-month summer job in Nice as a first-year student; one summer working in England during her second year.
*Tom** (NZ)	parents emigrated from Belfast to New Zealand; one family trip to Australia, Asia and Europe as a teenager; at 17, family repatriation to Northern Ireland[#]; undergraduate studies in Dublin; one summer working in Paris[#].
*Damien** (IRL)	born in the USA; international family travels; two school-exchanges in France for six weeks aged 12 and for four months aged 15; European trips as a student; one summer working in the USA.
Viktor (USSR)	one eight-month stay in Italy as a student.
*Christophe** (B)	born in England, lived there until 2; Flemish boarding school from the age of 12[#]; regular yearly holidays with his English family; European trips.
Thomas (D)	international family holidays; two months in Canada; six months working in the Club Med (Bahamas, Brazil); one year language-study in Aix; Brazilian girlfriend.
Josef (D)	many foreign holidays including two six-week trips to Asia and the United States.
Jürgen (D)	two weeks in France as a teenager; aged 17, one year school programme in an American college.
*Philip** (UK)	yearly holidays with his Italian family; family holidays in Europe; one school-exchange in Germany; inter-railing trip in Europe with English friends; trip to the United States with other European students; one summer camp with French students; one-year study period in France.
Kurt (D)	European holidays; aged 15, summer job in a French factory; one-year language-study programme in Paris[#]; many travels.
*Marina** (L)	yearly holidays with her Serbo-Croatian family; one two-week stay in Germany at the age of 10[#]; numerous trips within Europe; work-placements in England.
*Eric** (L)	yearly holidays with his Italian family; numerous trips within Europe, one to England[#].
Jose (P)	open house: international contacts at home from an early age;

visits to foreign friends or trips as a tourist; many international trips with AIESEC; one year as an Erasmus student in Paris.

Suzanne (IRL)   her family hosts foreign students; family trip to the United States aged 15; aged 18, one summer working in Strasbourg; aged 19, one summer working in the United States.

Christian (DK)   contacts with German visitors at home through his mother who teaches German; one three-week stay with German friends aged 12, followed by regular trips; several one–two-month sojourns in France.

Matthew (Scotland) several family holidays abroad when young; school trips; aged 16, one school-twinning programme; undergraduate studies in England; one year as an assistant in France as a third-year language student[#].

Iris (NL)   family trips; one language-study course; one work-placement; one summer in a kibbutz [#].

Franz (D)   holidays in France; one six-week work-placement as a student.

Bruno (I)   family trips to France; frequent visits to the Swiss and French Alps close to his hometown; trips with friends (Scotland).

Juan (E)   regular language-study courses in England since the age of 8; one month in the United States aged 14[#]; aged 16, one-year stay in an American college.

Annexe 8. Motivations of some Erasmus students

Daniel

1 a new personal experience;
2 to learn English;
3 to discover new people, a new culture.

Louis

1 an original experience (100%);
2 to encounter a new culture (50%);
3 to meet different people (70%).

Caroline

1 a new way of studying;
2 to encounter a new culture;
3 to improve my English.

Birgitta

1 to improve my language competence, particularly orally through socialising with Irish people;
2 personal interest in Irish culture, land and population;
3 specifically, to study the relations between Irish history and Latin (the Celts).

Ava

1 to learn the language;
2 to have new experiences;

3 to meet Irish people and see their way of life.

Hugo

1 to meet people and acquire long-term friends;
2 to learn the language and culture of another country from the inside;
3 to develop my own personality.

Marco

1 to improve my English;
2 an experience of autonomy: to live alone;
3 to meet different people;
4 to discover another way of studying.

Lucy

1 to study in a foreign university;
2 to see if my French, learnt as an au pair, would allow me to go beyond that linguistic level and allow me to follow lectures;
3 to get to know student life in another country;
4 to live alone… for the first time.

Amin

1 to improve my French;
2 to study abroad for a year;
3 to do something different.

John

1 to improve my Italian;
2 to go to Rome.

Annexe 9. Motivations of some EAP students

Elena

1 three European countries;
2 meeting students from other nationalities;
3 working in three countries.

Tom

1 going somewhere else than Ireland (in Europe);
2 living in the three countries;
3 languages.

Marina

1 experience in three countries;
2 degree from a '*grande école*';
3 a European school of management.

Jose

1 internationalisation;
2 diverse student body;
3 three totally new experiences.

Philip

1 continue with management studies;
2 learning German;

3 having a direct experience of Europe today.

Thomas

1 staying in France;
2 going to Oxford;
3 living in Berlin.

Jürgen

1 preparing for work abroad;
2 languages;
3 general interest in the countries.

Annexe 10. Forms of accommodation selected by the students

	1 Mixed or international cohabitation	*2 Cohabitation with natives*	*3 Ethnic or national cohabitation*	*4 Independent accommodation*
Erasmus	Daniel, Louis, Caroline, Birgitta, Ava, Ania, Marco (then 4), John, Lucy, Amin, Julie	Hugo, Hélène, Régine, Maria		Marco (at the end of his stay)
Assistants	Siobhan (Christine and Jannick in the middle of their stay)	Aoife (at first, then 4), Nicolas, Christine (then 1), Sophie, Valérie, Karine, Jannick (then 1), Mathilde, Sylvie, Edwige, Collette	Cecilia, Fiona, Emily	Aoife
EAP	Eric Viktor and Christian Later	Viktor (then 1), Christian (then 1), Thomas, Matthew, Franz (then 3)	Elena, Damien, Jürgen, Suzanne Franz	Tom, Josef, Philip, Kurt, Marina, Jose, Christian, Iris, Bruno, Juan

Note:
Numbers in parentheses indicate a change in form of accommodation

Notes

Introduction

1 European here has a political connotation and refers to students from EU member states.
2 Statistics must be read with caution since it is notoriously difficult to obtain reliable data about these highly volatile events. For example, definitions of an 'immigrant' vary between reporting countries, some recording non-nationals and nationals, others recording only non-nationals.
3 As a matter of fact, police or administrative interference, contravening Union legislation, too often reduces European citizens to a second-class ranking, long reserved for the traditional immigrant.
4 Though a great many are still excluded from this element of choice.
5 Some use the term 'sojourner', defined as 'temporary immigrants who reside for a specific purpose and time period and return to their home country' (Berry, 2000). But, in our study, this term refers to the original meaning Siu (1952) gave it.
6 The term 'origin' is meant to embrace different situations (birth, nationality, citizenship); emigration emphasises the movement outside one's own country and immigration the movement into a receiving country.
7 Statistics for example are difficult to get for UK students going out to EU countries (Admit, 2000).
8 For example, Greece has a long tradition of exporting its third-level students.
9 A case study may be unique or multiple, including one or several units of analysis (Yin, 1984). Case study is understood here as grouping several individuals in a similar situation.

1 The stranger's template

1 *The Stranger* belongs to a series of social types analysed by Simmel, such as *The Poor* or *The Adventurer*. The 'social type' is a sociological construction, like Weber's ideal type, whereby a human category is analysed in terms of the characteristics of their particular position in an interactional structure or in terms of the category of orientation to the world they embody (Levine, 1971). For the purpose of this study, we focus on the individual as type while remaining aware of the ambiguity of bald categorisations.
2 Inverted commas are generally used to denote reference to the original concept, a practice not strictly adhered to in this work.
3 The early texts on the stranger use the masculine grammatical gender. We tried to avoid this as far as possible in the remaining parts of the text, but this proved elusive in chapter 1.

4 Like itinerants, strangers are not fixed to a specific place. Unlike them, their ambit unifies the two opposite dimensions of dislocation and belonging.
5 This paradox haunted generations of readers according to Levine (1977), giving rise to studies attempting to measure social distance on different scales (Kadushin, 1962) or to quantify it.
6 It has even been suggested that Simmel's 'notion of strangeness and distance' in interaction serves to illuminate the experience of cyberspace communication (Bogard, 1996).
7 The last arrived is always more of a stranger in the social hierarchy designed by migrants. As a result, the first arrived may consider the newly arrived as usurping their place in the new society where they already see themselves as 'owners of soil'.
8 Simmel gives as an illustration the practice of choosing judges from the outside in certain Italian cities as well as the role of confidante easily bestowed on strangers.
9 Synthesised by Simmel's aphorism, echoed later by Weber: 'One need not be Cesar in order to understand Cesar' (Merton, 1972: 346).
10 Whereas political rights represent the stable demarcation line between citizens and foreigners.
11 'For the individual's self is an integral part of his social rôle, and when this social rôle is fundamentally changed the individual's self is forced through a similar transformation' (Stonequist, 1937: 6).
12 The French expression accounts for this as feeling '*dépaysé, déclassé, déraciné*'.
13 Their number varies, but the overall development seems to follow three main phases. In Goffman (1973) also, the career of the stigmatised actor involves three phases.
14 Besides, the move from a university environment to another provides a climate similar to that of the travelling medieval monks.
15 Stichweh (1997) assumes that a third status, neither 'friend' nor 'stranger', has become constitutive of everyday experience, which means that indifference to other individuals is the norm.

2 Narratives of student travellers

1 See annexe 1.
2 In the Weberian sense of the term.
3 The two terms are used interchangeably here.
4 These four strategies have been found to relate to other features of the acculturation process.
5 Which we refer to in chapter 10 in our discussion on the road travelled at the end of the stay.
6 As well as other more external areas such as academic and administrative support, study in the host country, accommodation, costs and financing, recognition, or determinants of academic progress abroad.
7 A principle which the hyphenated words 'language-and-culture' symbolise (Byram and Morgan, 1994).
8 A total of 3,212 Erasmus students answered the questionnaire in 1990–1991 out of the 25,835 given a grant.
9 The Federal Republic of Germany, France, Sweden and the United Kingdom.
10 An aspect developed in chapter 4.
11 The collective study involved an important number of researchers, particularly during data transcriptions.
12 The tendency though is to focus on the pedagogy of the period of residence abroad, as the three recent UK FDTL (Fund for the Development of Teaching and Learning) Languages Projects illustrate, rather than on research.
13 In different linguistic and national contexts, or indeed in a cross-European context.
14 See annexe 2.

15 See annexe 3.
16 Unfortunately, the single interview does not allow for a significant take on the progress of representations or practices.
17 The initials EAP refer to the previous name of the school, *Ecole des Affaires de Paris*. It has now merged with the *Ecole Supérieure de Commerce de Paris* (ESCP) and its name is now ESCP/EAP.
18 See annexe 4.
19 See annexe 5. The sample is representative of European diversity, but because of its size is not representative at a statistical level.
20 The thirteenth origin referring to Matthew's definition of himself as Scottish.
21 The names were nevertheless changed in the final narrative.
22 For example, in chapter 7, we deal with aspects of social entry which reoccur later on.

3 Mobility capital: a taste for living abroad

1 See annexe 6.
2 We come back to this point later.
3 Language students and more generally arts students are well represented in student mobility programmes.
4 Other factors besides educational choices, such as family resources either financial or social, may play a role as well. In this respect, the concept of mobility capital may be considered as an extension of their cultural capital.
5 But, not all students handed back their written questionnaires.
6 With the exception of Luxembourg where, as Marina who went on her first stay in Germany at the age of 10 points out, pupils start learning German in the first year of primary school and French in the second year.
7 In the written questionnaires, the multiple-choice question related to the amount of time spent abroad offered a choice between several durations.
8 Indicated in annexe 7 by a hash sign (#).
9 In the text, '*la pilule a passé*'.
10 As already mentioned in relation to the 'critical age hypothesis'.
11 See chapter 5.
12 We go back to this point in chapter 9.
13 Discussed in chapter 10.
14 As we will see in chapter 5.
15 Maria says: 'I had a good picture of Spain in my brain'.
16 Mathilde mentions two fears to be overcome – language apprehension and distance from friends and family (chapter 5).

4 An adventure into another time–space

1 As they dominate other data (Admit, 2000; Mübig-Trapp and Schnitzer, 1997).
2 See chapter 10.
3 Ideally, answers would be provided by investigating a few years on the professional careers of those who participated in programmes abroad as students.
4 See chapter 2.
5 In the list of twelve reasons influencing Erasmus students in 1993 (Maiworm *et al.*, op. cit), four come well ahead of the others: improvement in language learning (86 per cent); self-development (81 per cent); new studying experience in a different country (77 per cent); and improving one's knowledge of the foreign country (72 per cent).
6 Sometimes called 'reasonable' or 'functional' (Martineau, 1995).
7 The position afforded to motives related to studying, in many European studies of student mobility, reflects their institutional perspective.

8 Martineau mentions that students single out a first central motive around which they develop others which they link, formally or not, in causative chains (ibid.).
9 We come back to this point in greater detail in the next chapter.
10 See final chapters.
11 As we see in chapters 8 and 9.
12 We come back to this point later in the chapter.
13 Evocative of work on linguistic biographies (Coste *et al.*, 1997).
14 The phrases spoken in English, in an otherwise French interview, are in italics.
15 At the time of the interview, he was in Oxford for his second EAP year.
16 See annexe 8.
17 Since our intention in this study is not to carry out a comparative analysis of student life in various contexts, we do not dwell on this aspect of the data.
18 See chapter 8.
19 *Hugo*: (1) to meet people and acquire long-term friends; (2) to learn the language and culture of another country from the inside; (3) to develop my own personality.
20 In English in the student's text.
21 See Sylvie in chapter 5.
22 See also chapter 10.
23 An experience which is often missing in French academic life, where students are assigned a university close to their residence, resulting in a supplementary obstacle for outgoing French candidates.
24 We go back to this point in chapter 6.
25 '*Le métissage des modes de vie*'.
26 Discussed in chapter 6.

5 The arrival: a rite of passage

1 '... his position in this group is determined, essentially, by the fact that he has not belonged to it from the beginning' (Simmel, op. cit.: 402).
2 All the more so when the stranger does not anticipate the initiation process ahead.
3 See chapter 7.
4 'Social relationships are evolved in this way. We *feel* that we have certain obligations, that there are certain things that we ought or ought not to do; we *feel* that there are certain things which we have a right to do with respect to others. We also *feel* that others should behave in certain ways. As this manner of feeling becomes more definite and organized, it develops into a psychological state which may be referred to as an attitude, but which, under some circumstances, is perhaps better expressed by the term sentiment because of the nature of the emotional content which is present' (Wood, 1934: 30, emphasis added).
5 See chapter 4 where the first experience of adaptation is referred to as an initiation.
6 Besides, the issue remains as to the extent to which this aspect of a collective attitude may be identifiable or generalised from individual narratives.
7 Discussed in chapters 4 and 10.
8 Which they try and solve by offering university courses in English.
9 We return to this point in chapter 7.
10 The medical connotation illustrates the interpretation of culture shock as a cultural disease.
11 Influenced by 'the German notion of perfection', Josef feels like an infant because he dares not make a telephone call in French before March.
12 Elena recognised in the end that, even though she would have liked to have been aware of this type of difference before going, 'it's difficult to give advice out of context'.
13 In chapter 6.
14 'Mild psychosomatic complaints' are common (Furnham and Bochner, 1986: 49).

15 It is suggested that psychological interpretations obscured the sociological meaning Marx gave to the term and that in the end alienation indicated feelings of dissatisfaction with life among social actors (Abercombie *et al.*, 1994: 14) and a confusion of causes with symptoms.

16 The italics indicate that the student uses English in her otherwise French interview.

17 We will go back to this point in chapter 8.

6 Redefining culture shock in a European context

1 Amin, in the previous chapter, also mentioned preconceptions and how they impact on the travellers' mental representation of their host country.

2 Which he attributes to W.I. Thomas (in Schütz, 1971a: 96).

3 He says that in Luxembourg, 'there are no foreign cultures, rather… it's like a mixture between German cultures and francophone cultures'.

4 Kracke (1987) singles out three different conceptions of culture shock which each reflects a certain definition of culture, but all of them are negative because they focus on culture as difference.

5 Particularly Stonequist in chapter 5 on the life-cycle of the marginal man (1937).

6 As a Portuguese, he often finds himself as the only representative of his country.

7 Mentioned in chapter 5.

8 In a way, this result seems to validate Church's review of the U-curve literature (1982), summed up by Furnham and Bochner: 'not all sojourners start off in the phase of supposed adjustment, elation and optimism'. On the other hand, the majority of our students did not start off as 'unhappy, depressed and anxious right from the beginning' (1986: 132).

9 See chapters 7, 8 and 9.

10 See chapter 10.

11 The past is not always experienced as a sanctuary. Sylvie states that, in the first instance, she wanted to 'get rid of her French identity', was 'fed up with French mentality', and needed to distance herself from her life there. Spatial distance in her case supports the psychological and mental distance she seeks. At the end of her stay, she is frightened of going back home and delays the final date because she is afraid of losing what she has lived through in Ireland and fears that 'she will go back to square one'. She feels that what she is going back to is a restricted horizon.

12 From Homer's Ulysses to the modern migrants' voice, narratives of homecoming abound in literature.

13 This discovery represented her 'culture shock'.

7 New spaces, new places

1 This is dealt with in the next chapter.

2 The qualifier *comfortable* occurs as a leit-motiv, with the expression *at home*, to describe the adaptation process.

3 See chapter 5.

4 In English in the French text.

5 She speaks from experience, having spent a summer working in Bavaria.

6 As noted in chapter 5.

7 Referred to as 'middleman' in earlier discussions (Bonacich, 1973) and more recently as 'cultural intermediary' (Byram *et al.*, 1997).

8 Discussed further in chapter 9.

9 See chapter 5.

10 We go back to this point in chapter 10.

11 Though a temporary visitor may be welcomed inside a community more readily than a long-term settler.
12 A point not developed here.
13 In contrast with other metaphors used to account for spatial appropriation such as the onion, the bubble or the shell.
14 Certain places like Dublin, Bordeaux, Grenoble or Liège were perceived as more hospitable by students interviewed by Martineau (1995), a rating confirmed in part by our respondents.
15 See annexe 10.
16 The French *studios*.
17 Martineau points out that the issue of residence is present during the first interview, but is hardly mentioned in subsequent interviews when other aspects of the stay become more prominent.
18 Where she is moving the following year.
19 Marina explains that once students possess their own place, their home, and are no longer distracted by 'superficial' tasks, they can invest more in relations and go deeper into the culture.

8 The new social setting

1 The focus of chapter 9.
2 The notion of entry, alluded to in chapter 5, refers to the capacity to move in order to gain a position in society through socio-economic participation.
3 See chapter 4.
4 Extensive discussion of these issues is outside the realm of this work.
5 Already mentioned by Maria.
6 As Aoife does: 'we start school at 8.30 am and we don't finish until 4.30 pm... that was a big change and also the fact that there was a two-hour break at lunch time... it took me a long time to get used to that'.
7 The French term of *stage* refers to students' work placement in a company, often used as such in management courses.
8 Exceptions include those students who were living with a French family at the start of the year, like Viktor and Christophe who both mention the family and the work placement as the two experiences which afforded them an inside perspective on French society.
9 Hélène, for example, refuses to go out with her lodger. For personal reasons, she prefers to be on her own so as to have the opportunity to reflect on her life. As a result, she maintains a strictly functional relationship with most of the people who surround her.
10 Where culture is defined mainly in terms of high culture, the development of knowledge or aesthetic appreciation.
11 He suggested that practical advice about this aspect of social integration be mentioned in brochures for foreign students.
12 This is the case for many assistants and language students as well as for a few EAP students.
13 'Older' German students in Paris went regularly while 'younger' Irish students tended to mention nightclubs.
14 He recalls an 'awful woman treating us like slaves' during his work placement: 'some things I just could not believe and I thought I must have misunderstood and having her [his French flatmate] there, she understood, so that was very helpful'.
15 Asked the following question: 'After your year (in Paris), did you feel that you understood French culture better?', Thomas answered: 'Yes, especially the French, because we have a lot of French people and the way they work, they communicate with you,

the way they accept you and the way they are open inside the EAP and outside the EAP in Paris…'.

16 The *concours* is the competitive exam enabling a student to enter a *grande école*.

9 The creation of a new social fabric

1 See chapter 1.
2 See chapter 5.
3 Terms vary to designate these three networks, sometimes called co-national or mono-cultural, multicultural, and host, host-national or bicultural (Furnham and Bochner, 1986).
4 See chapter 4 for its role as motivation and chapter 10 for its role in the development of cross-cultural capability.
5 See mobility capital in chapter 3.
6 Stated by Klineberg and Hull in the following manner: 'the more contacts with natives, the more the experience of the stay will tend to be judged satisfying' (1979: 53).
7 Though Maria had two 'language compatriots' for intimate support.
8 The ethnic ghetto represents a place where contacts may be warm, spontaneous and intimate, by contrast with the outside where contacts are initially colder, more abstract and rational (Wirth, 1928).
9 See chapter 5 for details.
10 Trips back and forth between the new location and home, so tempting at the beginning of the experience, fulfil a similar function.
11 Reminiscent of Schütz's own words (1971a: 104).
12 See chapter 7.
13 We saw in chapter 7 that the students who stayed with a family throughout the year found it a powerful learning experience.
14 See chapter 7.
15 As discussed in chapter 7, Hugo, who understood this perfectly, decided to arrive two weeks before the start of the academic year to find accommodation with a group of natives.
16 'Not very many now, maybe four, five… I was maybe in four or five different Italian people's houses over the year' (John).
17 Régine had a long experience of life and travel abroad and explained in her interview that, having had difficulty readjusting to the French context after years in Hawaii, most of her friends in Paris were foreigners.
18 Short for *classes préparatoires*, where students prepare for the special examination or *concours* needed to enter a *grande école*.
19 Another French business *grande école*.
20 See chapters 7 and 8.
21 Though Elena recalls that 'when a French student had a *soirée*, the French friends invited would stay together'.
22 Julie finds the word 'to avoid' excessive: 'well, not avoided, I think more so like tended to be with German students as opposed to international students, but I didn't go out of my way to avoid them'.
23 See chapter 7.
24 Like Régine with her Irish flatmate.
25 She adds: 'they thought I was dressed like a tinker'.
26 Aoife used the basketball club in Arcachon with similar results.
27 See chapter 1.
28 See chapter 7.
29 See chapter 5.

30 Maria says: 'when I was tired of speaking Spanish, I always reverted back to her and we'd have a good few laughs together'.
31 See the discussion of the potential wanderer's personality features and mobility capital in chapter 3.

10 Adaptation: chameleon or clam

1   See chapter 6.
2   When going out with her Spanish friends in the evening, Marie would dress like them, but would return to her normal way of dressing during the day.
3   Sylvie gives the example of a friend who 'rejected France totally' and consequently, 'adopted the Irish mentality': 'I saw the transformations, her personality had completely changed... I didn't recognise her... even physical changes... the way she moved, even her very pronounced Dublin accent' (our trans.).
4   Jürgen, rightly, rejects the idea of no longer feeling that you are a foreigner, but he says that over time, the feeling of foreignness decreases.
5   As their plans for the future, discussed in chapter 4, reveal.
6   Discussed in chapters 7 and 8.
7   See chapter 5.
8   These responses were elicited in the written questionnaire by the question: 'List some factors which you consider as influencing one's integration into a foreign community.'
9   We also saw that access and resources play a role.
10 The question asked was: 'What is needed to be successful in adapting to a new culture/environment?'
11 As discussed in chapter 4.
12 His parents moved to a Paris suburb for professional reasons.
13 He instances having to eat something in Africa which did not appeal to him at all.
14 She used English in the French text.
15 Though food is obviously far from insignificant and the data contain many anecdotes about food as a contentious issue in cross-cultural relations.
16 That is, in her own culture.
17 This question was borrowed from a questionnaire used in the EAP in 1993, based on the acculturation stages defined by Acton and Walker de Felix (1986).
18 The EAP group is a special case since the period abroad observed here represents the first of three years abroad. Their position at the end of the three years would obviously be quite different.
19 Juan explains that, when he compares his life with that of his friends who stayed in Madrid, he thinks that they have no choice of where to go except where they are.

Conclusion

1   'Focusing on trustworthiness rather than truth displaces validation from its traditional location in a presumably objective, nonreactive and neutral reality, and moves it to the social world – a world constructed in and through discourse and actions, through praxis' (Mishler, 1990: 420).
2   Yet, Gurwitsch writes in a letter to Schütz, at the time the essay was published, that the characteristics of the réfugié, or indeed of the immigrant, and the crises they live through are 'incommensurable with those fundamentally harmless problems of adapting you describe' (Grathoff, 1989: 70).
3   Those which had been dealt with at length before, such as the issue of perceived cultural differences, are treated cursorily. One of the difficulties in such an investigation is the sheer volume of data, representing over 1,000 typed pages, which somewhat curtails an in-depth treatment of each area.

Annexes

1   The students' country of residence is indicated in brackets.
2   Asterisks refer to students with foreign or mixed families.
3   This hash symbol points to the first experience of adaptation, when explicitly identified as such by students.

Bibliography

Abercombie, N., Hill, S. and Turner, B. (1994) *Dictionary of Sociology*, London: Penguin.

Abou, S. (1990) 'L'insertion des immigrés. Approche conceptuelle', in Simon-Barouh, I. and Simon, P.-J. (eds) *Les étrangers dans la ville. Le regard des sciences sociales*, Paris: L'Harmattan.

Aciman, A. (ed.) (1999) *Letters of Transit. Reflections on Exile, Identity, Language and Loss*, New York: The New Press.

Acton, W. and Walker de Felix, J. (1986) 'Acculturation and mind', in Valdes, J. (ed.) *Culture Bound. Bridging the Cultural Gap in Language Teaching*, Cambridge: CUP.

Adler, P. (1975) 'The transitional experience: an alternative view of culture shock', *Journal of Humanistic Psychology*: 13–23.

—— (1977) 'Beyond cultural identity: reflections upon cultural and multicultural man', in Brislin, R. (ed.) *Culture Learning: Concepts, Applications and Research*, Honolulu: University of Hawaii Press.

Admit (1999) *International and EU Interest in Mobility and Higher Education*, Centre for Educational Research, London School of Economics.

—— (2000) *Mobility, Admissions and Common Curriculum Elements. Case Studies*, Centre for Educational Research, London School of Economics.

Adorno, T., Frenkel-Brunswick, D., Levinson, D. and Sanford, R. (1950) *The Authoritarian Personality*, New York: Harper.

Agar, M. (1980) *The Professional Stranger*, London: Academic Press.

Amir, Y. (1969) 'Contact hypothesis in ethnic relations', *Psychological Bulletin* 71: 319–342.

Ball-Rokeach, S. (1973) 'From pervasive ambiguity to a definition of the situation', *Sociometry* 36: 3–13.

Bauman, Z. (1992) *Intimations of Postmodernity*, London: Routledge.

—— (1995) 'Making and unmaking of strangers', *Thesis Eleven* 43: 1–16.

—— (1996) 'Assimilation into exile: the Jew as a Polish writer', *Poetics Today* 17, 4: 569–597.

Baumgratz-Gangl, G. (1993) *Compétence transculturelle et échanges éducatifs*, Paris: Hachette.

Becker, G. (1964) *Human Capital*, New York: Columbia University Press.

Beirao, D. (1999) *Les Portugais du Luxembourg. Des familles racontent leur vie*, Paris: CIEMI/L'Harmattan.

Berger, P., Berger, B. and Kellner, H. (1973) *The Homeless Mind. Modernization and Consciousness*, New York: Vintage Books.

Berry, J. (1990a) 'Psychology of acculturation', in Berman, J. (ed.) *Cross-Cultural Perspectives*, Nebraska: University of Nebraska Press.

—— (1990b) 'Psychology of acculturation. Understanding individuals moving between cultures', in Brislin, R. (ed.) *Applied Cross-Cultural Psychology*, London: Sage.

—— (2000) 'The sojourner experience: an international commentary', in MacLachlan, M. and O'Connell, M. (eds) *Cultivating Pluralism*, Dublin: Oak Tree Press.

Bochner, S. (1972) 'Problems in culture learning', in Bochner, S. and Wicks, P. (eds) *Overseas Students in Australia*, Sydney: New South Wales University Press.

—— (ed.) (1982) *Cultures in Contact: Studies in Cross-cultural Interaction*, Oxford: Pergamon.

Bogard, W. (1996) 'Simmel in cyberspace: distance and strangeness in postmodern communication', paper presented at the American Sociological Association.

Bonacich, E. (1973) 'A theory of middleman minorities', *American Sociological Review* 38: 583–594.

Bourdieu, P. (1980) *La distinction*, Paris: Les éditions de Minuit.

Brein, M. and David, K. (1971) 'Intercultural communication and the adjustment of the sojourner', *Psychological Bulletin* 76: 215–230.

Brislin, R., Bochner, S. and Lonner, W. (eds) (1975) *Cross-cultural Perspectives on Learning*, New York: Wiley.

Brown, D. (1980) *Principles in Language Learning and Teaching*, Englewood Cliffs: Prentice Hall.

Buijs, G. (ed.) (1993) *Migrant Women. Crossing Boundaries and Changing Identities*, Oxford: Berg.

Burn, B., Cerych, L. and Smith, A. (eds) (1990) *Study Abroad Programmes*, London: Jessica Kingsley Publishers.

Byram, M. (1993) *The 'Assistant(e) d'Anglais'. Preparing for the Year Abroad*, Durham: University of Durham School of Education.

—— (ed.) (1997a) *Face to Face. Learning 'Language-and-Culture' through Visits and Exchanges*, London: CILT.

—— (1997b) *Teaching and Assessing Intercultural Communicative Competence*, Clevedon: Multilingual Matters.

Byram, M. and Alred, G. (1993) *'Paid to be English'. A Book for English Assistants and the Advisers in France*, Durham: University of Durham School of Education.

Byram, M. and Morgan, C. (eds) (1994) *Teaching-and-Learning Language-and-Culture*, Clevedon: Multilingual Matters.

Byram, M., Zarate, G. and Neuner, G. (1997) *Sociocultural Competence in Language Learning and Teaching*, Strasbourg: Council of Europe Publishing.

Byrnes, F. (1966) 'Role shock: an occupational hazard of American technical assistants abroad', *Annals of the American Academy of Political and Social Science* 368: 95–108.

Carlson, J., Burn, B., Useem, J. and Yachimowicz, D. (1990) *Study Abroad. The Experience of Undergraduates*, Westport, CT: Greenwood Press.

Cassell, P. (1993) *The Giddens Reader*, London: Macmillan Press.

Castles, S. and Miller, M. (1993) *The Age of Migration*, London: Macmillan Press.

Chambers, I. (1994) 'Leaky habitats and broken grammar', in Robertson, G. *et al.* (eds) *Travellers' Tales. Narratives of Home and Displacement*, London: Routledge.

Chédemail, S. (1998) *Migrants internationaux et diasporas*, Paris: Armand Colin.

Church, A. (1982) 'Sojourner adjustment', *Psychological Bulletin* 91, 3: 540–572.

Claeys, A. (1999) *L'accueil des étudiants étrangers en France: enjeu commercial ou priorité éducative?*, Paris: Assemblée nationale.

Clarke, M. (1976) 'Second language acquisition as a clash of consciousness', *Language Learning* 26, 2: 377–389.

Clifton, H. (1993) 'Where we live', in Bolger, D. (ed.) *Ireland in Exile. Irish Writers Abroad*, Dublin: New Island Books.

Close, P. (1995) *Citizenship, Europe and Change*, London: Macmillan Press.

Coleman, J. (1995) 'The current state of knowledge concerning student residence abroad', in Parker, G. and Rouxeville, A. (eds) *The Year Abroad. Preparation, Monitoring and Evaluation*, London: AFLS/CILT.

—— (1997) 'Residence abroad within language study. State of the art article', *Language Teaching* 30: 1–20.

Convey, F. (1995) 'The stay abroad: objectives, strategies, outcomes', in Parker, G. and Rouxeville, A. (eds) *The Year Abroad. Preparation, Monitoring and Evaluation*, London: AFLS/CILT.

Corcoran, M. (1993) *Irish Illegals. Transients Between Two Societies*, London: Greenwood Press.

Coste, D., Moore, D. and Zarate, G. (1997) *Multilingual and Multicultural Competence*, Strasbourg: Council of Europe.

Delouche, F. *et al.* (1992) *Histoire de l'Europe*, Paris: Hachette.

Duenas-Tancred, M. and Weber-Newth, I. (1995) 'Profiling and crediting the year abroad', in Parker, G. and Rouxeville, A. (eds) *The Year Abroad. Preparation, Monitoring and Evaluation*, London: AFLS/CILT, pp. 110–126.

Elliot, D. (1997) 'United Kingdom', in Kälvemark, T. and van der Wende, M. (eds) *National Policies for the Internationalisation of Higher Education in Europe*, Stockholm: National Agency for Higher Education.

Eurostat (2000) 'International migration', Luxembourg: Office for Official Publications of the European Communities.

Fisher, G.-N. (1981) *La psychosociologie de l'espace*, Paris: PUF.

Flory, M. (1993) *Etudiants d'Europe*, Paris: La documentation française.

Freed, B. (ed.) (1995) *Second Language Acquisition in a Study Abroad Context*, Amsterdam: John Benjamins.

Freund, J. (1981) 'Introduction', in Simmel, G. *Sociologie et épistémologie*, Paris: PUF.

Friedman, J. (1995) 'Global system, globalization and the parameters of modernity', in Featherstone, M. *et al.* (eds) *Global Modernities*, London: Sage

Furnham, A. and Bochner, S. (eds) (1986) *Culture Shock. Psychological Reactions to Unfamiliar Environments*, London: Routledge.

Galland, O. (ed.) (1995) *Le monde des étudiants*, Paris: PUF.

Gareis, E. (2000) 'Intercultural friendship: five case studies of German students in the USA', *Journal of Intercultural Studies* 4: 67–91.

Geertz, C. (1973) *The Interpretation of Cultures*, New York: Basic Books.

Giddens, A. (1979) *Central Problems in Social Theory*, London: Macmillan Press.

Glaser, B. and Strauss, A. (1967) *The Discovery of Grounded-Theory*, Chicago: Aldine.

Goffman, E. (1973) *La mise en scène de la vie quotidienne: les relations publiques*, Paris: Les éditions de Minuit.

Goldring, M. and Mac Einri, P. (1989) 'La diaspora irlandaise', *Hérodote* 53, 2: 169–183.

Gordon, J. and Jallade, J.-P. (1995) *La mobilité étudiante au sein de l'Union Européenne: une analyse statistique*, Paris: Institut européen d'éducation et de politique sociale.

—— (1996) 'Spontaneous student mobility in the European Union: a statistical survey', *European Journal of Education* 31, 2: 133–151.

Grathoff, R. (ed.) (1989) *Philosophers in Exile. The Correspondence of Alfred Schütz and Aron Gurvitsch. 1939–1959*, Indianapolis: Indiana University Press.

Greenaway, D. and Tuck, J. (1995) *Economic Impact of International Students in UK Higher Education*, London: Committee of the Vice Chancellors and Principals of the Universities of the UK.

Gullahorn, J. and Gullahorn, J. (1963) 'An extension of the U-curve hypothesis', *Journal of Social Issues* 19, 3: 33–47.

Gurevitch, Z. (1988) 'The other side of dialogue: on making the other strange and the experience of otherness', *American Journal of Sociology* 93, 5: 1179–1199.

Guthrie, G. (1975) 'A behavioral analysis of culture learning', in Brislin, R., Bochner, S. and Lonner, W. (eds) *Cross-cultural Perspectives on Learning*, New York: Wiley.

Hannerz, U. (1983) *Explorer la ville. Eléments d'anthropologie urbaine*, Paris: Les éditions de Minuit.

Harman, L. (1988) *The Modern Stranger*, The Hague: Mouton de Gruyter.

Hen, C. and Léonard, J. (1998) *L'Union européenne*, Paris: Editions La Découverte.

Hoffman, E. (1989) *Lost in Translation. Life in a New Language*, New York: Penguin.

—— (1999) 'The new nomads', in Aciman, A. (ed.) *Letters of Transit. Reflections on Exile, Identity, Language and Loss*, New York: The New Press.

Hughes, E. (1949) 'Social change and status protest: an essay on the marginal man', *Phylon* 10, 1: 58–65.

Huston, N. (1999) *Nord perdu*, Arles: Actes Sud/Leméac.

Iyer, P. (1998) 'The nowhere man', *Prospect*: 6–7.

Jansen, S. (1980) 'The stranger as seer or voyeur: a dilemma of the peep-show theory of knowledge', *Qualitative Sociology* 2, 3: 22–55.

Joseph, I. (1984) *Le passant considérable. Essai sur la dispersion de l'espace public*, Paris: Librairie des Méridiens.

Kadushin, C. (1962) 'Social distance between client and professional', *American Journal of Sociology* 67, March: 517–531.

Kaufmann, N., Martin, J. and Weaver, H., with Weaver, J. (1992) *Students Abroad: Strangers at Home*, Yarmouth, MA: Intercultural Press.

Kelley, C. and Meyers, J. (1992) *The Cross-cultural Adaptability Inventory*, Yarmouth, MA: Intercultural Press.

Kim, Y. (1988) *Communication and Cross-cultural Adaptation: An Integrative Theory*, Clevedon: Multilingual Matters.

Kim, Y. and Gudykunst, W. (1988) *Cross-cultural Adaptation. Current Approaches*, London: Sage.

Klineberg, O. and Hull, W. (1979) *At a Foreign University: An International Study of Adaptation and Coping*, New York: Praeger.

Kohler Riessman, C. (1993) *Narrative Analysis*, London: Sage.

Koser, K. and Lutz, H. (eds) (1998) *The New Migration in Europe. Social Constructions and Social Realities*, London: Macmillan Press.

Kracke, W. (1987) 'Encounter with other cultures: psychological and epistemological aspects', *Ethos* 15, 1: 58–81.

Kramsch, C. (1993) *Context and Culture in Language Teaching*, Oxford: OUP.

Kristeva, J. (1991) *Strangers to Ourselves*, London: Harvester Wheatsheaf.

—— (1997) 'Français dans le texte', *Télérama* 2454: 40.

Kundera, M. (1997) *La lenteur*, Paris: Gallimard.

Kupferberg, F. (1998) 'Models of creativity abroad: migrants, strangers and travellers', *Archives Européennes de Sociologie* 39, 1: 179–206.

Le Bras, H. (1997) 'L'hospitalité comme relation: dilatation de l'espace et contraction du temps', *Communications* 65: 143–148.

Levine, D. (ed.) (1971) *Georg Simmel. On Individuality and Social Forms*, Chicago: University of Chicago Press.

—— (1977) 'Simmel at a distance: on the history and systematics of the sociology of the stranger', *Sociological Focus* 10, 1: 15–29.

Lofland, L. (1973) *A World of Strangers. Order and Action in Urban Public Space*, New York: Basic Books.

Lonner, W. (1986) 'Foreword', in Furnham, A. and Bochner, S. (eds) *Culture Shock. Psychological Reactions to Unfamiliar Environments*, London: Routledge.

Lynd, R. and Merrell Lynd, H. (1937) *Middletown in Transition. A Study in Cultural Conflict*, New York: Harcourt, Brace and Co.

Lysgaard, S. (1955) 'Adjustment in a foreign society: Norwegian Fullbright grantees visiting the United States', *International Social Science Bulletin* 7: 45–51.

Mac Einri, P. (1989) 'The New Europeans: the Irish in Paris today', in Mulholland, J. and Keogh, D. (eds) *Emigration, Employment and Enterprise*, Cork: Hibernian University Press.

Maffesoli, M. (1997) *Du nomadisme. Vagabondages initiatiques*, Paris: Le livre de poche.

Maiworm, F., Steube, W. and Teichler, U. (1991) *Learning in Europe. The Erasmus experience*, London: Jessica Kingsley Publishers.

—— (1992) *ECTS in its Year of Inauguration: The View of the Students*, Kassel: Universität Gesamthochschule.

—— (1993) *Experiences of Erasmus Students 1990/91*, Kassel: Universität Gesamthochschule.

Makine, A. (1995) *Le testament français*, Paris: Mercure de France.

Martin, J. (ed.) (1989) 'Intercultural communication competence', *International Journal of Intercultural Relations*, special issue 13, 3.

Martineau, M., with Lusato, L. (1995) *Regards étudiants sur les échanges: cinéma et communication en Europe*, Paris: INRP/Corlet/Télérama/SFSIC.

Mauger, G. (1995) 'Jeunesse: l'âge des classements. Essai de définition sociologique d'un âge de la vie', *Recherche et prévisions* 40: 19–36.

Merton, R. (1996/1972) 'Insiders and outsiders: a chapter in the sociology of knowledge', in Sollors, W. (ed.) *Theories of Ethnicity. A Classical Reader*, London: Macmillan.

Meyer, J. (1951) 'The stranger and the city', *American Journal of Sociology* 56, March: 476–483.

Milton, J. and Meara, P. (1995) 'How periods abroad affect vocabulary growth in a foreign language', *ITL Review of Applied Linguistics* 107–108: 17–34.

Mishler, E. (1990) 'Validation in inquiry-guided research: the role of exemplars in narrative studies', *Harvard Educational Review* 60, 4: 415–442.

Morin, E. (1987) *Penser l'Europe*, Paris: Gallimard.

Mübig-Trapp, P. and Schnitzer, C. (1997) *Gearing Up for Europe via Mobility and Internationalization of Study*, Hannover: HIS-Hochschul-Informations-System GmbH.

Mukherjee, B. (1999) 'Imagining homelands', in Aciman, A. (ed.) *Letters of Transit. Reflections on Exile, Identity, Language and Loss*, New York: The New Press.

Murphy-Lejeune, E. (1995) 'The student strangers: aspects of cross-cultural adaptation in the case of international students', in Parker, G. and Rouxeville, A. (eds) *The Year Abroad. Preparation, Monitoring and Evaluation*, London: AFLS/CILT.

—— (1996) 'Images of other cultures', *Proceedings from the Intercultural Education-Celebrating Diversity Conference*, Dublin: Teacher Education Centre, 66–80.

—— (1997) 'Language and culture crossing: the ethnographic bridge', in Coulson, T. (ed.) *Exiles and Migrants: Crossing Thresholds in European Culture and Society*, Brighton: Sussex Academic Press.

—— (1998) 'The vicissitudes of the modern "stranger" or the adventures of a concept', paper presented at the Dublin City University and Saint Patrick's College Joint Faculty of Humanities Conference, Dublin.

—— (2000a) 'Autour d'un mot "étranger"', in Paganini, G. (ed.) *Proximités et différences culturelles: L'Europe*, Paris: L'Harmattan.

—— (2000b) 'La formation à l'interculturel par l'interculturel', in Barbot, M.-J. and Grandmangin, M. (eds) *De nouvelles voies pour la formation*, Paris: Cahiers de l'ASDIFLE.

—— (2001) 'Mapping the territory: insights from the sociology of the stranger', in Killick, D. and Parry, M. (eds) *Mapping the Territory: The Poetics and Praxis of Languages and Intercultural Communication*, Glasgow: Glasgow French and German Publications.

Murphy-Lejeune, E., Cain, A. and Kramsch, C. (1996) 'Analysing representations of otherness using different text-types', *Language, Culture and Curriculum* 9, 1: 51–65.

Musgrove, F. (1963) *The Migratory Elite*, London: Heinemann.

NARIC (1993) *Academic Recognition of Higher Education Entrance, Intermediate and Final Qualifications in the European Community*, Brussels: NARIC.

Nash, D. (1963) 'The ethnologist as stranger: an essay in the sociology of knowledge', *Southwestern Journal of Anthropology* 19: 149–167.

Nash, D. and Schaw, L. (1962–3) 'Personality and adaptation in an overseas enclave', *Human Organization* 21: 252–263.

Oberg, K. (1960) 'Culture shock: adjustment to new cultural environments', *Practical Anthropology* 7: 177–182.

Opper, S., Teichler, U. and Carlson, J. (1990) *Impacts of Study Abroad Programmes on Students and Graduates*, London: Jessica Kingsley Publishers.

Park, R. (1928) 'Human migration and the marginal man', *American Journal of Sociology* 33, 8: 881–893.

Park, R. and Burgess, E. (1921) *An Introduction to the Science of Sociology*, Chicago: University of Chicago Press.

Parker, G. and Rouxeville, A. (eds) (1995) *The Year Abroad. Preparation, Monitoring and Evaluation*, London: AFLS/CILT.

Pearson-Evans, A. (2000) 'A grounded theory approach to the analysis of cross-cultural adjustment: case-studies based on the diaries of six Irish university students in Japan', unpublished doctoral dissertation, Trinity College Dublin.

Pels, D. (1999) 'Privileged nomads. On the strangeness of intellectuals and the intellectuality of strangers', *Theory, Culture and Society* 16, 1: 63–86.

Personal Narratives Group (eds) (1989) *Interpreting Women's Lives: Feminist Theory and Personal Narratives*, Indianapolis: Indiana University Press.

Plummer, K. (1983) *Documents of Life. An Introduction to the Problems and Literature of a Humanistic Method*, London: Unwin Hyman.

Raphael, F. (1986) '"L'étranger" de Georg Simmel', in Watier, P. (ed.) *Georg Simmel. La sociologie et l'expérience du monde moderne*, Paris: Méridiens Klinksieck.

Regan, V. (1995) 'The acquisition of sociolinguistic native speech norms: effects of a year abroad on L2 learners of French', in Freed, B. (ed.) *Second Language Acquisition in a Study Abroad Context*, Amsterdam: John Benjamins.

Roselle, D. and Lentiez, A. (1999) *Le Programme Erasmus 1987–1995. Une rétrospective qualitative, un regard vers le futur…*, Lille: Pôle Universitaire Européen.

Said, E. (1999a) 'No reconciliation allowed', in Aciman, A. (ed.) *Letters of Transit. Reflections on Exile, Identity, Language and Loss*, New York: The New Press.

—— (1999b) *Out of Place. A Memoir*, London: Granta Books.

Schild, E. (1962) 'The foreign student, as stranger, learning the norms of the host-culture', *Journal of Social Issues* 18: 41–54.

Schumann, J. (1978) *The Pidginization Process: A Model for Second Language Acquisition*, Rowley, MA: Newbury House.

Schütz, A. (1944) 'The stranger. An essay in social psychology', *American Journal of Sociology* 49: 499–507.

—— (1971a) 'The stranger. An essay in social psychology', in Bordersen, A. (ed.) *Collected Papers II. Studies in Social Theory*, The Hague: Martinus Nijhoff, pp. 91–105.

—— (1971b) 'The homecomer', in Bordersen, A. (ed.) *Collected Papers II. Studies in Social Theory*, The Hague: Martinus Nijhoff, pp. 106–119.

Simic, S. (1999) 'Refugees', in Aciman, A. (ed.) *Letters of Transit. Reflections on Exile, Identity, Language and Loss*, New York: The New Press.

Simmel, G. (1908) 'Exkurs über der Fremden', *Soziologie*, Leipzig: Dunker and Humblot.

—— (1950) 'The stranger', in Wolff, K. (ed.) *The Sociology of Georg Simmel*, New York: Free Press of Glencoe.

—— (1971) 'The stranger', in Levine, D. (ed.) *Georg Simmel. On Individuality and Social Forms*, Chicago: University of Chicago Press.

Singleton, D. (1989) *Language Acquisition. The Age Factor*, Clevedon: Multilingual Matters.

Siu, P. (1952) 'The sojourner', *American Journal of Sociology* 58, 1: 34–44.

Slama, S. (1999) *La fin de l'étudiant étranger*, Paris: L'Harmattan.

Small, A. (1905) *General Sociology*, Chicago: University of Chicago Press.

Smalley, W. (1963) 'Culture shock, language shock and the shock of self-discovery', *Practical Anthropology* 10: 49–56.

Sollors, W. (1996) *Theories of Ethnicity. A Classical Reader*, London: Macmillan.

Sorti, C. (1997) *The Art of Coming Home*, Yarmouth, MA: Intercultural Press.

Stichweh, R. (1997) 'The stranger – on the sociology of indifference', *Thesis Eleven* 51: 1–16.

Stonequist, E. (1937) *The Marginal Man: A Study in Personality and Culture Conflict*, New York: Russell and Russell.

Teichler, U. (1991) *Experiences of ERASMUS Students 1988/89*, Kassel: Universität Gesamthochschule.

Thomas, W. I. and Znaniecki, F. (1918–1920) *The Polish Peasant in Europe and America. Monograph of an Immigrant Group*, Chicago: University of Chicago Press.

Tiryakian, E. (1973) 'Sociological perspectives on the stranger', in TeSelle, S. (ed.) *The Rediscovery of Ethnicity*, New York: Harper and Row.

Torbiörn, I. (1982) *Living Abroad. Personal Adjustment and Personnel Policy in the Overseas Setting*, New York: John Wiley and Sons.

van Gennep, A. (1960/1909) *The Rites of Passage*, Chicago: University of Chicago Press.

Van Hear, N. (1998) *New Diasporas. The Mass Exodus, Dispersal and Regrouping of Migrant Communities*, London: UCL Press.

Wagner, A.-C. (1998) *Les nouvelles élites de la mondialisation. Une immigration dorée en France*, Paris: PUF.

Walsh, R. (1994) 'The year abroad – a linguistic challenge', *Teanga* 14: 48–57.

Ward, C. and Rana-Deuba, A. (1999) 'Acculturation and adaptation revisited', *Journal of Cross-cultural Psychology* 30, 4: 422–442.

Wirth, L. (1928) *The Ghetto*, Chicago: University of Chicago Press.

Wiseman, R, Hammer, M. and Nishida, H. (1989) 'Predictors of intercultural communication competence', *International Journal of Intercultural Relations* 13, 3: 349–371.

Wollen, P. (1994) 'The cosmopolitan ideal in the arts', in Robertson, G., Mash, M., Tickner, L., Bird, J., Curtis, B. and Putnam, T. (eds) *Travellers' Tales. Narratives of Home and Displacement*, London: Routledge.

Wood, M. (1934) *The Stranger. A Study in Social Relationships*, New York: Columbia University Press.

Yin, R. (1984) *Case Study Research. Design and Methods*, London: Sage.

Zajonc, R. (1952) 'Aggressive attitudes of the "stranger" as a function of conformity pressures', *Human Relations* 5: 205–216.

Znaniecki, F. (1934) *The Method of Sociology*, New York: Farrar and Rinehart.

Index